1 CORINTHIANS

CHARLES L. CAMPBELL

WJK WESTMINSTER
JOHN KNOX PRESS
LOUISVILLE · KENTUCKY

© 2018 Charles L. Campbell

First edition
Published by Westminster John Knox Press
Louisville, Kentucky

18 19 20 21 22 23 24 25 26 27—10 9 8 7 6 5 4 3 2 1

Unless otherwise indicated, Scripture quotations are from the New Revised Standard Version of the Bible, copyright © 1989 by the Division of Christian Education of the National Council of the Churches of Christ in the U.S.A., and used by permission. Scripture quotations marked NEB are taken from *The New English Bible*, © The Delegates of the Oxford University Press and The Syndics of the Cambridge University Press, 1961, 1970. Used by permission.

Excerpts from Oscar Romero, *The Violence of Love* (Maryknoll, NY: Orbis Books, 2004). Used by permission of Orbis Books. Excerpts from Charles L. Campbell and Johan H. Cilliers, *Preaching Fools: The Gospel as a Rhetoric of Folly*, 50. © 2012. Reprinted by permission of Baylor University Press. Excerpts from "River inside the River," from *River inside the River: Poems* by Gregory Orr. Copyright © 2013 by Gregory Orr. Used by permission of W. W. Norton & Company, Inc.

Book design by Drew Stevens
Cover design by Lisa Buckley
Cover illustration: © David Chapman/Design Pics/Corbis

Library of Congress Cataloging-in-Publication Data
Names: Campbell, Charles L., 1954- author.
Title: 1 Corinthians / Charles L. Campbell.
Other titles: First Corinthians
Description: First edition. | Louisville, KY : Westminster John Knox Press,
   2017. | Series: Belief: a theological commentary on the Bible | Includes
   bibliographical references and index.
Identifiers: LCCN 2017047275 (print) | LCCN 2017048184 (ebook) | ISBN
   9781611648430 (ebk.) | ISBN 9780664232535 (pbk. : alk. paper)
Subjects: LCSH: Bible. Corinthians, 1st--Commentaries.
Classification: LCC BS2675.53 (ebook) | LCC BS2675.53 .C35 2017 (print) | DDC
   227/.207--dc23
LC record available at https://lccn.loc.gov/2017047275

In memory of my father,
Charles C. Campbell,
and
for my mother,
Johnsye Campbell

Contents

Publisher's Note

William C. Placher worked with Amy Plantinga Pauw as a general editor for this series until his untimely death in November 2008. Bill brought great energy and vision to the series and was instrumental in defining and articulating its distinctive approach and in securing theologians to write for it. Bill's own commentary for the series was the last thing he wrote, and Westminster John Knox Press dedicates the entire series to his memory with affection and gratitude.

William C. Placher, LaFollette Distinguished Professor in Humanities at Wabash College, spent thirty-four years as one of Wabash College's most popular teachers. A summa cum laude graduate of Wabash in 1970, he earned his master's degree in philosophy in 1974 and his PhD in 1975, both from Yale University. In 2002 the American Academy of Religion honored him with the Excellence in Teaching Award. Placher was also the author of thirteen books, including *A History of Christian Theology*, *The Triune God*, *The Domestication of Transcendence*, *Jesus the Savior*, *Narratives of a Vulnerable God*, and *Unapologetic Theology*. He also edited the volume *Essentials of Christian Theology*, which was named as one of 2004's most outstanding books by both *The Christian Century* and *Christianity Today* magazines.

Series Introduction

Belief: A Theological Commentary on the Bible is a series from Westminster John Knox Press featuring biblical commentaries written by theologians. The writers of this series share Karl Barth's concern that, insofar as their usefulness to pastors goes, most modern commentaries are "no commentary at all, but merely the first step toward a commentary." Historical-critical approaches to Scripture rule out some readings and commend others, but such methods only begin to help theological reflection and the preaching of the Word. By themselves, they do not convey the powerful sense of God's merciful presence that calls Christians to repentance and praise; they do not bring the church fully forward in the life of discipleship. It is to such tasks that theologians are called.

For several generations, however, professional theologians in North America and Europe have not been writing commentaries on the Christian Scriptures. The specialization of professional disciplines and the expectations of theological academies about the kind of writing that theologians should do, as well as many of the directions in which contemporary theology itself has gone, have contributed to this dearth of theological commentaries. This is a relatively new phenomenon; until the last century or two, the church's great theologians also routinely saw themselves as biblical interpreters. The gap between the fields is a loss for both the church and the discipline of theology itself. By inviting forty contemporary theologians to wrestle deeply with particular texts of Scripture, the editors of this series hope not only to provide new theological resources for the church but also to encourage all theologians to pay more attention to Scripture and the life of the church in their writings.

We are grateful to the Louisville Institute, which provided funding for a consultation in June 2007. We invited theologians, pastors, and biblical scholars to join us in a conversation about what this series could contribute to the life of the church. The time was provocative, and the results were rich. Much of the series' shape owes to the insights of these skilled and faithful interpreters, who sought to describe a way to write a commentary that served the theological needs of the church and its pastors with relevance, historical accuracy, and theological depth. The passion of these participants guided us in creating this series and lives on in the volumes.

As theologians, the authors will be interested much less in the matters of form, authorship, historical setting, social context, and philology—the very issues that are often of primary concern to critical biblical scholars. Instead, this series' authors will seek to explain the theological importance of the texts for the church today, using biblical scholarship as needed for such explication but without any attempt to cover all the topics of the usual modern biblical commentary. This thirty-six-volume series will provide passage-by-passage commentary on all the books of the Protestant biblical canon, with more extensive attention given to passages of particular theological significance.

The authors' chief dialogue will be with the church's creeds, practices, and hymns; with the history of faithful interpretation and use of the Scriptures; with the categories and concepts of theology; and with contemporary culture in both "high" and popular forms. Each volume will begin with a discussion of *why* the church needs this book and why we need it *now*, in order to ground all the commentary in contemporary relevance. Throughout each volume, text boxes will highlight the voices of ancient and modern interpreters from the global communities of faith, and occasional essays will allow deeper reflection on the key theological concepts of these biblical books.

The authors of this commentary series are theologians of the church who embrace a variety of confessional and theological perspectives. The group of authors assembled for this series represents more diversity of race, ethnicity, and gender than most other commentary series. They approach the larger Christian tradition with a critical respect, seeking to reclaim its riches and at the same time to acknowledge its shortcomings. The authors also aim to make available to readers a wide range of contemporary theological voices from many parts of the world. While it does recover an older genre of writing, this series is not an attempt to retrieve some idealized past. These commentaries have learned from tradition, but they are most importantly commentaries for today. The authors share the conviction that their work will be more contemporary, more faithful, and more radical, to the extent that it is more biblical, honestly wrestling with the texts of the Scriptures.

William C. Placher
Amy Plantinga Pauw

Acknowledgments

Because this book draws on work I have been doing for over twenty-five years, there are too many people to thank by name. Countless conversation partners and previous editors have helped me develop my thinking and refine my ideas. I am grateful to them all.

More directly related to this book, there are numerous people to thank. I am grateful to Westminster John Knox Press, including the late William Placher, for inviting me to contribute to this series. The current editors, Amy Plantinga Pauw and Donald McKim, were endlessly patient as I missed one deadline after another, and they improved and sharpened the manuscript through their careful editorial work. The anonymous outside reader commissioned by WJK also provided helpful suggestions and saved me from a few missteps. Finally, Julie Tonini—the production manager—and her team graciously transformed my manuscript into a book. I appreciate all their efforts on behalf of this commentary.

I am also grateful to several New Testament scholars, some of whom I have never met, on whose work I depended while writing this book. Alexandra Brown's *The Cross and Human Transformation* has been especially formative for my thinking, and her personal support and encouragement have been invaluable. Indeed, this commentary has largely been an attempt to explore the implications of Brown's insights into the first two chapters of 1 Corinthians for the remainder of the letter. The work of other scholars has also influenced this book, as the numerous footnotes will indicate: Richard B. Hays, Dale B. Martin, J. Louis Martyn, and L. L. Welborn. While none of these scholars is responsible for the directions I take, and while each of them will undoubtedly disagree with some of my conclusions, their work has been important for my interpretation of Paul's letter.

I also want to thank my South African colleague, Johan Cilliers, with whom I coauthored *Preaching Fools: The Gospel as a Rhetoric of Folly*. Our work on that book informed this one. Neither book would have come to press without the extensive and creative theological conversations I have enjoyed with Johan. In addition, I have twice team-taught a class on preaching Paul's apocalyptic gospel with my Duke colleague, Susan Eastman; her insights and support have been invaluable over the past few years. Another colleague, Lauren Winner, read the entire manuscript and made helpful substantive and stylistic suggestions. Katrina Schaafsma, a Duke doctoral student, provided remarkable assistance with the copyediting and proofreading, making the manuscript much more precise, consistent, and accurate.

I developed portions of this book through lectures and workshops at Saint Meinrad Seminary and School of Theology, Lancaster Theological Seminary, Hazelip School of Theology at Lipscomb University, Leipzig University in Germany, the University of Copenhagen, and the Swedish Preaching Program. I am grateful for the feedback I received from participants on these occasions. I am especially thankful for the responses and encouragement offered by several colleagues with whom I have taught in these programs: Alexander Deeg, Carina Sundberg, Tina Johansson, Anne Gidion, and Marlene Ringaard Lorensen.

As always, I thank my wife, Dana, for over forty years of unending patience, daily encouragement, honest critique, and theological wisdom. What a blessing our life together has been.

Finally, I thank my parents, Johnsye Campbell and the late Charles C. Campbell. They first introduced me to the Bible, and I dedicate this book to them.

Introduction
Why 1 Corinthians? Why Now?

Creative theological thinking, Mary McClintock Fulkerson has noted, "originates at the scene of a wound."[1] Moreover, this theological thinking is not brought in after the wound is described, as if theology had a full-blown doctrine of God or church that is neatly applied to the wound. There is not a linear movement from theology to wound but rather a dynamic relationship between theological reflection and the wound that needs to be addressed. Theology interprets the wound and may even help one perceive the wound. But the wound also informs and shapes the theological reflection. "Theologies that matter," Fulkerson writes, "emerge out of dilemmas—out of situations that matter. . . . Wounds generate new thinking"; they generate an impulse toward creativity and change.[2]

Paul's creative theological thinking in 1 Corinthians has this character; it "originates at the scene of a wound." The entire letter represents Paul's theological wrestling with the deep wound of division in the Corinthian church. This wound is not simply an intellectual dilemma or a contested idea, though differing ideologies appear to be part of the problem. Rather, the wound takes shape in the embodied practices of the community, whether it be the practices of baptism, the Lord's Supper, and preaching; the acts of taking others to court and eating meat at elite banquets; or the exercise of different spiritual gifts.

1. Mary McClintock Fulkerson, *Places of Redemption: Theology for a Worldly Church* (Oxford: Oxford University Press, 2007), 13.
2. Ibid., 13–14.

1

The character of the divisions in Corinth has been dissected by countless scholars. Because we know about these divisions only through Paul's response to them, any conclusions we might draw are limited. Whatever the specifics may be, however, we can discern through the letter some general outlines. First, there were social and economic divisions, creating a hierarchy of "high" and "low," "weak" and "strong" in the church. Consequently, there were tensions between the elites and those of lesser status. Indeed, this social hierarchy appears to be a central issue in the community that contributes to other divisions.[3] Second, related to the hierarchical divisions, there were philosophical differences in the community. More than likely, these divisions revolved around popular philosophical trends that were "in the air" rather than more formal, developed philosophical systems (e.g., Gnosticism).[4] The elites in the community were probably more knowledgeable of these philosophical trends and more responsive to them, which led to convictions about human bodies and spiritual knowledge that were not shared by others in the community.[5] Third, ironically, these divisions often emerged around different spiritual gifts, as Paul notes at the beginning of the letter and addresses repeatedly. Both cultural assumptions about social hierarchy and philosophical assumptions about spiritual knowledge shaped some members' approach to spiritual gifts, leading to hierarchy and division in that area as well. Finally, add to all these divisions the community's conflict with Paul himself, who not only preaches the "weak" and "foolish" cross, but does so in an unimpressive rhetorical manner. The wound in Corinth is deep.

Contemporary churches in North America are currently dealing with some analogous wounds. Christian communities find themselves in a time of transition and division. And some of the divisions are not unlike those in Corinth. Tensions continue in many churches around the ordination of women. As a professor of preaching, I talk to women seminarians every year who are called to preach

---

3. Dale B. Martin emphasizes the central role of hierarchy in *The Corinthian Body* (New Haven: Yale University Press, 1995). My interpretation of the letter is deeply indebted to Martin's work.
4. Most scholars today reject the role of Gnosticism. See Martin, *Corinthian Body*, 70–71.
5. See ibid., 71–76.

but not allowed into pulpits in their denomination—a prohibition often grounded in interpretations of 1 Corinthians itself. Similarly, matters of sexuality continue to divide churches, again sometimes shaped by readings of Paul's letters, including his epistle to Corinth. How may LGBTQ+ persons participate in church leadership? Who can preach and celebrate the Lord's Supper? Who can marry whom? Denominations and churches have split over precisely these questions, and resolution and reconciliation seem to be a long way off in many contexts.

Moreover, adding to these divisions, and sometimes shaping the response to them, contemporary churches are in a time of profound transition, which often feels like a wound. Many churches are experiencing a significant decline in both membership and influence. Demographic changes have created a new context for churches, one that is far more ethnically, culturally, and religiously diverse. Contemporary churches may in fact now be able to relate better to that miniscule church in Corinth seeking to live out its life in a wildly diverse and cosmopolitan city. In this context, the comfortable old ecclesial patterns and assumptions are dying, while it is not clear what the shape of the new will be. The church finds itself in-between, in an unsettled, liminal space. As a result, anxiety, and even fear, ooze from the church's wound. And often, as in Corinth, this conflict and anxiety comes to full expression in worship—the heart of the church's life. Music. Worship leadership. Wedding services. All these have become the occasion for "worship wars" in an unsettled church.

Paul thus invites not only the Corinthians but also the contemporary church to engage in creative, transformative theology at the scene of a wound. Unfortunately, all too often interpreters have focused on Paul's specific directives (e.g., about women or marriage), isolating them from Paul's theology and writing them in stone. When one looks beneath the specific "presenting issues" in Corinth, however, one discovers in Paul's letter not only theological affirmations but also a theological orientation that can be generative for the contemporary church. In response to this wound, Paul's theology has a distinctive and instructive character; it is practical, apocalyptic, hermeneutical, and fragmentary.

Practical Theology

Theology at the site of a wound is necessarily practical theology. It is theological reflection on a particular situation. Such theology, first of all, attends to the shape and demand of the situation; the structure of the wound is "as much a part of the analysis as the presence of biblical and doctrinal elements."[6] Second, in addressing the wound, practical theology seeks to change the situation. It is not theology for the sake of theology; it is not a purely abstract intellectual exercise. Rather, it is theological reflection "shaped by a logic of transformation."[7]

Paul's practical theology in 1 Corinthians has both these characteristics. Throughout the letter Paul addresses the wound at the heart of the community, which is enacted in specific, divisive practices. The issues emerging from the scene of the wound have come to Paul in written or oral form as questions or requests. In response, Paul does not write neat, systematic theology. Rather, he engages in the messy work of practical, even pastoral, theology. His theology is in the service of the being-saved church (1:18; 15:2), not the academy or the theological guild. He speaks in medias res, as all busy pastors do. And he seeks redemptive change; he writes theology in service of the common good (e.g., 12:7); he seeks to build up the community of faith (e.g., chapters 3, 14). In so doing, he consistently seeks to discern the dynamic relationship between theology and wound.

Throughout the letter, Paul engages in the kind of practical theology described by theologian Serene Jones. The apostle is not specifically focused on one of the practical disciplines, such as pastoral care or homiletics. Rather, he approaches theology itself as a practical discipline. As Jones writes,

> It has always seemed to me that any responsible Christian theologian should be, in fact, a practical theologian because— isn't it obvious—the faith we teach is through and through a practical faith. It lives only insofar as it lives in the tissue of our everyday comings and goings, in our practices, and in our

---

6. Fulkerson, *Redemption*, 21.
7. Ibid., 14, 23.

is the character, as Boeve notes, of interruptions. There is a twofold dynamic at work—both continuity and discontinuity. What is interrupted—in this case, the old age—does not cease actively and even persuasively to exist. At the same time, however, what is interrupted does not continue as if nothing had happened.[12] There is thus a conflictual dynamic to apocalyptic because of the unsettled, tensive relationship between the old age and the new creation.

> The shortest definition of religion: interruption.
>
> Johan Baptist Metz, *Faith in History and Society: Toward a Fundamental Practical Theology*, trans. J. Matthew Ashley (New York: Crossroad, 2007): 158.

As a result of the apocalyptic interruption, Christians stand at the "juncture of the ages" or the "turn of the ages."[13] We stand "in-between," in a kind of liminal or threshold space where the two ages overlap, where the old is passing away while the new has not yet fully come. This space, like all liminal spaces, is an unsettled space; it is a dynamic, fluid space of movement from one place to another, in this case movement from the old age to the new. And this movement is never complete until the final coming of the new creation.[14]

In this tensive, liminal space, apocalyptic imagination—and theology—is born. Central to this imagination is discernment, which is, according to Paul, the primary gift of the Spirit (2:6–16). Apocalyptic theology, in particular, calls for a kind of bifocal vision—or bifocal discernment.[15] Such discernment holds continuity and discontinuity together in tensive relationship;[16] it *simultaneously* perceives *both* the old-age powers of death continuing their work in the world *and* the life of the new creation, which often remains *hidden* to those who lack the perception to recognize it.

---

12. Boeve, *God Interrupts History*, 42–43.
13. Martyn, "Epistemology," 89, 92; Brown, *Cross and Human Transformation*, 124.
14. For a helpful discussion of liminality, see Charles L. Campbell and Johan H. Cilliers, *Preaching Fools: The Gospel as a Rhetoric of Folly* (Waco, TX: Baylor University Press, 2012), 39–43.
15. The image of bifocal vision comes from J. Louis Martyn. See, for example, Martyn, "From Paul to Flannery O'Connor," 284. The spirituals offer a profound example of bifocal vision. See Luke A. Powery, *Dem Dry Bones: Preaching, Death, and Hope* (Minneapolis: Fortress Press, 2012).
16. Boeve, *God Interrupts History*, 42.

This kind of discernment or perception is inherent in apocalyptic theology. In the New Testament, the Greek term *apokalyptō* involves an unveiling, an uncovering, an unmasking of the invasion of God that has taken place. In English we translate it as "to reveal." Apocalyptic is thus a new kind of discernment, a new kind of imagination. In John's Apocalypse, for example, that is what the "seer" of Patmos offers in the midst of his grotesque, shocking imagery: new perception. The almighty Empire, which claims to be the divine giver of life, is unmasked and revealed to be a violent, dominating, death-dealing beast. And the martyrs killed by the Empire are actually triumphantly singing praises to God. The slaughtered Lamb—the one crucified by the Empire—is actually the one who reigns. The future belongs not to Caesar but to the slaughtered lamb who paradoxically sits on the throne. John is engaged in a battle, to be sure, but a battle for discernment, perception, imagination. And he must have appeared quite foolish to those under the spell of the Empire. For it's not just John's imagery that is wild and crazy. His perception of the world is even more profoundly foolish.

> Discerning signs has to do with comprehending the remarkable in common happenings, with perceiving the saga of salvation within the era of the Fall. It has to do with the ability . . . to see portents of death where others find progress or success but, simultaneously, to behold tokens of the reality of the Resurrection or hope where others are consigned to confusion or despair.
>
> William Stringfellow, *An Ethic for Christians and Other Aliens in a Strange Land* (Waco, TX: Word, 1973; repr. Eugene, OR: Wipf & Stock, 2004), 138–39.

In 1 Corinthians Paul engages in this same kind of apocalyptic imagination. He is uncovering, unveiling God's hidden interruption of the old age in the crucified and risen Christ.

Paul disrupts the conventions and rationalities of the Corinthians. He turns his culture's hierarchies upside down by lifting up folly and weakness in a culture that elevated wisdom (including the mind above the body) and strength (including the male body above the female). Paul seeks a perceptual or imaginative transformation of the Corinthian church, which requires him first to interrupt and dislocate their old-age perceptions in order that new discernment might be born.[17] He seeks to create the liminal space in which those who are "being saved" may discern the new creation in the midst of the old and journey together as an odd, new community.

Apocalyptic imagination is the critical theological context for Paul's emphasis on the folly of the gospel. The radical, disruptive *incongruity* between the in-breaking new creation and the continuing old age creates the foolishness of the Christian witness and life. On the one hand, if the old age had never been interrupted, there would be no gospel folly; people would simply continue to live within the old hierarchies, conventions, and rationalities. On the other hand, if the new creation had fully arrived, there would be no incongruity; the way of Christ would not appear foolish at all but would be fully discerned as the way of life. The apocalyptic context sets the stage for the incongruity between the old age and the new, which is the theological context for the foolish word Paul proclaims.

Similarly, apocalyptic liminality—like apocalyptic incongruity—is the breeding ground for folly. Unsettled, liminal spaces are the very places where fools live and thrive. For fools both instigate and sustain liminality. They "melt the solidity of the world," just as the in-breaking new creation "dissolves" the old age.[18] Fools do not allow life to become narrow or settled or secure. They are all about keeping things fluid and open and on the move. In Paul's terms, they continually remind believers that we are simply "being saved"; we are on the way.

In this threshold space of the fool, Paul's apocalyptic theology not only interrupts the assumptions of the Corinthians, it also unsettles theology itself. Theology at the threshold of the ages is necessarily "double-voiced;" it is bi-vocal as well as bifocal. It will necessarily be characterized by tensions, and even contradictions, as the theologian seeks to negotiate the liminal space where the old age and the new creation overlap and conflict with each other. It should not be surprising if aspects of the apocalyptic theologian's thought remain captive to the old age hierarchies, even as he or she seeks to affirm and proclaim the new. The "powers of this age" (2:6) have

---

17. Brown, *Cross and Human Transformation*, 14, 65–104, 158.
18. Enid Welsford, *The Fool: His Social and Literary History* (Gloucester, MA: Peter Smith, 1966), 223; Brown, *Cross and Human Transformation*, 13.

been interrupted but not yet overcome, and the theologian lives in this tension as much as any other believer.[19] The apocalyptic theologian's insights appear as glimpses of the new creation, even as they often simultaneously remain captive to the assumptions of the old age. Apocalyptic theology lives in the liminal space at the turn of the ages; it sees in a mirror dimly until that day when the old age is fully overcome, and we see face to face (13:12).

Paul's apocalyptic theology is thus a foolish and weak undertaking; it is not fixed or final but unsettled and fluid. It too is on the way from the old age to the new. Tensions and even contradictions need not be avoided or denied but can be recognized with an eye to the glimpses of the new creation that can inform theological reflection today. In a variety of ways—from his own bi-vocal rhetoric to the disclaimers in his letter—Paul signals the tensive character of theology at the turn of the ages, and he highlights the necessary humility of the theologian. Though often not approached in this manner, Paul's theology offers an important challenge and corrective to rigid "iron theologies" that remain unshakeable in their certainty and finality. Paul reminds believers that we need not fear unsettled, transitional times; we need not circle the wagons or shore up the boundaries. At the turn of the ages, such liminal existence is the very character of the Christian life. "Fear not," Paul proclaims to the church. Rather, step boldly and humbly into the liminal space and seek to discern the implications of the new creation in ever new contexts.

Hermeneutical Theology

Paul's apocalyptic theology is also hermeneutical theology.[20] That is, Paul consistently seeks to interpret different "texts"—whether the Hebrew Scriptures or the story of Jesus or Christian experience— for the contemporary situation in Corinth. Here too, Paul's theology

19. "Powers of this age" is my translation. I will explain it further in Chapter 2.
20. Richard B. Hays, First Corinthians, Interpretation: A Bible Commentary for Teaching and Preaching (Louisville, KY: John Knox Press, 1997), 12. Hays has thoroughly examined Paul's hermeneutical theology, particularly his use of texts from the Hebrew Scriptures, both in 1 Corinthians and more broadly. See also Richard B. Hays, Echoes of Scripture in the Letters of Paul (New Haven, CT: Yale University Press, 1989).

lives and moves in an unsettled space known to all preachers—the space between text and context. The hermeneutical character of Paul's theology deepens the liminal character of Paul's apocalyptic theological claims. Indeed, the Greek god Hermes, the god of interpretation, from whom the term "hermeneutics" derives, was an ancient trickster figure, inhabiting the liminal, unsettled space between humans and the gods.[21] He was, in fact, the messenger of the gods; he was the patron "of heralds and what heralds pronounce, their *kērygma*."[22] For Hermes, like other trickster figures, the liminal space is an improvisational, creative, imaginative space—a space where transformation becomes possible. And that is the space of hermeneutics as well, which always moves in-between text and context.

As a hermeneutical theologian, heralding his *kērygma*, Paul aligns himself with Hermes and the figure of the trickster. Working at the unsettled threshold between

> I came to this earth to rearrange it.
> —Winnebago Trickster
>
> Paul Radin, *The Trickster: A Study in American Indian Mythology* (New York: Schocken Books, 1972), 52.

the ages, Paul himself is a kind of trickster figure, crossing cultural boundaries and employing metaphor, hyperbole, parody, and paradox to create a space in which something new might be imagined and a new kind of community might come to life. Paul "rearranges the world," which is the classic work of trickster figures.[23]

Paul's hermeneutical theology is thus simply one more facet of his liminal theology between the ages. Hermeneutical theology is necessarily unsettled theology. It does not begin with universal philosophical foundations but with particular texts that are polyvalent and open to multiple interpretations. Hermeneutical theology is

---

21. Henry Louis Gates Jr. has argued that the West African Trickster, Esu (or Eshu), also a messenger of the gods, is likewise a hermeneutical figure who embodies the indeterminacy of interpretation. Esu becomes the "Signifying Monkey" when he passes from Africa through the middle passage into the liminal situation of Africans in the "New World." See Henry Louis Gates Jr., *The Signifying Monkey: A Theory of African-American Literary Criticism* (New York: Oxford University Press, 1988).

22. Frank Kermode, *The Genesis of Secrecy: On the Interpretation of Narrative* (Cambridge, MA: Harvard University Press, 1979), 1.

23. Further aspects of Paul's role as a trickster will be discussed in chapter 9.

likewise practical theology, which seeks to discern a "fitting word" in ever-new situations.

Although Paul's primary "text" is the story, and, indeed, the body of Jesus, he also interprets the Hebrew Scriptures as he develops his theological claims for the Corinthians.[24] Paul does not tend to use these Scriptural references in the way a contemporary Protestant preacher would use them, as the exegetical source of the sermon. Rather, while he does cite texts as warrants for some of his theological claims, the Hebrew Scriptures function more often as "echoes" that help to frame his theological affirmations.[25] Paul hermeneutically creates figural and metaphorical connections between the Hebrew texts and the Corinthian community. Repeatedly, Paul interprets Jesus and the Christian life through specific texts or more general allusions to Hebrew Scripture.

Importantly, while Paul uses Hebrew Scripture to interpret Jesus throughout his letter, he does not use Jesus to negate or overcome this Scripture. The gospel does not supersede Hebrew Scripture, but these texts themselves proclaim the trajectory of the gospel. Like a good preacher, Paul is a lively, imaginative interpreter, seeking to read the current situation through the lens of certain texts. The character of God, for Paul, is revealed in these Scriptures, so it should not be surprising that Jesus embodies the divine character. Paul thus witnesses in an unsettled liminal space, seeking to hold together his Jewish heritage and the disruptive Messiah he has encountered.

Paul's practice of hermeneutical theology, like all such theology and preaching, is risky, even dangerous, and never final. In claiming the Hebrew Scriptures for the proclamation of the gospel, Paul runs the risk of distorting them in the service of Jesus Christ and the church. And Christian preachers today all too often inappropriately turn the Hebrew Scriptures and Israel into mere preludes to the fulfillment of Jesus and the Christian community. And, of course, Christian preachers also distort the New Testament texts as we seek to interpret them for the present context. Hermeneutical

24. For a discussion of Jesus' body as "text" in both Paul and Julian of Norwich, see Donyelle C. McCray, "The Censored Pulpit: Julian of Norwich as Preacher." (PhD diss., Duke University Divinity School, 2014), 92–136, ProQuest (3681865).
25. See Hays, *Echoes of Scripture.*

theology is always unsettled, developing, changing in new and different contexts; it always risks distortion and even damage, as Paul's use of the creation stories in 1 Corinthians 11:7–10 indicates. Such theology calls for humility and an openness to new insights and interpretations.

The hermeneutical character of Paul's theology, however, is not simply limited to his use of the Hebrew Scriptures. Paul also seeks to interpret other texts for the Corinthian community: the story of Jesus, the crucified and risen body of Jesus, his own experience, and the experience of the Corinthians themselves. Drawing on all these "texts," Paul seeks to relate the gospel to the life of the Corinthian church. Here too, like all good preachers, he stands "in-between" certain texts and the context, and he seeks to speak a fitting word. The hermeneutical character of Paul's theology becomes evident in the fact that Paul's fitting word is never really settled within the Corinthian community itself. Indeed, at times he declares that he does not even have a word from the Lord (e.g., 7:12, 25), and he invites the Corinthians to "judge for yourselves" (e.g., 10:15; 11:13). Of course, he has to write a second letter, and possibly more, to the church.

Hermeneutical theology between the ages involves communal conversation and disagreement, as the dialogical and contentious character of Paul's letter makes clear. Hermeneutically, as well as soteriologically, the Christian community, including Paul, is "being saved" as it seeks to discern the character of the gospel and the Christian life at the turn of the ages. Hermeneutical theology requires the discernment of the Spirit in the in-between places; it calls for humility, rather than rigidity—an important reminder for contemporary theologians and pastors in a divisive time of transition.

Fragmentary Theology

First Corinthians is a theological fragment. The letter is one fragment amid the polyphonic witness of Scripture. Indeed, it is even a fragment within the larger Pauline corpus of letters. In addition, the letter is a theological fragment in the long history of the church's theology. It has contributed to the development of Christian theology and ethics, but its emphases and perspectives are particular and fragmentary—at points probably heretical—within the larger theological traditions of the church.[26] Moreover, this fragmentary nature of the letter is inherent in its character as practical theology. The letter was written in dialogical fashion in response to concerns and issues in the Christian community in Corinth. Paul's theology engages the practices of the Corinthian Christians. He is not attempting to write systematic or dogmatic theology. Rather, he is an active, overworked pastor doing practical theology "on the fly," with, I suspect, little sense that he is writing the final word or, especially, Scripture.

> As a descriptive category, polyphony is a useful model for understanding the nature of the biblical text, one that can avoid some of the distortions of the various attempts to grasp its unity in terms of center, system, and abstract summary. . . . The Bible certainly is not a monologic text. There is no single "author" who coordinates and controls meaning across the whole. One can easily identify a plurality of unmerged voices in the Bible.
>
> Carol A. Newsom, "Bakhtin, the Bible, and Dialogic Truth," *The Journal of Religion* 76, no. 2 (Apr. 1996), 296.

The fragmentary character of the letter, however, exists at an even deeper level. The letter is not simply a theological fragment, but it actually fragments theology itself. The very character of the theology in 1 Corinthians refuses system. Although portions of the letter have often been read as providing order and clarity and even rigid rules for the Christian community, Paul's theology and ethic are in fact quite unsettling. For both crucifixion and resurrection, which frame the letter in chapters 1 and 15, are disruptive, apocalyptic events, which inherently resist systems and fracture wholes. Together, crucifixion and resurrection interrupt old-age structures and create a liminal, threshold space between the ages in which the Spirit freely moves to form and re-form the community. Consequently, Paul's theology, by its very nature, cannot become a system. As New Testament scholar

---

26. Paul, for example, despite some suggestive proto-Trinitarian elements in the letter, appears in places to have a subordinationist Christology (e.g., 11:3, 15:28). See Hays, *First Corinthians*, 192.

Roy Harrisville writes, "The apostle could not master his theology in any ultimate way because it never existed as a system; in fact, it could not, since the event at its core [crucifixion] spelled the death of system."[27]

Paul "writes neither system nor treatise, nor even really a book." Rather, his letters are interventions, and he propounds a speech of "interruption" and "rupture." The folly of Paul's message is the "deadlock" of language. For conventional language, the event of the cross is "genuinely unnamable."

Alain Badiou, *Saint Paul: The Foundation of Universalism*, trans. Ray Brassier (Stanford: Stanford University Press, 2003), 23, 31, 46–47.

Such is the character of Paul's theology of interruption. For Paul, the gospel is not a settled reality that we can bring under the control of our thought or our rhetoric. Rather, as Lieven Boeve notes, the gospel shatters the boundaries of closed narratives and seeks to open us to others: "The whole metaphor and dynamic of the Christian narrative appears to be permeated with the *interruption* of its own narrative, its own identity, and the confrontation with the other, God.... The Christian narrative simply may not become a closed narrative. For precisely then God will break it open again."[28] Paul's gospel interrupts and fractures closed traditions, systems, and narratives (including Christian ones) and simultaneously claims and confounds believers. The cross and resurrection interrupt believers whenever we are tempted to settle down and secure ourselves over against others.[29]

First Corinthians is thus a theological fragment that fragments theology. It is a theological fragment within the polyphonic Scripture, the Pauline corpus, and the long history of Christian theology. It fragments theology through its disruptive, apocalyptic understanding of the crucifixion and resurrection. I will approach the letter from this theological perspective. My interpretation will explore the letter in its fragmentary particularity rather than trying to fit it

---

27. Roy A. Harrisville, *Fracture: The Cross as Irreconcilable in the Language and Thought of the Biblical Writers* (Grand Rapids, MI: William B. Eerdmans Publishing Co., 2006), 108.
28. Lieven Boeve, "The Shortest Definition of Religion: Interruption 3," *The Pastoral Review* 5, (Sept./Oct. 2009): 18–19; italics mine.
29. Boeve, *God Interrupts History*, 48.

> The Christian narrative is
> never allowed to close itself.
> When it does, then the God
> of love breaks the narrative
> open.
>
> Boeve, *God Interrupts History*, 46.

into a more encompassing "Pauline theology" or "biblical theology" or "systematic theology." In part, this approach reflects my orientation and priorities as a homiletician and preacher. I believe preachers are called to engage texts in their radical and odd particularity, without trying to smooth them out by plac-ing them in a larger theological system. In this sense, every sermon, because it grows out of a particular text, is a fragment, a small piece of an ever-evolving mosaic.[30] In their exegetical and homiletical particularity biblical texts interact with each other, both informing and contradicting each other, to make up the polyphonic witness of the Bible. In their particularity these texts inform the larger projects of dogmatic and systematic theology, at times possibly fracturing those projects at their very core. The odd, unsettling particularity of these texts, that is, takes priority over the theological systems within which they are often interpreted and to which they are often subordinated. As preachers and theologians, we approach the texts first in their specificity and then bring them into interaction with the countless other fragments of Scripture and with larger—always frag-mentary—theological projects. From this perspective, one discerns 1 Corinthians to be a more unsettling witness than many might like it to be. But in this destabilizing, unsettling form, 1 Corinthians may also be a most important witness to the contemporary church.

Playing with Élan

In this commentary I seek to engage Paul's practical, apocalyptic, hermeneutical, fragmentary theology. The commentary itself is a fragment, in which I am seeking to discern the dynamic, theological

---

30. Carina Sundberg, "The Sermon as a Fragment of God's Communication," in Lucy Hogan and Theo Pleizer, eds., *Preaching as Picturing God in a Fragmented World*, Studia Homiletica 8 (Delft: Eburon Academic Publishers, 2012), 207–14. My reflection on Paul's letter as a fragment was stimulated by Sundberg's essay.

trajectories in Paul's letter, even as I too stand apocalyptically at the threshold of the ages and hermeneutically between Paul's letter and the contemporary church. In this space, one lives, like Paul, within one further tension: the tension between boldness and humility.

I have written this commentary with the words of the classical pianist Hélène Grimaud echoing in my head: "A wrong note that is played out of élan, you hear it differently than one that is played out of fear."[31] Grimaud's words suggest the spirit called for in this commentary. Like others writing in this Belief series, I am not a technical, biblical scholar. I undoubtedly know just enough to get myself into trouble with the scholarly guild. But the invitation of this series (I hope!) is to write with élan, not with fear, humbly recognizing there will be wrong notes but confidently hoping even wrong notes might stimulate conversation. The series itself is a lively adventure, and I hope this volume will reflect that spirit.

In this way I believe I am simply engaging the character of Paul's own theology. Paul is like a jazz musician who knows well his vital chords and scales and themes. He is always improvising, though, for the particular challenges of his diverse congregations, in this case the church in Corinth. In so doing, he plays with élan, not with fear. Along the way (to speak with élan!), I believe the apostle hits some wrong notes—or at least some inconsistent ones. Indeed, I suspect wrong notes are inevitable when one is engaged in the new and daring theological improvisation Paul undertakes. How would any of us like to write Christian theology with no New Testament, no Rule of Faith, no volumes of Christian ethics? As in jazz, even Paul's "wrong notes," played with passion and conviction, can lead us into new insights, new dialogue, new trajectories. The wrong notes keep us humble and keep us moving, which is the necessary character of theology at the turn of the ages.

So in this commentary I seek to reflect theologically in conversation with Paul's theological vision, rather than simply interpreting Paul's letter. I seek to explore the in-between space of his theology, rather than drawing out specific rules or principles. At times I will explore a chapter in a verse-by-verse or, more often,

---

31. D. T. Max, "Her Way: A Pianist of Strong Opinions," *The New Yorker*, November 7, 2011, http://www.newyorker.com/magazine/2011/11/07/her-way-d-t-max.

section-by-section manner. At other times I will engage a chapter or section through a kind of theological essay. At all times, I will be trying to keep alive Paul's practical, apocalyptic, hermeneutical, fragmentary theology by focusing more on underlying theological trajectories than on specific solutions to presenting problems. From this perspective, Paul's letter to the Corinthians becomes a radical word to the church, both in its theological insights and in its challenge to rigid theological systems and narrow ethical rules.

1:1–2:5
The Apocalyptic Word

River inside the river
World within the world

All we have is words

To reveal the rose
That the rose obscures.
—Gregory Orr[1]

The primary theological interruption in the letter is the foolish, unsettling word of the cross (1:17–25), which radically disrupts the hierarchies, rationalities, and conventions of the old age with the in-breaking new age of God. The folly of the cross interrupts the world's fundamental presuppositions about status, power, and wisdom like the fool in the Roman theater interrupts the neat plot and respected actors on the stage.[2] The word of the cross profoundly "troubles the waters," and the unsettling ripples flow back to the opening words of the letter and forward to all that follows. Moreover, this opening interruption of the cross is matched at the conclusion of the letter by Paul's equally disruptive proclamation of the *resurrection of the body* in chapter 15. Both crucifixion and resurrection create incommensurable realities: *crucified Messiah* and *resurrected body*. Each "perceptually unbalances" the Corinthians and potentially contemporary readers as well.[3] Making things even more complex, crucifixion and resurrection, each disruptive in its own way, are held together in a

---

1. Gregory Orr, "River inside the River," in *River inside the River: Three Lyric Sequences* (New York: W. W. Norton and Company, 2013), 124.
2. L. L. Welborn, *Paul, the Fool of Christ: A Study of 1 Corinthians 1–4 in the Comic-Philosophic Tradition* (London: T. & T. Clark, 2005), 36–37, 149.
3. Alexandra R. Brown, *The Cross and Human Transformation: Paul's Apocalyptic Word in 1 Corinthians* (Minneapolis: Fortress Press, 1995), 158.

tensive relationship as the letter's bookends; neither one ever erases the other. The tension between a "theology of the cross" and a "theology of glory" remains unresolved until the final consummation, the hope for which shapes life at the threshold of the ages.

Through these theological interruptions, Paul creates a liminal space at the threshold of the ages, and he opens the possibility for a new community that transcends the cultural hierarchies and theological divisions tearing apart the church in Corinth. Within this tension between Christ's crucifixion and resurrection, Paul develops the dynamic ecclesiology that shapes his letter: the church is on the way, "being saved" (*sōzomenois*, 1:18; *sōzesthe*,15:2) in the unsettled liminal space between the ages where the Spirit moves to form and re-form the church in the mind of Christ.[4]

The rhetoric of the opening chapter enacts Paul's apocalyptic theology of interruption; form and content reinforce each other. Paul uses "conventional language unconventionally."[5] He employs "destabilizing pairings of opposites": crucified Messiah; wisdom/folly; power/weakness; power/folly.[6] Paul proclaims the gospel with irony and sarcasm, parody and paradox, even laughable incongruities. Through his double-voiced, bi-vocal rhetoric Paul often says two things simultaneously, preventing his hearers from settling down defensively into any one, secure position. Unable to capture or control the disruptive gospel he proclaims, Paul employs rhetoric that is unsettled and open, creating space at the threshold of the ages for the Spirit to move with power. From the incongruities of his words about God's call (1:1; 1:26–31) to his ironic affirmation of the Corinthians' gifts (1:4–9) to his central, paradoxical affirmations about the cross (1:17–25), Paul proclaims God's disruptive grace, which cannot be managed through "eloquent wisdom" (1:17) or human achievements (1:31).

4. *Sōzomenois and sōzesthe* are connected with both crucifixion (1:18) and resurrection (15:2) at the beginning and end of the letter; as will be emphasized throughout this commentary, being saved depicts the dynamic character of the Christian life in the liminal space at the turn of the ages. The term highlights the "futuristic nuance of the present tense;" "salvation is now, but it is also in process, to be completed at the Day of the Lord." See Gordon D. Fee, *The First Epistle to the Corinthians*, The New International Commentary on the New Testament (Grand Rapids, MI: William B. Eerdmans Publishing Company, 1987), 720, n. 32.
5. Brown, *Cross and Human Transformation*, 20.
6. Ibid., 30.

Too often, Paul's theology of interruption has been neglected as the church has interpreted 1 Corinthians. Sections of the letter have been lifted out as final words or clear rules of guidance for the universal church through the ages. Or readers have searched for doctrinal truths or propositions that can be abstracted from the letter for a theological system. But in the threshold space between the ages, the gospel repeatedly interrupts; it is open and on the move. There can be no closed, dogmatic systems. Theological truth here is not univocal or systematic but bi-vocal and dialogical, emerging at the threshold of the ages within the ongoing dialogue of the community of faith, as the dialogical character of Paul's letter suggests. In 1 Corinthians we stand in the liminal, threshold space between the ages, where the Spirit is moving, language is ironic and paradoxical, and believers are being saved while living in hope. Chapter 1, focusing on the folly and weakness of the cross (1:17–25), theologically and rhetorically dislocates the hearers and opens up that space for the remainder of the letter.

> The heteroglossic nature of [Paul's] rhetoric . . . reflects his need to inject the truth of an apocalyptic realm and its discourse into the mist and delusion of a supposedly unified and monolithic discourse of "this world," the world of Greco-Roman, upper-class ideology.
>
> Dale B. Martin, *The Corinthian Body* (New Haven, CT: Yale University Press, 1995), 57.

1:1–3
God's Disruptive Call

The first three words of the letter, easily passed over as a polite introduction, are themselves a radical theological and rhetorical interruption. The very order of the words enacts the interruption of God's call: *Paulos klētos apostolos.* "Paul called apostle." Many of us have read Paul's address so often that his words no longer shock us. But shocking and disruptive they are. Paul-Apostle. By themselves, these are incommensurable realities, as Paul himself confesses toward the end of the letter: "Last of all, as to one untimely born, [the risen

Christ] appeared also to me. For I am the least of the apostles, unfit to be called an apostle, because I persecuted the church of God" (15:8–9). Paul, the violent persecutor of Christians who terrorized the church—Paul, an Apostle of Jesus Christ? It is impossible. If one did not know better, one might burst out laughing at the incongruity of the claim. "Paul" and "Apostle" simply do not belong together in the same sentence according to human possibilities. They can be conjoined in no natural way. Rather, these incommensurable realities—Paul-Apostle—come together only because of a disruptive "call" initiated by God—an interruption of Paul's life and identity reflected in the very order of the words themselves: *Paulos klētos apostolos.*

Paul's identity and mission are thus given by the unsettling, disruptive call of God. The initiative is God's, not Paul's. From the opening words of the letter Paul points to the activity of God as the key to his own and the Corinthians' lives. As his opening words signal, God's call is not simply in continuity with our human stories, providing us with a secure affirmation of our own positions. Rather, God's call is an interruption. As an interruption, God's call does not annihilate Paul's previous identity or tradition or theology; what is interrupted does not cease to exist. However, as an interruption, God's call intrudes on Paul's identity, theology, and mission. The interruption is radical; it cannot be captured by Paul's previous story but reshapes the boundaries and trajectory of that story. God's surprising otherness intrudes in the form of a crucified Messiah and a mission to the Gentile other. Paul thus occupies a tensive, in-between space, no longer possessing the security devices to protect him against God's disruptions. Paul's opening words unsettle the world: *Paulos klētos apostolos.*

Moreover, God's disruptive call creates a profound and unsettling irony in Paul's apostleship. As an apostle, Paul now serves a God who is other than he had imagined; he serves people he could only perceive as enemies. Paul is sent to proclaim the very one he had persecuted. He is sent to serve the very people he had tried to destroy. The call that gives Paul his authority also reminds him of his own misperception and of God's interruption. Paul's authoritative call requires openness to further interruptions, and it prevents the security of boasting. Paul's call from God entails humility. In this humility Paul now calls Sosthenes "our brother," echoing the words of Ananias, whom God sent to Paul and who initially called Paul "brother" (Acts 9:17).

The identity of the Corinthian Christians is likewise grounded in God's disruptive call (1:2). God's call to the church in Corinth carries the same resonance as God's call to Paul. As will be evident throughout the letter, that call invites the church to be interrupted by an unsettling God whose power and wisdom are other than they imagine. That call invites members of the church to be interrupted by others who are different from themselves and may in fact change their understanding of what it means to be faithful. As with Paul, God's call to the Corinthians invites an unsettled openness to change and the vulnerable humility required for relationship. Paul's ecclesiology is not shaped by clear or rigid rules and guidelines but by the unsettling, calling God.

In this liminal space of God's disruptive call, the Corinthians, Paul suggests, live in the theological tension between God's indicative and God's imperative. Paul begins with the indicative. The church at Corinth *is* the church of God, and those called by God *are* sanctified—set apart, made holy—in Christ Jesus (1:2). As a people sanctified in Jesus Christ, the Corinthians are *already* a reconciled people, a set-apart, holy people—an extraordinary affirmation in light of the fractious divisions among them. Paul does not stop there, though. The members of the church in Corinth are called *to be* saints (1:2). Their sanctified life, grounded in the call of God, brings expectations. The Corinthians are called to live into the sanctification that is already their reality in Jesus Christ. They are called to *be* who they *are*. Indeed, it is in this unsettled, dynamic space—the space between the ironic indicative and the challenging imperative—that the church lives into the call of God. In this God-shaped space, as the church is being saved, believers learn to trust in and live by the grace and peace that come "from God our Father and the Lord Jesus Christ" (1:3). Only that word of grace and peace from God will sustain the church in the liminal space at the threshold of the ages.

FURTHER REFLECTIONS
Paul, the Prophet

In this opening chapter, in which Paul emphasizes the proclamation of the Word, his initial emphasis on God's call should be interpreted within the prophetic tradition. Like the prophets before him, Paul's ministry is grounded not in his own wisdom or power but in the call of God.[7] In addition to this apostolic calling, the gift of the Spirit, central to the calling and ministry of the prophet, also plays an essential role in Paul's discernment and proclamation throughout the letter. Moreover, the role of interruption, not only in terms of calling but also in terms of the Word itself, is central to prophetic ministry. Indeed, the prophets were in many ways primarily interrupters, whether they interrupted with a word of judgment or a vision of hope; they too were seeking transformation at the scene of wounds.[8]

In addition, in the opening two chapters, in which Paul holds together the prophetic emphases of call, Word, and Spirit, the apostle directly aligns himself with the prophets by repeatedly citing texts from Isaiah. While these texts provide warrants for Paul's arguments, at a deeper level they align him with the prophetic tradition. For example, at the beginning of his proclamation of the folly of the cross, Paul quotes Isaiah 29:14: "I will destroy the wisdom of the

> In his presentation of his apostolic vocation, [Paul] shares with the classical prophets two characteristics: he is called by the God of Israel to communicate a specific message, and he is "sent" (*apostellō*) in God's name.
>
> Eastman, *Recovering Paul's Mother Tongue*, 68–69.

---

7. On Paul in the tradition of the prophets, see Susan Eastman, *Recovering Paul's Mother Tongue: Language and Theology in Galatians* (Grand Rapids, MI: Wm. B. Eerdmans, 2007), 67–80. Eastman provides a detailed discussion of the various ways, including Paul's suffering, that Paul aligns himself with the prophets, as well as the ways in which his focus on Jesus Christ differentiates him in some ways from the prophets. While focused on Galatians, many of Eastman's insights would also apply to 1 Corinthians, particularly the emphasis on being called and sent.

8. Jennifer Lord has noted that prophetic preaching fundamentally interrupts; see *Finding Language and Imagery: Words for Holy Speech*, Elements of Preaching Series (Minneapolis: Fortress Press, 2010), 24–25.

wise, and the discernment of the discerning I will thwart" (1:19). In chapter 2, where he emphasizes the work of the Spirit between the ages, Paul alludes to Isaiah 64:4 (v. 9)[9] and concludes his discussion of the mind of Christ with words from Isaiah 40:13: "Who has known the mind of the Lord so as to instruct him?" (v. 2:16). All the texts from Isaiah emphasize the necessity of discernment, which is central to Paul's emphasis on Word and Spirit in the opening two chapters. Drawing creatively on these texts, Paul interprets his ministry as prophetic. Called by God and given the gift of the Spirit, Paul speaks a prophetic word to the Corinthians. Like the prophets before him, he seeks to discern and speak a fitting word to address the wound among God's people.

This early alignment of Paul with the prophets is important. Later in the letter, in chapter 14, Paul will emphasize the importance of prophecy over speaking in tongues in the gathered assembly. So at the outset Paul frames his letter and his preaching as prophecy, which is the primary spiritual gift of speech in the community's worship. Paul thus invites the Corinthians to hear his letter in a specific way. And *hear* it they would. The epistle would have been read out loud in the assembly; it would have served as a form of preaching for the community.[10] Indeed, in the understanding of epistolary communication at that time, Paul himself would have been seen as an "absent presence" with the community through the reading of his letter. Paul, that is, would have been prophesying as an "epistolary presence" in the Corinthian church's worship (see 5:3).[11] So Paul at the beginning, anticipating his later emphasis on prophecy, places himself among the prophets. His letter offers a prophetic word for the Corinthian church.

9. "What no eye has seen, nor ear heard, nor the human heart conceived, what God has prepared for those who love him."
10. Richard B. Hays, *The Faith of Jesus Christ*, Society of Biblical Literature Dissertation Series, no. 56 (Chico, CA: Scholars Press, 1983), 264–65. As Hays notes, though they are not identical to sermons, Paul's letters bear a close relationship to preaching.
11. Margaret M. Mitchell, *The Heavenly Trumpet: John Chrysostom and the Art of Pauline Interpretation* (Louisville, KY: Westminster John Knox Press, 2002), 47–49.

1:4–9
Paul's Unsettling Thanksgiving

The tensive character of Paul's message, grounded in the call of God, continues as the apostle gives thanks for the church at Corinth (1:4–9). Paul's thanksgiving has generated conflicting interpretations. Does Paul genuinely praise the Corinthians as being enriched in speech and knowledge of every kind, not lacking in any spiritual gift? (1:5–7) Or does Paul speak ironically, knowing full well that the fractious Corinthians fall far short of the Spirit-inspired "mind of Christ" to which he will call them in chapter 2? In light of the unsettled, disruptive dynamic of the letter, it seems best to view Paul's thanksgiving as both-and. It is true that in Christ the Corinthians have been enriched in speech and knowledge and spiritual gifts. It is also true, however, that these words of thanksgiving can be said only ironically, with a tone that subverts the Corinthians' trust and assurance in these gifts, which have themselves become divisive. That is, the words mean what they say but also mean just the opposite of what they say. Martin Luther might speak here of the paradox of *simul iustus et peccator*—at the same time justified and a sinner. Maybe such an ironic, paradoxical sense of identity is essential not only for the Christians in Corinth but also for Christians today. Because we serve a God who is other than we imagine, who interrupts our certainties and securities, and who calls us to engage with others different from ourselves, we dare not boast. Rather, we affirm our spiritual gifts and accomplishments with humility.

Paul's tone of irony, which he will repeatedly use in relation to both the Corinthians and himself, is an important tone for theology. For theology itself is, like the Corinthians, always being saved; it remains open to interruptions, always moving between the old age and the new. Theology too is *simul iustus et peccator*. Paul actually highlights this character of theology in the closing words of his thanksgiving. He reminds the Corinthians that we wait for the revealing (the apocalypse) of our Lord Jesus Christ (1:7). Christ is not yet fully revealed, as Paul will remind the Corinthians later when he tells them "we see in a mirror, dimly" (13:12). Theologians, like all believers, depend on the assurance that Christ will strengthen us for the journey and present us blameless at the end (1:8). Ultimately, one promise alone forms the goal and end of the Christian journey: the God who has called us is faithful (1:9). God's call and God's faithfulness, not our systems or securities, sustain us on the way.

1:10–17
Paul's Parodic Appeal

Only after his unsettling greeting and thanksgiving does Paul directly address the community's wound and begin to make his appeal. Things are a mess in the Corinthian church. The community of faith is divided: high and low, superior and inferior, honored and shamed, strong and weak. The Corinthians had been blessed with spiritual gifts and knowledge, but these blessings had contributed to the divisions. Sides had formed. Different groups claimed their own superior certainties and securities. "Our gifts are more important than yours." "We have attained a higher wisdom than you." The groups actually began to cluster around different leaders: followers of Apollos, Peter, and Paul. So Paul interrupts the church dynamics. He seeks to unsettle the sides. He calls the Corinthians ever more deeply into the odd reality of God and an open relationship with others.

In appealing for unity among the divided Corinthians (v. 10), Paul rhetorically parodies their cultural complicity, putting into their mouths claims more appropriate for the disciples of popular orators than the followers of Christ. Members of the church remain captive to the hierarchies and status of the old age, clinging to their own securities, rather than trusting the disruptive faithfulness of God. So layer by layer, Paul peels away the securities and certainties dividing the community. Using sarcasm, irony, and paradox, Paul holds a not-so-flattering mirror up to the community so the Corinthians can see what they look like.[12] He is intrusive and irritating as

---

12. Fools regularly employ the metaphor of the mirror, both to puncture people's preconceptions and to reverse their perception of reality. See Charles L. Campbell and Johan

he seeks to interrupt and destabilize the opposing camps and their circled wagons.

Paul begins sarcastically, recounting the claims of the Corinthians: "What I mean is that each of you says, 'I belong to Paul,' or 'I belong to Apollos,' or 'I belong to Cephas.'" Then with a final sarcastic twist, he adds: "or 'I belong to Christ,'" as if Christ is simply one more leader among the others (v. 12). Then he turns to some rhetorical questions dripping with irony: "Has Christ been divided? Was Paul crucified for you? Or were you baptized in the name of Paul?" (v. 13). Through these comments, Paul actually subverts his own authority; he takes himself out of competitive game. He will not participate in the sides.

Then Paul proceeds to disrespect baptism. The sacrament of unity has become divisive, just as the sacraments of baptism and Eucharist continue to be divisive today. People were claiming allegiance to the various leaders who had baptized them. Paul's rhetoric is shocking here. He speaks of one of the sacraments as if it is insignificant. One should imagine Paul's words spoken in mockery: "I thank God that I baptized none of you except Crispus and Gaius, so that no one can say that you were baptized in my name." So there! Oh yeah, he continues in a parenthetical comment, "I did baptize also the household of Stephanas; beyond that, I do not know whether I baptized anyone else" (vv. 14–16). The apostle is not simply forgetful but intentionally dismissive. Baptism becomes an afterthought. It is so unimportant Paul does not even remember the baptisms he performed. Paul thus unmasks and subverts the ridiculous factions dividing the Corinthian community.

Finally, after peeling back the layers of division, the apostle gets to the heart of the matter. He arrives, literally, at his "come-to-Jesus" moment. Paul sets the cross right in the middle of the community. The cross interrupts everything, for there is nothing more unsettling or destabilizing than the cross.

For Christ did not send me to baptize but to proclaim the

H. Cilliers, *Preaching Fools: The Gospel as a Rhetoric of Folly* (Waco, TX: Baylor University Press, 2012), 81–82.

gospel, and not with eloquent wisdom, so that the cross of
Christ might not be emptied of its power.
    For the message about the cross is foolishness to those who
are perishing, but to us who are being saved it is the power of
God. (vv. 17–18)

Paul's rhetoric punctures the presuppositions of the Corinthians
and exposes their cultural captivity. Then Paul turns their gaze away
from themselves and their leaders so they might perceive what God
has done in Jesus Christ. What God has done in Christ is radically
to interrupt the hierarchies, rationalities, and conventions of the old
age through the folly and weakness of a crucified Messiah.

1:18–25
The Apocalyptic Interruption: The Folly and Weakness of the Cross

The folly of the cross proclaimed by Paul is inseparable not only
from an apocalyptic theological context, as was noted earlier, but
also from the scandal of particularity. Only by beginning with the
radical particularity of Jesus, rather than general religious or cultural
assumptions, can Paul proclaim the paradoxical folly of the crucified
Messiah with its full disruptive power. In contemporary theological terms, Paul's theo-logic is what theologian Hans Frei has called
"ascriptive logic."[13] This logic is the link between the story of Jesus
and theological argument in Paul's letter. According to ascriptive
logic, one does not begin with generally acknowledged understandings or categories and then *describe* Jesus through them. Jesus does
not illustrate or refer to general truths—including "truths" about
the Messiah—that people know through other means. Rather, Jesus'
identity is constituted by what he says, does, and undergoes in the
stories. One begins with the particular identity of Jesus rendered
through the stories about him—in this case, his crucifixion. Then
theological categories are ascribed to Jesus in his particularity, often
with radically new meanings. Ascriptive theo-logic is a way of affirming the scandal of particularity.

13. See, for example, Hans Frei, *Types of Christian Theology*, ed. George Hunsinger and William
C. Placher (New Haven, CT: Yale University Press, 1992), 125–26, 142.

This logic leads to Paul's "foolish" proclamation of the cross. In the midst of a culture based on hierarchies of wisdom and honor and power, Paul proclaims the crucified Christ. Theologically, it was unimaginable that the Messiah— the Christ—would be crucified. Philosophically, it was unthinkable that the divine could hang in the flesh on a cross. Politically, it was inconceivable that the Messiah would liberate Israel through crucifixion by the very Empire from which liberation was expected. Culturally, it was impossible that one shamed on the cross could be honored as the Christ.[14] Messiah-Cross. These were incommensurable realities—the ultimate destabilizing pair of opposites. Neither the theological nor philosophical nor political nor cultural imagination could entertain such an idea. It was a scandalous, even blasphemous paradox.[15] It was, in short, foolishness. Indeed, according to some scholars, the translation, "foolishness," is actually too tame. It was, rather, "madness."[16]

> [Jesus] is the subject of his personal predicates and his doings and sufferings, and holds them together, essentially, rather than they him; he is the subject to whom descriptions are ascribed.
>
> Frei, *Types of Christian Theology*, 142.

For Paul, the cross is an apocalyptic interruption or invasion of the old age—the old hierarchies and conventions and rationalities of the world—by the new.[17] As such, the cross unmasks the powers of this age for what they are: not the divine regents of life, but the agents of death.[18] The cross inaugurates the new age or new creation right in the midst of the old. By interrupting the old age with the new, the cross creates a liminal space where people may be liberated from the powers, both to resist their deadly ways and to begin living

14. For a concise description of these issues, see Martin Hengel, *Crucifixion: In the Ancient World and the Folly of the Message of the Cross*, trans. John Bowden (Philadelphia: Fortress Press, 1977), 6–7.
15. Welborn, *Paul, the Fool of Christ*, 23.
16. Hengel, *Crucifixion*, 1.
17. Though their work contains different nuances, see, for example, J. Christiaan Beker, *Paul's Apocalyptic Gospel: The Coming Triumph of God* (Philadelphia: Fortress Press, 1982); J. Louis Martyn, "Epistemology at the Turn of the Ages" and "From Paul to Flannery O'Connor with the Power of Grace," in *Theological Issues in the Letters of Paul* (Nashville: Abingdon Press, 1997), 89–110 and 279–97; and Brown, *Cross and Human Transformation*.
18. The "powers of this age" will be discussed fully in chapter 2.

in the new creation. Discernment is essential. People have to learn to look, to discern the wisdom and power of God in the foolishness and weakness of the cross. People must learn to discern with apocalyptic imagination. In the midst of the old age, the power and wisdom of the cross remain hidden; the cross still appears as weakness and folly. In this threshold space, people of faith must discern with a kind of bifocal vision.[19] Believers must simultaneously perceive the unmasked old age for what it is— the enslaving way of death opposed to God—and the unveiled new age as the liberating, life-giving way of the future. Indeed, the interruption of the cross creates a crisis of perception, dividing those who discern with such bifocal vision (those who are called and being saved) from those who continue to perceive according to the ways of the world (those who are perishing) (vv. 18, 24).[20] People, that is, must discern the cross that the cross obscures. Through his foolish preaching, Paul seeks to create the space in which such discernment may happen.

> "Much Madness is divinest Sense—
> To a discerning Eye—
> Much Sense—the starkest Madness—
> 'Tis the Majority
> In this, as All, prevail—
> Assent—and you are sane—
> Demur—you're straightway dangerous—
> And handled with a Chain—"
>
> Emily Dickinson, *Final Harvest: Emily Dickinson's Poems*, ed. Thomas H. Johnson (Boston: Little, Brown, and Company, 1961), 101.

A closer look at Paul's context reveals more fully the character and depths of the scandalous folly he proclaims through the word of the cross. In Roman society, the cross was understood as a "coarse and vulgar joke," a fact that itself probably sounds scandalous to many

---

19. "Apocalypse" (*apokalyptō; apokalypsis*) means to reveal, unveil, disclose, bring to light. It is distinctively concerned with perception. However, while the emphasis here is on "looking," and while I will employ Martyn's metaphor of "bifocal vision," discernment is *not* simply a visual matter. Many people who cannot physically see are gifted with discernment. Indeed, discernment and perception may come through a variety of senses, and the foolishness of the cross could be captured through various senses. For example, the odor of the cross is rarely mentioned, but the stench of that event surely captures the foolishness of the cross just as powerfully as the sight or the sound of it. How does one smell the fragrant incense of God in the stench of the cross? By "perception" and "discernment" I refer to the entire way in which one observes life, with all the senses at one's disposal.

20. Martyn, "From Paul to Flannery O'Connor," 284.

contemporary Christians.[21] The cross and jokes seem as incommensurable today as "crucified Messiah" seemed at the time of Paul. Crucifixion jokes were prevalent in Paul's day.[22] Crucifixion actually generated different kinds of laughter. For those in positions of privilege and power, for whom crucifixions reinforced their status, the cross invited mocking laughter that trivialized the horrific instrument of execution through which elites maintained their dominance. For the "low and despised," however, the cross created an uneasy laughter, a kind of gallows humor that helped to blunt the horror of the punishment.[23]

Moreover, this grotesque relationship between the cross and the comic went deeper than these different kinds of laughter. A joke was inherent and explicit in the act of crucifixion itself. Crucifixion was intentionally a parody; it was a form of "parodic exaltation"—literally a coarse and vulgar joke.[24] Crucifixion occurred in a society that was fixated on matters of hierarchical rank. The wealthy and powerful elites were considered to be "high"; the poor, the slaves, and the marginalized were viewed as "low," as Paul's own description of such people as "*low* and despised" suggests (1 Cor. 1:28). Maintaining these hierarchical rankings, along with the honor and shame associated with them, was central to the ordering of Greco-Roman society—the very order that was shaping aspects of the Christian community in Corinth. If the "low and despised" overstepped their bounds and got "*above* themselves," crucifixion was the appropriate punishment. Crucifixion intentionally served as a grotesque parody of this inappropriate breach of the hierarchy by those, such as rebellious slaves, who would not stay in their place.

In this gruesome form of punishment, the crucified one is "lifted up" on the cross in a form of mocking exaltation. In this way crucifixion unmasked, in a deliberately grotesque manner, the pretension

---

21. Welborn, *Fool of Christ*, 2.
22. On crucifixion jokes, see Justin Meggit, "Laughing and Dreaming at the Foot of the Cross: Context and Reception of a Religious Symbol?," in *Modern Spiritualities: An Inquiry*, ed. Laurence Brown, Bernard C. Farr, and R. Joseph Hoffmann (Amherst, NY: Prometheus Books, 1997), 63–70.
23. Welborn, *Fool of Christ*, 2, 101.
24. Joel Marcus, "Crucifixion as Parodic Exaltation," *Journal of Biblical Literature* 125, no. 1 (2006): 73–87. The following discussion of the parodic character of crucifixion relies on Marcus's work.

and arrogance of those who had dared to "raise themselves" above their station. Crucifixion mocked the victims' pretensions by raising and fixing them in a tortuously *elevated* state until they died—driving the last nail (and a pun is actually appropriate here) into their lofty pretensions. This ironic raising up of the crucified was the intention of crucifixion; the cross "was designed to mimic, parody, and puncture the pretensions of insubordinate transgressors by displaying a deliberately horrible mirror of their self-elevation."[25]

In addition, as a form of parodic exaltation, crucifixion was often explicitly or implicitly linked with a kind of mock kingship. A common understanding of crucifixion was "enthronement," and the connection between the raising up of the crucified and the raising up of the king made for a good joke. Mocking the crucified as a kind of royal figure was often part of the crucifixion itself. Jesus himself was mocked by the soldiers as a king; they put a robe and crown on him and saluted him: "Hail, King of the Jews!" Then they knelt down in homage to him (Mark 15:17–20). At the cross, a sign was placed above his head reading, "King of the Jews" (Mark 15:26). While on the cross, Jesus was mocked by the passersby, as well as by the religious leaders: "Let the Messiah, the King of Israel, come down from the cross now, so that we may see and believe" (Mark 15:32). Such mockery was not only directly related to the charge against Jesus; it was intrinsic to the act of crucifixion itself. The mocking crowd enacted the parody; they were part of the public performance. The soldiers and the crowds all participated in the coarse and vulgar joke.

The crucifixion of Jesus, however, interrupts this parodic exaltation and calls people to discern something more happening on this particular cross. Moreover, Jesus' crucifixion interrupts his parodic exaltation not with an act of worldly power, which would have simply reinforced the ways of the old age, but in the way of the fool—that is, with irony. With Jesus, there is a double irony at the heart of the cross. The irony of the mock enthronement, intrinsic to crucifixion, is itself ironically mocked. The one who is parodied as "King of the Jews" in his crucifixion is, according to the New Testament witness, in fact the Royal Figure. The cross is his throne. While the degrading

25. Marcus, "Parodic Exaltation," 78.

slave's death of crucifixion seems to be the decisive contradiction of the claim that Jesus is king (indeed, a mockery of that claim), the opposite is in fact true. Jesus' crucifixion is his coronation. In a radical reversal of cultural hierarchies, the "low and despised," weak and foolish one actually reigns. His kingship involves precisely *not* saving himself, as the crowds taunt him to do, but dying on the cross. As the centurion says at the foot of the cross (whether in genuine faith or in a mocking, satiric way we do not know), "Truly this man was God's Son!"—a foolish proclamation if there ever was one (Mark 15:39). This story of Jesus underlies Paul's witness: the foolishness and weakness of the cross is the wisdom and power of God. Through Paul's witness, people must now discern the cross that the cross obscures. For those who *do* discern with the bifocal vision of faith, the real joke is on the powers of this age, who mocked and crucified Jesus (1 Cor. 2:8) but who have unwittingly become participants in his enthronement.

At the heart of this proclamation of the cross is a classic rhetorical trick of the fool: ironic literalism. Through ironic literalism, the fool (a jester, for example) adheres to the *letter* of the language and ignores the *spirit*. By taking the words literally, the fool actually turns the intended meaning on its head—the meaning may even become the *opposite* of what was intended. Fools engage in this rhetorical maneuver all the time. One of the masters of ironic literalism was the German jester/trickster Till Eulenspiegel. Time and time again in the Eulenspiegel tales, as numerous scholars have noted, Eulenspiegel's tricks simply involve taking language literally when other people were using it figuratively. Here is one example: A king once rewarded Eulenspiegel for a trick by telling him he could get his horse "the very best horseshoes." Eulenspiegel then went to the goldsmith and had his horse shod with gold shoes and silver nails. When the king objected to the cost, Eulenspiegel simply replied, "Gracious Sire, you said they were to be the best horseshoes, and that I ought to take you at your word."[26]

Consider a more contemporary example: the housekeeper in the well-known children's books, Amelia Bedelia. Amelia Bedelia is

26. Paul Oppenheimer, ed. and trans., *Till Eulenspiegel: His Adventures* (New York: Routledge, 2001), 43–45.

a master of ironic literalism, though, unlike most fools, she doesn't intend to trick anyone. For example, Amelia's employer tells her to "dust the furniture." So Amelia gets some powder and throws dust all over the tables and chairs. Or Amelia is told to "draw the drapes," so she takes out a pencil and sketchpad and proceeds to draw them. She's told to "pitch a tent," so of course she throws all the poles and nylon into the bushes.[27] Goethe's comment about the tales of Till Eulenspiegel also applies to the stories of Amelia Bedelia: "All the chief jests of the book depend on this: that everybody speaks figuratively and Eulenspiegel takes it literally."[28]

Goethe's comment also describes the rhetorical character of the New Testament witness to Jesus' crucifixion. The empire employs crucifixion figuratively as a parody of exaltation. But Paul, like the other New Testament witnesses, *takes the parody literally*. The meaning of the cross becomes the *opposite* of what the empire intended. The parodic exaltation of empire proclaimed in a figurative way that Jesus was *not* a royal figure worthy of enthronement—no one shamed on the cross could be royalty. Paul, however, takes the parody of exaltation literally and proclaims Jesus' crucifixion as his Messianic enthronement. Paul interrupts the empire's parody with ironic literalism. As New Testament scholar Joel Marcus writes, "Here the mockery that has transformed kingship into a joke encounters a sharper mockery that unmasks it, so that the derision of kingship is itself derided and true royalty emerges through negation of the negation. For many early Christians, this reversal of a reversal, which turned penal mockery on its head, was probably the inner meaning of Jesus' crucifixion."[29] Through ironic literalism, Paul interrupts the old categories and assumptions about hierarchical power and rule. He subverts the claims of the powers of this age through an extreme rhetoric that "pushes the limits of knowing and explodes thinking's border zones. . . ."[30] A "gallows-bird" embodies the divine.[31]

---

27. Peggy Parish, *Amelia Bedelia* (New York: Harper & Row, 1963). See "Amelia Bedelia (book)," Wikipedia, http://en.wikipedia.org/wiki/Amelia_Bedelia_(book), accessed January 20, 2014. I am indebted to several former students for pointing me to Amelia Bedelia.
28. Cited in Oppenheimer, *Till Eulenspiegel*, lxiv.
29. Marcus, "Parodic Exaltation," 87.
30. D. Diane Davis, *Breaking Up [at] Totality: A Rhetoric of Laughter* (Carbondale: Southern Illinois University Press, 2000), 8.
31. Welborn, *Fool of Christ*, 180.

The gospel in 1 Corinthians turns on a complex, coarse, and vulgar joke. The parodic exaltation of crucifixion is, in Jesus' case, literally affirmed. For those who discern with bifocal vision a new kind of laughter is born—the laughter of those who are in on the joke that Jesus plays on the powers of this age. At the deepest level, this laughter is the profoundly theological laughter of unsettled irony. Such laughter signals the inexpressible incongruities at the heart of the gospel. It is the unsettled laughter of those who discern that the cross simultaneously confounds us and claims us. It is laughter in the midst of scandalous paradox, laughter that recognizes the impossibility of ever capturing or controlling the cross in human words or systems. As theologian Jacqueline Bussie writes, such "laughter functions as an apposite extra-linguistic resource for expression of a theology of the cross because a theology of the cross is inherently paradoxical, resistant to linguistic expressibility, and resultant from a collision of narratives." [32]

This network of parodies and ironies is what Paul gestures toward in his stammering, paradoxical proclamation about the foolishness and weakness of the cross: wisdom is folly and folly is wisdom; weakness is power and power is weakness; and, even, foolishness is power (vv. 18–25). The cross invades the world like a fool who can never be controlled by human wisdom or rhetoric but is always disorienting us and humbling us, inviting us to rely on its odd power rather than our own. The liminal space created by Paul's destabilizing pairs of opposites is always unsettling; it is never something we can master. That is why Paul cannot preach with "eloquent wisdom" (v. 17). Such preaching would limit the "power of the cross." For such rhetoric seeks to manage the liminal space created by the interruption of the cross; it seeks to make the cross reasonable and effective by human efforts, often by plugging it into a theological system or atonement theory. When that happens, the cross becomes dependent on the theologian or the preacher, who is so busy trying to "save" the cross that it can no longer save us. As Paul discerns, only in its out-of-control foolishness, its paradoxical weakness, and its nonsensical otherness does the cross have real power. Only as

---

32. Jacqueline Bussie, *The Laughter of the Oppressed: Ethical and Theological Resistance in Wiesel, Morrison, and Endo* (New York: T. & T. Clark, 2007), 122.

it fools us can the cross save us. So Paul must give up a rhetoric of control for a rhetoric of risk.[33] Such rhetoric can create the possibility for new perception. It can create a space in which people can begin to move from the old age to the new. Finally, however, Paul, like every other preacher, is left with no other foundation than the event of Jesus Christ and the "power of the cross."

1:26–31
The Folly of God's Call

At the end of this opening chapter Paul returns to God's call to the Corinthians, now refracted through the lens of the folly of the cross.

> What is my word, what is
>   human wisdom
>   but a noise that reaches the
>   outer ear?
> But from that ear to the heart
>   lies a road
>   that only God can travel.
> Blessed the preacher
>   who does not put his trust
>   in the noise of his own words,
>   even though they come
>   wrapped in great human
>   wisdom.
>
> Oscar Romero, *The Violence of Love* (Maryknoll, New York: Orbis Books, 2004), 36.

Through this lens, the radical, surprising, and disruptive character of God's call becomes even more apparent. In fact, God's call to the Corinthians serves as a kind of experiential "proof" of the disruptive and paradoxical wisdom and power of God enacted on the cross:

> Consider your own call, brothers and sisters: not many of you were wise by human standards, not many were powerful, not many were of noble birth. But God chose what is foolish in the world to shame the wise; God chose what is weak in the world to shame the strong; God chose what is low and despised in the world, things that are not, to reduce to nothing things that are, so that no one might boast in the presence of God. (vv. 26–29)

Just as Jesus Christ was elevated on the cross as one of the low and despised in the world, so God has called the low and despised to be the church, the Body of Christ. God's call to the Corinthians

---

33. This dichotomy is adapted from Sharon Welch, who distinguishes between an ethic of control and an ethic of risk. Sharon D. Welch, *A Feminist Ethic of Risk*, rev. ed. (Minneapolis: Fortress Press, 2000).

interrupts the hierarchies, presuppositions, and conventions of the old age as radically as the folly of the cross. Those whom the world would shame are in fact honored and called by God. Indeed, the very categories of honor and shame, so central to Roman culture, are radically interrupted and subverted. The call of the low and despised actually shames the wise and powerful elites whom the culture holds in honor (vv. 27–28). Though there are clearly culturally elite people in the church ("not many of you," Paul says, were wise or powerful or of noble birth; v. 26), God does not simply call the wise and power-ful. Rather, God also calls those whom the world considers foolish and weak to make up the Body of Christ. Just as this call disrupts cul-tural hierarchies and conventions, so it will interrupt the Corinthian church wherever it remains complicit with and captive to those hier-archies and conventions.

God, in fact, accomplishes in God's call precisely what hap-pens on the cross. The church itself embodies an interruption of the culture's hierarchical categories of high and low, honored and shamed, wise and foolish, powerful and weak. The very ones who could have been parodically lifted up on the cross for "step-ping above their station" have now been lifted up by the call of God. The Body of Christ itself is a "coarse and vulgar joke" that interrupts the rigid hierarchies of the body politic. Because of the disruptive call of God, the church itself becomes the fool in the Roman theater who interrupts the elite actors on the stage and disorients the drama.

As in Paul's case, there is also a deep irony at the heart of this calling. God's call, which elevates the foolish and weak, simultane-ously reminds the church of the source of its life: God in Jesus Christ (v. 30). The elevation of the low and despised by God is the very act that precludes all boasting. Christ is the source of life; Christ is, indicatively, the Corinthians' righteousness, sanctification, and redemption (v. 30). In Christ the Corinthians *are* in right relation-ship with God (righteousness); in Christ the Corinthians *are* holy (sanctification); in Christ the Corinthians *have been* set free from the powers of this age to live in the new creation of God (redemp-tion). These extraordinary indicatives, however, bring with them an inescapable imperative: humility. No boasting. Indeed, how could one boast following the cruciform interruption of God, who is the very source of life?

Paul's theology of interruption, grounded in God's disruptive call and Christ's ironic crucifixion, is a theology that prevents boasting. Paul's theology of interruption counters the kind of secure, closed theological boundaries that create hierarchies and victims. Though Paul's rhetoric at times seems simply to invert who is honored and shamed, in fact Paul ultimately seeks to break down the oppositional binaries that divide people and create "sides" within the Christian community. In the liminal space between the ages, where believers are being saved, there is no room for boasting and no place for "sides." This space is the space of a new form of community, as Paul will develop throughout the letter. Paul's theology keeps the church on the way, constantly reminded of the "dangerous memory" of God's cruciform interruption, which calls for an ongoing openness to ever new interruptions by God and by other people. Through this apocalyptic theology, Paul begins to address the wound at the center of the Corinthian church.

> A drunk, so the story goes, crossed the street to accost a perplexed pedestrian and asked, "I shay, which is the other shide of the street?" Nonplussed the pedestrian replied, "That side of course!" "Shtrange," said the drunk, "when I wash that shide, they shaid it was thish shide."
>
> Desmond Tutu, *Hope and Suffering: Sermons and Speeches* (Johannesburg: Skotaville, 1983), 111.

2:1–5
Paul's Parody of the Orator

Having reminded the Corinthians of their own call, Paul now reminds them of his preaching among them. He begins by reminding them that he came proclaiming (*katangellōn*) "the mystery of God" (*to mystērion tou theou*) (2:1). The term for "proclaim" here is different from the more familiar terms used earlier (*euangelizō*, 1:17; *kērygma* [proclamation], 1:21; *kēryssō*, 1:23). *Katangellō* implies an over-against-ness, a conflict, even a battle; it is a polemical term for

Paul.[34] It is a disruptive word, reflecting the apocalyptic interruption that Paul proclaims. And what disrupts is the *mystery of God*. This genitive construction should probably be read both as an objective and a subjective genitive. As an objective genitive God is the object of the mystery; the mystery concerns God. As the subjective genitive, God is the subject of the mystery, the agent of the mystery, which is equally important for Paul. God's apocalyptic in-breaking takes the form of a mystery, which has a hidden quality to it and calls for discernment and new perception.

Moreover, the mystery of God is not to be understood in some general way, as if God were some unfathomable, transcendent reality to be explored by human wisdom. Indeed, Paul here is probably challenging the spiritual inclinations of some of the elite Corinthians who trust in human wisdom to penetrate divine mysteries. According to Paul, however, the mystery of God is enacted on the cross. To proclaim (*katangellō*) this mystery involves knowing nothing but Jesus Christ and him crucified (2:2). Paul's conception of mystery is paradoxical; it disrupts cultural uses of the term. This mystery is embodied in Jesus Christ on the cross; it is a scandalously particular action of God. Yet, precisely in its particularity, it remains a destabilizing mystery, not solvable by human wisdom. Indeed, Paul here undercuts all confidence in human wisdom to rise to the divine.

God's apocalyptic interruption of the old age invites a reconsideration of God's transcendence. Theologians often speak of God's transcendence as if God were simply some mysterious "Other" whom we humans can never understand. For Paul, however, the mystery of God, God's transcendence, invades the world in the very scandal of the cross. God's embodied power-in-weakness and wisdom-in-folly interrupt human assumptions about God with a mystery beyond our conception, calling for ever new discernment. God's transcendence is not somehow beyond the human or earthly but is revealed (apocalypsed) precisely within the particular, embodied humanity of Jesus Christ. As a result, Paul cannot proclaim this mystery with "lofty words or wisdom" (v. 2:1); that would reflect the culture's presuppositions about mystery and the way to enter into it. Rather, Paul

34. Brown, *Cross and Human Transformation*, 101.

can only preach Jesus Christ and him crucified—for he is the very embodied, enacted mystery of God.

Moreover, the mode of Paul's proclamation, his presence as a preacher, also enacts the mystery he proclaims. As an orator, Paul embodies the gospel he preaches; he comes not with a wisdom and power of his own but in the foolishness of the cross and a weak rhetorical presence (2:3–4). Just as God's call to the low and despised interrupts the wisdom and power of the old age, so Paul's presence and preaching among the Corinthians interrupt cultural conceptions of the orator. In describing his presence among the Corinthians, Paul actually parodies the confident figure of the popular rhetorician, who speaks with lofty words of plausible wisdom, persuading his audience through his impressive person and rhetorical skill. Paul, on the other hand, comes with a most implausible message and presence (v. 4). He speaks only a weak and foolish word: Christ crucified. He does not display the culturally honored kind of ethos or character that enables a speaker to be trusted, to win a hearing, and thereby to persuade his audience.

Rather, Paul comes in weakness and fear and trembling (v. 3). As homiletician Andre Resner argues, Paul embodies a kind of "reverse-ethos" or "ironic ethos." His character is shaped not by cultural norms but by the criteria of the gospel.[35] Paul is in fact a living parody of the popular orator.[36] His scandalous rhetorical presence, one might say, is an enacted mystery. His person and his message are one. Just as the foolishness of the gospel requires bifocal vision and discernment, so Paul himself, the parodic orator, calls for discernment on the part of his hearers. Just as believers must see the ironically literal truth of

> Paul's strategy . . . in reestablishing his own authority as a preacher to whom the Corinthians should listen, is to reframe their categories of orator evaluation by way of a new framework for discernment which has been revealed in the cross.
>
> Resner, *Preacher and Cross*, 99.

---

35. See Andre Resner, *Preacher and Cross: Person and Message in Theology and Rhetoric* (Grand Rapids, MI: Wm. B. Eerdmans Publishing Co., 1999), 83–131. Resner provides a thorough treatment of the various understandings of the orator's ethos or character.
36. Welborn, *Paul, the Fool of Christ*, 90–99.

Jesus' parodic exaltation on the cross, so Paul's hearers must similarly discern in Paul the orator that the orator obscures.

That discernment happens only in the power of the Spirit, whom Paul first mentions in 2:4. Paul's preaching is powerless apart from the Spirit. Once again, the theology of interruption that shapes the opening section of Paul's letter leads back to God's initiative and activity. Just as there is no room for boasting among those whom God has called, there is no room for boasting by the preacher. The preacher comes in weakness with a foolish gospel. Faith can thus never rest on the rhetorical skills or charismatic person of the preacher. Rather, the bifocal vision and discernment of faith depend solely on the power of God through the work of the Spirit.

Paul thus opens his letter with a wild and disruptive apocalyptic Word. Theologically and rhetorically he unsettles the Corinthian church with the gospel. Such an interruption is critical for addressing the community's wound. In his initial words, Paul seeks to break through the destructive old-age ways of the Corinthians. He seeks to create the possibility for new theological imagination, discernment, and perception. So he interrupts the old-age hierarchies and conventions that were dividing the church in Corinth. He creates a threshold space between the ages in which the Spirit might move to form and re-form the church. Having come onto the stage at the conclusion of Paul's opening theological interruption, the Spirit now takes center stage in Paul's theological vision and will continue to move disruptively and creatively throughout the rest of the letter.

2:6–16
The Power of the Spirit

In the opening chapter Paul develops a dynamic apocalyptic theology of interruption. First, he proclaims an apocalyptic gospel that *interrupts* the hierarchies, rationalities, and conventions of the old age with the new age that has invaded the world in the call of God and the cross of Jesus Christ. Second, Paul interrupts the old-age *perceptions* of the Corinthians in order to call them to radically new imagination and perception shaped by the new age that has broken into the world. Finally, through this gospel interruption, Paul rhetorically creates a *liminal, threshold space* between the ages, in which the church is being saved as it lives in the tension between the old age and the new.

In the second chapter, Paul delineates the theological dynamics of the liminal space in which the church is called to perceive and live anew. That space is shaped by a struggle between two competing, even battling, realities: the powers of this age and the Spirit of God. In the unsettled, liminal tension between these two realities, the initial gift of the Spirit is the gift of discernment.

The Powers of This Age

The "powers of this age" (*tōn archontōn tou aiōnos toutou*; 2:6, 8) are an active presence throughout Paul's letter, sometimes referred to by explicit terms for the powers (e.g., *archontōn, exousia, dynamis*; see 15:24), though at other times implicitly referred to as "the world" (*kosmos*; 2:12) or "flesh" (*sarx*; 5:5) As was noted earlier, although the new age has interrupted the old, the old age has not yet been fully overcome but continues its deadly work through the activity of the powers of this age. Paul first mentions the powers of this age here at the beginning of his treatment of the threshold space between the ages, making clear their important, ongoing role. He emphasizes their direct opposition to the way of Christ and their consequent conflict with the Spirit of God who moves in the threshold space between the ages. The continuing activity of the powers becomes clearer in chapter 15, where Paul proclaims that Christ overcomes these powers only at the end before handing the reign over to "God the Father" (15:24). The activity of the powers and Christian resistance to them in the power of the Spirit is thus the central dynamic of life at the threshold of the ages.

Paul highlights several dimensions of the *archontōn tou aiōnos toutou* in his brief reference to them in 2:6–8. First, the powers have a structural, systemic, institutional dimension.[1] *Archontōn* as a term refers to the structural organization of power. The root of the word, *arch*, is still used in English for various organizations of power: for example, mon*arch*y, patri*arch*y, and hier*arch*y. In 1 Corinthians hier*arch*ical structures represent a central aspect of the powers work that Paul confronts. The NRSV's translation, "rulers," is thus inadequate, giving the sense that *archontōn* refers to individual persons serving as rulers. That is not the case; even if a particular ruler is in mind, he or she is always a person in an office within a structure or organization of institutionalized power. That structure often exercises more power than the person occupying the office, as can be seen in people who begin to change when they assume an office. I have thus chosen to use the more general term, "powers," which encompasses the work of the various *archontōn tou aiōnos toutou*.

Second, the powers are plural: *archontōn*. They are *legion*.[2] Paul does not speak here of the single, unified power of "empire." He speaks of a multiplicity of powers that impinge on people, including

---

1. Walter Wink, *Naming the Powers: The Language of Power in the New Testament* (Philadelphia: Fortress Press, 1984), 13–15. For a fuller discussion of the powers of this age, see Charles L. Campbell, *The Word before the Powers: An Ethic of Preaching* (Louisville, KY: Westminster John Knox Press), 2002. My work relies on that of Walter Wink and William Stringfellow. See, for example, Walter Wink, *The Powers That Be: Theology for a New Millennium* (New York: Doubleday, 1998); and William Stringfellow, *An Ethic for Christians and Other Aliens in a Strange Land* (Waco, TX: Word, 1973; repr. Eugene, OR: Wipf & Stock, 2004).

2. Stringfellow, *Ethic for Christians*, 77–78.

believers, and seek to hold them captive. The powers are "potent, mobile, and diverse."[3] Their activity is akin to Foucault's understanding of power, which is omnipresent, "not because it embraces everything, but because it comes from everywhere."[4] The result is chaos, as the legion of powers struggle for survival and domination.

> [People] are veritably besieged, on all sides, at every moment simultaneously by these claims and strivings of the various powers, each seeking to dominate, usurp, or take a person's time, attention, abilities, effort; each grasping at life itself; each demanding idolatrous service and loyalty. In such tumult it becomes very difficult for a human being even to identify the idols which would possess him [or her].
>
> Stringfellow, *Ethic for Christians*, 90.

Third, the *archontōn tou aiōnos toutou* are not simply human structures and systems. While a case can be made that Paul is referring to human agents in 2:6–8, and while such agents certainly participate in Jesus' crucifixion, the powers of this age have a spiritual, even demonic, dimension to them.[5] The individual rulers of Jesus' day who participated in his crucifixion (e.g., Pilate, the religious leaders, etc.) simply cannot carry the weight of the phrase, "powers of this age." Those rulers are either no longer in office or dead by the time Paul writes. According to Paul these powers are still active in the present—and will continue to be until the end. They have both a structural dimension and a spiritual aspect. Although various interpreters have sought to emphasize one dimension to the exclusion of the others, there is a both-and character to the *archontōn*: they are both material and spiritual.

So we speak correctly, for example, of the "spirit of capitalism." Capitalism not only is embodied in institutions but also has a spirit or driving force that animates it, often directing institutions and holding captive individuals. One of John Steinbeck's characters in

3. Ibid., 79.
4. Michel Foucault, *The History of Sexuality*, vol. 1, *An Introduction*, trans. Robert Hurley (New York: Vintage Books, 1990), 93. See also David Toole, *Waiting for Godot in Sarajevo: Theological Reflections on Nihilism, Tragedy, and Apocalypse* (Boulder, CO: Westview Press, 1998), 220–22.
5. See Wink, *Naming the Powers*, 40–45.

The Grapes of Wrath describes this spiritual force that drives the bank and holds captive even those in "power":

> If a bank or a finance company owned the land, the owner man said, The Bank—or the Company—needs—wants—insists—must have—as though the Bank or the Company were a monster, with thought and feeling, which had ensnared them. These last would take no responsibility for the banks or the companies because they were men and slaves, while the banks were machines and masters all at the same time. Some of the owner men were a little proud to be slaves to such cold and powerful masters.

The owner continues his explanation of the bank's driving spirit:

> A man can hold land if he can just eat and pay taxes; he can do that.
>
> Yes, he can do that until his crops fail one day and he has to borrow money from the bank.
>
> But—you see, a bank or a company can't do that, because those creatures don't breathe air, don't eat side-meat. They breathe profits; they eat the interest on money. If they don't get it, they die the way you die without air, without side-meat. It is a sad thing, but it is so. It is just so.[6]

In dealing with the *archontōn tou aiōnos toutou*, one must not only engage the structural, systemic, and institutional embodiments of power but also the spiritual forces behind and within them. Paul will engage the powers of this age in precisely this way, not only in his emphasis on the Spirit of God in chapter 2, but also in chapter 12, where he interrupts the driving hierarchical spirit of the Roman "body politic" with the different Spirit that forms the Body of Christ.

This spiritual dynamic of the powers can be discerned not simply in the character of the powers themselves but in the ways they operate on people. As Paul notes, the powers seek to instill their own "wisdom" (2:6), which is opposed to the wisdom of the gospel. The powers work on human minds, spirits, and imaginations, seeking to hold human beings captive to their "wisdom." Indeed, this spiritual

---

6. John Steinbeck, *The Grapes of Wrath*, Penguin Great Books of the Twentieth Century (New York: Penguin Books, 1999), 31–32.

captivity is often the deepest form of human captivity. If the powers control human spirits and imaginations, they do not need to exercise control in more physical ways. If the spirit of capitalism, for example, becomes common wisdom, shaping imaginations so that everything, including persons, becomes a commodity, and power is understood in terms of wealth and status, then no other forms of control are necessary. Everyone already goes along with the powers. In this sense, captivity to the powers of this age is the fundamental reality from which people need to be redeemed (1:30). Indeed, for Paul, sin itself is a form of this captivity; sin is not primarily bad individual actions but rather a power that holds people in its grip. This is why it is so important for Paul to interrupt the "wisdom" of the *archontōn tou aiōnos toutou* with the gospel that the powers consider foolish. Only then will freedom from captivity and new perception be possible.

Paul highlights this spiritual dimension of the powers when he writes about the "spirit of the world" (*to pneuma tou kosmou*) that is opposed to the Spirit of God (2:11–12). The term for "world," *kosmos*, is itself tensive and bi-vocal. It can and does mean God's creation in the broadest sense, and it does carry that sense here, reminding readers that, despite Paul's dualistic apocalyptic emphasis on the two ages, there is no ultimate dualism at work. Nothing is outside God's creation or God's purposes. In this instance, however, *kosmos* also carries a more specific and negative meaning. In 2:12 Paul refers to the world in its rebellion against God's ways.[7] *Kosmos* is the system organized and driven by the powers of this age; it is what Walter Wink has called the "Domination System."[8] In this sense, *kosmos* reflects the will of the powers to dominate human beings, as well as the hierarchical arrangements that develop among human beings themselves. The *kosmos* is a world of honored and shamed, high and low, superior and inferior, strong and weak. It is the system that engages in the parodic exaltation of crucifixion in order to reinforce the hierarchical power arrangements and punish those who step out of place. In the Corinthian church captivity to the *kosmos* inevitably

---

7. Walter Wink, *Engaging the Powers: Discernment and Resistance in a World of Domination* (Minneapolis: Fortress Press, 1992), 51–59.
8. Ibid., 51.

leads to boasting in one's more honored, superior status, whether that status is claimed for social or spiritual reasons.

Although embodied in structures and institutions, the *kosmos*, as Paul recognizes, also has a spiritual dimension. The *pneuma tou kosmou* ("spirit of the world") is the "spiritual atmosphere" that drives the world in rebellion and takes human spirits captive.[9] The spirit of the world shapes and limits human perception. It becomes the air people breathe, so they cannot even imagine alternatives to its dominating and destructive ways. As Walter Wink writes, the *pneuma tou kosmou* is "the 'surround' constellated by fields of forces in rebellion against God . . . a pseudo-environment that ascribes to itself absoluteness and permanence and thus, by simply appearing to be, wins from all who submit to it their total and unwitting obedience." Indeed, the spirit of the world "'kills' us precisely because we 'breathe' it in before we even realize it is noxious. Like fish in water, we are not even aware that it exists, much less that it determines the way we think, speak, and act."[10] In the *kosmos* the cross as power and wisdom is simply an impossibility. A crucified Messiah is an unimaginable reality. So the spirit of the world must itself be interrupted by another Spirit, by the fresh air of God breathed into believers, setting us free, giving us life, and enabling new discernment at the threshold of the ages.

Fourth, the *archontōn tou aiōnos toutou*, driven by the spirit of the world, crucified Jesus—an extraordinary affirmation (2:8). God did not crucify Jesus. Individual human beings did not crucify Jesus. Rather, the powers of this age crucified Jesus. Unable to discern the foolish wisdom of God hidden in Jesus because of their own rebellious wisdom and perception, the powers kill him. This one little sentence contains some huge theological implications. To begin with, although Paul does not tell the story of Jesus' life and ministry, the apostle suggests that Jesus' death in some way results from his resistance to the powers of this age. The *archontōn*, in both their material and spiritual manifestations, only crucify someone who threatens them, who "steps out of his place" and challenges their authority and dominion. Only for such a person is the parodic exaltation of

9. Ibid., 53.
10. Ibid., 84.

crucifixion necessary. Jesus, Paul implies, lives free from the powers of this age; they cannot capture his spirit. He interrupts their dominion. So the powers must put him to death.

In addition, this interpretation of Jesus' crucifixion suggests that understandings of the atonement that implicate the first person of the Trinity in Jesus' death, as if God required a vicarious sacrifice or a substitutionary victim, are theologically misguided, not to mention pastorally dangerous. Here Jesus' crucifixion is a result of his *conflict* with the powers of this age, not the consequence of God's demanding bloody justice or filial sacrifice or legal satisfaction. The powers of this age, not God, crucify Jesus. To the extent that Jesus' death is a sacrifice, it is because of his active resistance to the powers in order to interrupt them and set people free from their captivity.

Through his death, moreover, Jesus "fools" the powers, as Paul proclaims in chapter 1 (see 1:17–25). Some early theological interpretations of the cross captured this understanding of Jesus' crucifixion. In these interpretations, Jesus is presented as a kind of trickster, who lures the devil into crucifying him in order to expose the devil and overcome him in a surprising and unexpected way.[11] In crucifying Jesus the powers of this age are themselves exposed for what they are—not the divine regents of life, as they would like to claim, but the opponents of God and the purveyors of death. Their moment of triumph is in fact ironically the beginning of their end. Their wisdom is unmasked as folly, their power as weakness. Those who have the Spirit of discernment are set free from captivity.

Fifth, as the crucifixion of Jesus reveals, the powers of this age rely on violence. Indeed, a central dimension of the spirit of the world is what Walter Wink calls the "myth of redemptive violence."[12] According to this myth, the way to bring order out of chaos is through

---

11. See Gustav Aulén, *Christus Victor: A Historical Study of the Three Main Types of the Idea of the Atonement*, trans. A. G. Hebert (New York: MacMillan, 1951), 47–55. Jesus lures the devil into his trap by playing on the devil's uncontrollable "appetite" for human beings, which causes the devil to overstep his bounds and crucify Jesus. These are classic themes in trickster narratives. See Lewis Hyde, *Trickster Makes This World* (New York: North Point Press, 1998), 17–80. Strikingly, Gregory of Nyssa even refers to Jesus as a kind of "fish-hook," or "bait" used to catch the devil on the cross (Aulén, *Christus Victor*, 52). In Homeric Greek, "trick" is *dolos*, and the oldest known use refers to a quite specific trick: baiting a hook to catch a fish (Hyde, *Trickster Makes This World*, 18). The link between this understanding of Jesus' work on the cross and the figure of the trickster is intriguing.
12. Wink, *Engaging the Powers*, 13–31.

violence; the way to deal with threatening enemies is ultimately to kill them. This myth is not simply an ancient one; it continues to hold imaginations captive today. *New York Times* columnist Maureen Dowd reflected our captivity to this myth (as well as the folly of the cross!) after the killing of Osama Bin Laden. "Only fools or knaves," she wrote, "would argue that we could fight Al Qaeda's violence non-violently."[13] Following the mass killing at the elementary school in Newtown, Connecticut, Wayne LaPierre, the executive vice president of the National Rifle Association, stated the myth of redemptive violence in its starkest form: "the only thing that stops a bad guy with a gun is a good guy with a gun."[14] So wars and drone strikes and special tactical units become woven into the fabric of our lives, and over thirty thousand people a year are killed with guns in the United States (then some of the killers are executed). The spiral of violence continues. The title of a recent book sums it up succinctly: *How Everything Became War and the Military Became Everything*.[15] The violent spirit of the world not only crucified Jesus but continues to hold people captive today.

Paul himself understood the myth of redemptive violence all too well, not only as he witnessed the violence of the *Pax Romana*, including crucifixions, but also in his own life. He himself had tried to deal with the chaos created by followers of Christ by violently persecuting them (15:9; Gal. 1:13). His own imagination had been captive to the spirit of the world. But God's call interrupted Paul and set him free from the myth of redemptive violence. After his call, Paul no longer resorted to persecution but relied solely on the Word (Acts 9:20; Gal. 1:23).

Sixth, as the crucifixion of Jesus also reveals, the *archontōn tou aiōnos toutou* are the powers of death, not life. In chapter 15, where Paul returns to the powers of this age, he speaks of death as the "last enemy" (15:26), for death is the ultimate weapon and sanction

13. Maureen Dowd, "Killing Evil Doesn't Make Us Evil." *New York Times*, May 7, 2011, http:// www.nytimes.com/2011/05/08/opinion/08dowd.html?_r=1&ref=maureendowd.
14. Wayne LaPierre, "NRA Press Conference, December 21, 2012," http://www.npr .org/2012/12/21/167824766/nra-only-thing-that-stops-a-bad-guy-with-a-gun-is-a-good -guy-with-a-gun.
15. Rosa Brooks, *How Everything Became War and the Military Became Everything: Tales from the Pentagon* (New York: Simon and Schuster, 2016).

of the powers; they will put to death any who oppose their desire for domination. Importantly, the death wielded by the powers is broader than mere physical death. At times, the powers will crudely and directly resort to physical death—as they did on the cross, and as they did, apparently, with Paul himself. But this death also takes more subtle forms. It includes the death of our humanity, the death of our "moral conscience," the death of our imagination, the death of the creation God intends us to be.[16] Like the owners described by Steinbeck, people become servants of the powers, doing what they hate but unable or unwilling to resist. They go along, give up, stay busy, become numb. In so doing, they die. The spirit of the world kills people. In the deepest sense the powers of this age are the powers of death.[17]

Finally, Paul proclaims, the *archontōn tou aiōnos toutou* are "doomed to perish" (2:6). The powers of this age, though in rebellion against God, are not outside God's purposes; they cannot ultimately defeat God's way. In the end, God will overcome them; they will perish. *How* God overcomes them remains open at this point and will be addressed only in chapter 15. Theologically, however, we should assume that the means by which God overcomes the rebellious powers will be consistent with the foolish wisdom and weak power enacted in Jesus Christ. Having refused at the cross to resort to the means of death employed by the *archontōn,* Jesus Christ will surely not resort to those means as he overcomes the powers at the end. While difficult to imagine—possibly because our imaginations have become so captive to the myth of redemptive violence—we should expect the powers to "perish" in an odd and ironic way at the end, overcome by the "foolish" and "weak" way of Jesus, rather than by a resort to their own means of death.

At the threshold of the ages, the *archontōn tou aiōnos toutou,* although exposed and ultimately overcome by Jesus, continue actively to pursue their deadly ways. Paul is under no illusions: the old age has been interrupted but not yet been fully overcome; the

---

16. Stringfellow, *Ethic for Christians,* 106; Sharon Welch speaks of the death of the moral imagination; see *A Feminist Ethic of Risk,* rev. ed. (Minneapolis: Augsburg Fortress Press, 2000), 11–64.
17. Stringfellow, *Ethic for Christians,* 67–94.

powers continue to impinge on believers. Nevertheless, in Jesus Christ the new age has broken into the old, interrupting it and creating the possibility for new perception, new life, and new forms of community. The active agent of this new creation, who moves at the threshold of the ages and creates the possibility for this new life, is the Spirit. In this tension—this battle—between the powers of this age and the power of the Spirit, the Christian life is lived. So the other reality proclaimed by Paul in chapter 2 is the Spirit of God.

The Power of the Spirit

Paul's proclamation of the Spirit, like his emphasis on God's call and Christ's crucifixion in chapter 1, serves to emphasize the initiative and activity of God, on which the faithful depend. Faith, Paul declares, rests "not on human wisdom but on the power of God" (2:5). Indeed, in the context of what he has said about the activity of the powers, such an emphasis is critical; human beings simply cannot set themselves free from the overwhelming powers of this age and spirit of the world. Divine interruption is necessary. Indeed, the boasting of the Christians in Corinth simply reveals their captivity to the hierarchical powers of this age. The spiritual gifts about which they boast have become expressions of the spirit of the world, as Paul's ironic description of these gifts in chapter 1 suggests. So strong is the grip of the old age that even expressions of Christian faith may become captive and need to be interrupted.

The Spirit of God is the ongoing agent of interruption. Just as Christ's crucifixion physically exposes and interrupts the powers of death, so the Spirit of God interrupts the spirit of the world that holds people captive to the old age. Indeed, Paul inextricably links Christ's crucifixion and God's Spirit in his opening reference to the Spirit in 2:1–5. The Spirit makes the message of the cross real and powerful for believers. The "Spirit refigured in light of the cross . . . brings the work of the Word to completion."[18] The work of the Spirit creates a community set free from the spirit of the world to resist the powers of this age.

18. Alexandra R. Brown, *The Cross and Human Transformation: Paul's Apocalyptic Word in 1 Corinthians* (Minneapolis: Fortress Press, 1995), 103.

Paul's rhetoric actually performs the disruptive work of God's Spirit. Paul employs the terminology of the philosophies of the day: knowledge (*gnōsis*), mystery (*mystērion*), spirit (*pneuma*), wisdom (*sophia*), unspiritual (*psychikos*), spiritual (*pneumatikos*).[19] He declares that among the mature he does speak wisdom (v. 6); and he highlights "God's wisdom, secret and hidden," a wisdom that exists "before the ages" (v. 7). Indeed, some of this terminology was probably used by the higher status members of the church, who would have been more familiar with various philosophical commonplaces.[20] The powers of this age can take captive the language of the gospel for their own purposes, just as the serpent can use God's words in Genesis 3 or Satan can use the Bible at Jesus' temptation.[21] So Paul challenges the misused language. He takes up popular terminology but interrupts it by refiguring the Spirit through the lens of the cross (2:1–5). By so doing, he rhetorically "brings one set of meanings into conflict with another; the symbolic world defined by God's revelation at the cross challenges a worldview that is centered elsewhere."[22] Both theologically and rhetorically, the work of the Spirit, like the word of the cross, continues to interrupt the spirit of the world.

In this space between the ages, the primary work of God's Spirit involves discernment (*anakrinō*; 2:14–15). While other gifts of the

---

Paul's letters demonstrate that, for him, the enemy forces often hold territory by skillfully subverting the language of the gospel he preaches. It is perhaps for this reason that his writing in 1 Corinthians 1–2 is filled with double entendre, irony, and sometimes biting sarcasm. By such means he seeks to expose the false logos of his opponents and thus to win people back to the territory already claimed by God.

Brown, *Cross and Human Transformation*, 108.

---

19. For a thorough exegetical study of these terms, see Brown, *Cross and Human Transformation*, 105–48. My interpretation relies on her work.
20. On the relationship between high status and knowledge of philosophical ideas and commonplaces, see Dale B. Martin, *The Corinthian Body* (New Haven, CT: Yale University Press, 1995), 70–73.
21. See Matt. 4:5–7; Luke 4:9–12.
22. Brown, *Cross and Human Transformation*, 109.

Spirit will be highlighted later in the letter, Paul's initial presentation of the Spirit highlights the Spirit's role in perception, which is essential in the context of the apocalyptic interruption at the turn of the ages.[23] The revealing work of the Spirit alone enables people to "comprehend" (ginōskō; v.11) what is truly God's and to understand (oida; v.12) the gifts of God (contrary to the powers of this age, which did not ginōskō; v. 8).[24] The new creation has broken into the world in Jesus Christ, interrupting the old age with the new. That has been done; humans, as Paul has proclaimed, have nothing to contribute to this accomplished event. What is necessary now is new perspective that enables believers to discern the power and wisdom of God that the world considers weak and foolish.

This apocalyptic perception is central to Paul's pneumatology. The initial work of the Spirit is "to reveal" (apokalyptō). The Spirit has revealed (apekalypsen) "these things" to us, Paul declares (v. 10). The aorist tense of the verb locates the revelation in the past, probably reminding the Corinthians not only of their own reception of the Spirit but also specifically linking the work of the Spirit to the crucifixion of Christ, which has happened once and for all. The work of the Spirit, as Paul has affirmed, cannot be disconnected from Christ. There is no general, spiritual knowledge to be attained by human wisdom. What has been revealed through the Spirit is Jesus Christ, in all his scandalous particularity. As Paul has proclaimed so powerfully and paradoxically in chapter 1, the wisdom of Jesus Christ is hidden in the weakness and folly of the cross. This divine wisdom, hidden in the revelation (apocalypse) itself, must be unveiled through the power of the Spirit. The apocalypse of the Spirit interrupts the spirit of the world in order to reveal the cross that the cross obscures. Consequently, the "mature" among whom Paul speaks wisdom (2:6) are ironically the fools who discern God's power and wisdom in the weakness and folly of the cross.

Word and Spirit thus belong inseparably together. Even the words through which new perception comes about are not "taught

23. In 2:6–16, consistent with the centrality of perception in apocalyptic epistemology, there are thirty-one perception related terms. See Brown, Cross and Human Transformation, 107.
24. All the Greek terms are related to perception. See Brown, Cross and Human Transformation, 107n7.

by human wisdom but taught by the Spirit" (v. 13). The "foolishness of our proclamation" (1:21) interprets (*synkrinō*; 2:13) God's revelation (*apokalypsis*), which must be discerned (*anakrinō*) by those who have received the gift of the Spirit (vv. 14–15).[25] Proclamation, interpretation, and discernment work together. Only through the Spirit do human words reveal the power and wisdom of the cross. The words given by the Spirit and received through the Spirit are thus the bridge to "perceptual transformation" among Paul's hearers. The words of Paul's bi-vocal gospel rhetoric not only interrupt the powers of this age but, through the Spirit, also have the power (2:4–5) to move believers from the perspective of the old age, in which the cross is a "symbol of suffering, weakness, folly, and death," to the perspective of the new creation, in which the cross is the "transforming symbol of power and life."[26]

Moreover, the Spirit's gift of discernment is intimately related to the other primary work of the Spirit, the "more excellent way" of love (12:31–13:13). Revelation is not for the "knowers of God" but for the "lovers of God" (2:9), certainly a destabilizing affirmation for those who valued knowledge (*gnōsis*) as the superior attainment.[27] Love (*agapē*) is essential for the discernment of the Spirit; one cannot perceive the wisdom and power of the cross apart from the love embodied there. At the beginning of his letter, Paul thus foreshadows the central role of love as "the proper alternative to elitism and boasting in knowledge."[28]

All these emphases are affirmed in Paul's culminating affirmation about life in the liminal space between the ages: through the Spirit, "we have the mind [*nous*] of Christ" (v. 16). The radical character of this claim becomes clear through Paul's allusion to a text from Isaiah: "For who has known the mind of the Lord so as to instruct him?" (2:16; see Isa. 40:13)—the presumed answer to which is "no one." Paul, however, follows this rhetorical question with a disruptive, antithetical "but": "But we have the mind of Christ" (2:16).

25. All the Greek terms highlighted in this paragraph are also related to perception. See *Cross and Human Transformation*, 107, n. 7. Note also the link between interpretation (*synkrinō*) and discernment (*anakrinō*).
26. Brown, *Cross and Human Transformation*, xii, 14.
27. Ibid., 120–21.
28. Ibid., 121.

Those who have been given the Spirit not only know the mind of the Lord but actually *have* the mind of Christ, the Lord. Every dimension of this concluding sentence has enormous implications.

First, this mind does not belong to believers; it is the mind *of Christ*, the gift of the Spirit. Like God's call, the mind of Christ cannot bring with it the arrogance of those who claim superior knowledge for themselves. Indeed, Paul's claim actually breaks down the social hierarchies that divide the community. The notion of mind was deeply rooted in the hierarchical assumptions of Paul's world. After the spirit, the mind was the highest ranking member of the human body; it represented a superior activity of a human being.[29] In addition, understandings of the mind also reinforced social hierarchies, including gender hierarchies. Only the highest male, social elites would be expected to exercise the full capacities of the mind.[30] Co-opting this language of the mind, however, Paul claims this gift for "*we*"—that is, for *all* the members of the Christian community. No longer are the gifts of the mind reserved for the social elites in the Corinthian community, who take it upon themselves to scrutinize others (v. 15). The mind of Christ is given to the entire community of believers, including those who are considered "low and despised."

Second, the mind of Christ foreshadows what Paul will say later about the church as Christ's body. The church is the body governed by the mind of Christ. The mind of Christ is not simply given to any one person but is a gift for the church. The Spirit moves in the new community, and discernment with the mind of Christ becomes a communal process within Christ's body. Paul's "we" encompasses not only the persons within the community, but the life of the community as a whole.

Third, the mind Paul proclaims is not that of the philosophers or the rhetoricians; it is the mind of *Christ*, which "fools" the wisdom and power of the world. The folly and weakness of Christ are here elevated to the high status of the mind. The activity of the mind celebrated by the top-ranking people in the social hierarchy now belongs

---

29. Martin, *Corinthian Body*, 96–103. The mind rules over the inferior members of the body. See Brittany Wilson, *Unmanly Men: Refigurations of Masculinity in Luke–Acts* (New York: Oxford University Press, 2015), 49.
30. Wilson, *Unmanly Men*, 49, 54.

to the "low and despised" one who was executed on a cross. Through this mind, believers are able to discern the truth of Christ's crucifixion. The folly and weakness of the cross are indeed the wisdom and power of God. The crucified one is the Lord of Glory (v. 8). The mind of this curious *Kyrios*, not the mind of the elite philosophers, shapes the life and discernment of the community of faith.

FURTHER REFLECTION
Trinitarian Trajectories

While Paul's affirmation that "we have the mind of Christ" marks the culmination of his theological exploration of the liminal space at the threshold of the ages, one more theological aspect of the first two chapters needs to be noted. In these chapters there is a Trinitarian dynamic in Paul's theology. Uninterested in systematic theology, Paul offers no doctrine of the Trinity. Nevertheless, a proto-Trinitarian dynamic remains. The Spirit is the Spirit *of* God, searching the depths of God, as the human spirit searches the depths of a human being (vv. 10–11). And the Spirit is *"from* God," and gives comprehension of "what is truly God's" (vv. 11–12). In addition, the Spirit is inextricably linked to the work of Jesus Christ, and the Spirit gives believers nothing other than the "mind of Christ" (v. 16). In fact, the Spirit should be understood as the continued activity of the crucified and risen Christ in the Christian community and the world. In addition to these dynamics among God, Christ, and Spirit, there is Paul's earlier greeting to the Corinthians: "Grace to you and peace from God our Father and the Lord Jesus Christ." The greeting is further developed in Paul's thanksgiving: "I give thanks to my God always for you because of the grace of God that has been given you in Christ Jesus" (1:3–4).

Such affirmations are the fertile soil out of which will later grow doctrines of the Trinity. At this point, however, Paul makes no formal attempt to systematize the relationship between God (the Father), Jesus Christ, and the Spirit. The dynamic relationship among them remains open. That is theologically appropriate for Paul's theology of interruption at the threshold of the ages. The God Paul proclaims is no more manageable than the gospel he declares. Even God is not univocal but lives and works somehow in the unsettling dynamic of "God the Father"—"Lord Jesus Christ"—"Spirit." Like Jesus' crucifixion, God's very person fractures all human attempts at neat, univocal theology. Like the Spirit, God's very person keeps us unsettled, on the move, inviting us into the dynamics and dialogue of living community.

3:1–4:21
Building Up the Church

Paul's opening treatment of Word and Spirit leads him to the church. Chapters 3 and 4 develop general implications of the Word of the cross and the power of the Spirit for the life of the community of faith. In other terms, Paul's Christology and pneumatology move to ecclesiology, which will occupy Paul through the rest of the letter. Continuing the emphases in chapters 1 and 2, chapters 3 and 4 present a dizzying array of ironic reversals of social hierarchies. Unsettling conventional understandings of leadership, including his own, Paul seeks to help the larger community learn to "look" so they might move beyond the divisions in the church toward life in the Spirit at the turn of the ages.

This section of the letter is framed by two unsettling parental images, in which Paul addresses the Corinthians as infants and children. The section opens with Paul depicting his leadership through maternal imagery. He is the one who breastfeeds the infant Corinthians (3:2). In likening himself to a nursing mother or wetnurse, Paul places himself toward the bottom of the social hierarchy, refusing to identify with prevailing masculine ideals. He depicts himself not with the hard boundaries of the male body but with the soft, porous body of a breastfeeding woman.[1] He presents the church leader through a relational, nurturing role rather than as the authoritative—or authoritarian—person.[2]

1. For an overview of the understanding of male and female bodies in Greco-Roman culture, see Brittany Wilson, *Unmanly Men: Reconfigurations of Masculinity in Luke–Acts* (Oxford: Oxford University Press, 2015), 49–54.
2. On maternal images in Paul, see Susan Eastman, *Recovering Paul's Mother Tongue: Language and Theology in Galatians* (Grand Rapids, MI: Wm. B. Eerdmans Publishing Co.,

At the end of the section, Paul depicts himself as a father who will discipline his children (4:14–21). By this point in the letter, however, the multiple reversals of status that have taken place change the image of the father as leader. That image can no longer be interpreted through the hierarchical lenses of Paul's culture but is reinterpreted by the folly of those who follow the crucified Christ. Indeed, Paul's use of the image suggests a rather comical, anxious father who is not in complete control of his children.[3] Throughout this chapter, with its unsettling parental framing and repeated status reversals, Paul's primary concern is arrogance, which destroys the community Paul seeks to form.

3:1–4

People of the Flesh

Paul begins with disruptive, paradoxical critique. The divisions and quarreling about church leaders (vv. 3–4) provide evidence that the Corinthians are not the spiritually mature people that they claim to be. Paul's words are dripping with sarcasm and irony; they are almost comical. Rather than having attained the spiritual heights many thought they had attained, the Corinthians are in fact mere infants who are not ready for solid food (v. 2). The image is insulting. The proud, spiritually mature believers who think they have arrived at the apex of their spiritual journey are depicted as helpless babes whose journey has only begun; they are not ready for anything beyond mother's milk. Indeed, Paul even suggests that the Corinthians have not grown any since he first preached to them. Just as they were not ready for solid food earlier, they are "still not ready" (v. 2). They remain "infants in Christ" (v. 1).

The "jealousy and quarreling" result because the Corinthians are people "of the flesh" (v. 3). Paul is not denigrating human creatureliness or fleshly human existence, much less focusing on human

---

2007); Beverly Roberts Gaventa, *Our Mother Saint Paul* (Louisville, KY: Westminster John Knox Press, 2007).

3. L. L. Welborn, *Paul, the Fool of Christ: A Study of 1 Corinthians 1–4 in the Comic-Philosophic Tradition* (London: T. & T. Clark, 2005), 86–90.

sexuality. Rather, *sarx* is an image for life that is captive to the powers of death.[4] In "the flesh," the Christian community in Corinth is characterized by the very realities that animate the powers: jealousy, divisions, quarreling, all driven by a hierarchical framework of honored and shamed, high and low, powerful and weak, wise and foolish. Shaped by the standards of the old age, by life in the flesh, leadership inevitably becomes divisive and conflictual. It is captive to the powers of this age rather than shaped by the Spirit of God. The Corinthians have been born into the new creation of God's Spirit but remain infants as they continue to live according to the standards of the hierarchical and divisive "Domination System." Paradoxically, yet again, the claim to be powerful and wise according to the ways of the powers of this age is actually the weakness and ignorance of an infant. It is not freedom and life but captivity to the flesh, the opposite of the Spirit.

Life lived "according to the flesh" (*kata sarka*) denotes the self externalized and subjugated to the opinions of others. It is the self socialized into a world of inauthentic values, values that lead it away from its own centeredness in God. It is the beachhead that the Domination System establishes in our beings. *Sarx* means more than "the pursuit of the merely human, the earthly-transitory"; it is pursuit of the values of the Domination System.

Wink, *Engaging the Powers*, 61–62

3:5–15
Servant Leaders: Farmhands and Construction Workers

3:5–9 *Farmhands*

In response to the infantile, "fleshy" divisions in Corinth, Paul proceeds comically to put all church leaders in their place. He actually pokes fun at the leaders, including himself. Church leaders, he proclaims, are nothing more than common laborers—farmhands (vv. 6–9) and construction workers (vv. 10–15). "What are these great

---

4. Walter Wink, *Engaging the Powers: Discernment and Resistance in a World of Domination* (Minneapolis: Fortress Press, 1992), 61–62.

leaders of yours?" he asks. "Servants" (v. 5). We are just farmhands, planting and watering the field. We are just laborers constructing a building. In Greco-Roman society, all these folks were low-class people whom the elites mocked and degraded. There were even plays in the Roman theater making fun of buffoons in the various crafts. Poking fun at such "low" characters made for a good laugh from the rich and powerful folks in the audience. No eloquent and respectable leader would ever want to be compared to such folks.[5]

Paul's emphasis is sharply stated in verses 5–9. Everything depends on God, not on the leaders. As farmhands, Paul and Apollos—and any other leader—merely plant and water. But *God* gives the growth. The ones who plant and water have important but subordinate parts, for growth depends on God alone. Moreover, as laborers, they should not be divided, for they have a common purpose. Whether planting or watering, they labor together so God may grow the church. Paul sharply makes his point in verse 9: *God's* servants. *God's* field. *God's* building. Paul repeats his emphasis in verses 16–17: *God's* temple. *God's* temple. *God's* temple. God's. God's. God's. As Paul has stressed from his opening words, both the church and its ministers belong to God. God is the central actor. God is the one who calls the workers, the one who gives the growth in the field, the one who has provided the foundation for the building, the one who dwells in the temple. For Paul, the minister is not like the wise orator who seeks distinction and acclaim in the rhetorical games of the Roman culture. Nor is the minister one who seeks to gather followers in competition with others. Rather, all are merely servants (3:5), coworkers (3:9), seeking together to build up the Christian community.

Oikodomein

The metaphor of *building up* the church lies at the heart of this text, and it will play a role throughout Paul's letter. *Epoikodomein* (to build upon) occurs four times in the text (vv. 10, 12, 14). *Oikodomein* (to build up) is a theologically rich and multifaceted metaphor in Paul's

5. Welborn, *Paul, the Fool of Christ*, 234–47.

letter to the Corinthians, providing an essential understanding of Christian ministry.[6] First of all, *oikodomein* holds together both the divine and human aspects of ministry. Building up is the work of God through the Holy Spirit. But it is also the task of the community of faith through the gifts of the Spirit (see 1 Cor. 14). Ministers never go "solo" but are at best, as has been noted, God's coworkers (*theou synergoi*, v. 9), serving God, who alone gives the growth and "builds the house" (see Ps. 127:1). *Oikodomein* reminds Christian ministers that their own work is important but is always carried out in communion with and service to God. The divine-human character of *oikodomein* is inescapable.

Second, *oikodomein* focuses on the *community* of faith; the primary concern is not meeting the needs of individuals but building up the *church*. Through the Spirit, God is an active subject building up a people whose life together witnesses to Jesus' presence in the world. Christian ministry participates in God's work of building up such a community. From beginning to end, the text is not about individuals but about building up the *community* of faith. In many Western, individualistic contexts, *oikodomein* invites a significant shift from preaching, teaching, and ministry that focus almost exclusively on the needs of individuals. "What is the Spirit saying to the *church?*" That is the key question for ministry.

Third, *oikodomein* has an eschatological, apocalyptic aspect. Building up is an end-time activity. The new creation has broken into the world

> "Let anyone who has an ear listen to what the Spirit is saying to the churches."
>
> Rev. 3:22

in Jesus Christ. This apocalyptic interruption of "Christ crucified" is the foundation on which Christian *oikodomein* takes place. God seeks to build up a people who embody the new creation *now* and live toward its future fulfillment. Ministry as *oikodomein* is an activity of the new age that has come and is coming in Jesus Christ; it participates

---

6. On *oikodomein*, see Otto Michel, "*oikodomeō*," in Gerhard Friedrich, ed., *Theological Dictionary of the New Testament*, vol. 5, trans. Geoffrey Bromiley (Grand Rapids, MI: Wm. B. Eerdmans Publishing Co., 1967), 136–44; also Gerhard Lohfink, *Jesus and Community*, trans. John P. Galvin (Philadelphia: Fortress Press, 1982), 99–106.

in the unsettling work of God's new creation that interrupts the world through the crucified and risen Messiah. In 3:13 Paul highlights the apocalyptic character of *oikodomein*. The quality of one's building will be "revealed" (*apokalyptetai*) through fire on the final day of the Lord. Until that day Christians must use the gifts of discernment to perceive what is faithfully built on the foundation of Christ.

Fourth, *oikodomein* is intimately related to the "household" (*oikos/ oikia*), which was one of the fundamental building blocks of the social order in Paul's context. Consequently, as becomes clear in the remainder of the letter, *oikodomein* includes the social, economic, and political dimensions of the community of faith. The up-building of the church should not simply be considered a spiritual matter but rather involves building up a concrete, publicly enacted community with distinctive social practices—practices shaped not by the culture's presuppositions but by the folly of the cross. The Christian community is called to be a public alternative to the institutional, ideological, and systemic powers of this age, which crucified Jesus (2:6, 8).

Finally, *oikodomein* is not simply the work of a few leaders or ordained ministers. It is the work of the entire community, among whom the gifts of the Spirit are shared (1 Cor. 14). Just as there is no solo ministry apart from God, there is no solo ministry apart from others in the community of faith. Ministers are not only coworkers with God but also coworkers with each other (*theou synergoi* in v. 9 can be interpreted with both emphases). The whole people of God is the temple within whom God's Spirit dwells. Paul's communal, cooperative understanding of *oikodomein* itself interrupts the divisiveness among the leaders and factions in Corinth.

3:10–11 *The Church's Odd Foundation*

Just as Paul emphasizes ministry as *oikodomein*, so he repeatedly stresses the foundation on which ministers build. Indeed, the form of *oikodomein* used in this text is *epoikodomein* (to build on), which highlights the centrality of the foundation. Christian ministry "builds on" something that is already given. In stressing this foundation, Paul again employs irony and paradox to undermine the Corinthians' reliance on human wisdom. In verse 10, Paul pointedly and craftily refers to himself as the "wise" (*sophos*) architect who has laid the foundation of the building "according to the grace of God given to me" (v. 10).[7] In this one sentence he unsettles the claims and presuppositions of the church in Corinth. In using the term *sophos*, he employs the idiom of the wisdom-loving Corinthians but radically reconfigures it. As has become clear in the opening two chapters, *sophos*, as used by Paul, is not the human wisdom so valued in Corinth but the "foolish wisdom" of God, which is enacted on the cross. Moreover, even as Paul describes himself as a "wise" architect, he reminds the Corinthians (and himself!) that such wisdom is not his own but a gracious gift from God. There is no room for boasting but only reliance on the initiative of God, which Paul has stressed from his opening words about God's call (1:1–2).

Paul repeatedly emphasizes the foundation on which everyone must build. He states clearly that this foundation is Jesus Christ, the crucified one (v. 11). Paul, the "wise" architect, paradoxically lays a foundation that the world and many of the Corinthians consider "weak" and "foolish" (1:18–31). Paul lays a destabilizing foundation that unsettles the certainties and securities on which Roman society was constructed. In the midst of a culture built on wisdom and honor and power, Paul absurdly lays the foundation of the crucified Christ. The crucified Messiah is the odd, unsettling foundation on which Christians in Corinth must build up the community of faith. Not surprisingly, most people considered Paul to be a very foolish architect.

Paul's proclamation, however, converges with the conclusion to Jesus' Sermon on the Mount. In his sermon, which begins with destabilizing pairs of opposites—blessed poor, blessed mourners, blessed meek (Matt. 5:3–5)—Jesus, like Paul, lays a destabilizing foundation on which believers are to build. His preaching would certainly have seemed as foolish as Paul's proclamation of the cross. And at the end of his sermon, Jesus, like Paul, reconfigures wisdom and folly using the metaphors of foundations and buildings:

7. *Sophos* often means "skilled" in relation to craftspersons. But in the context of 1 Corinthians, Paul's use of the word contains a double entendre. The translation "wise" highlights the subversive character of Paul's argument. See Richard B. Hays, *First Corinthians*, Interpretation: A Bible Commentary for Teaching and Preaching (Louisville, KY: John Knox Press, 1997), 54.

Everyone then who hears these words of mine and acts on
them will be like a wise man who built his house on rock. The
rain fell, the floods came, and the winds blew and beat on that
house, but it did not fall, because it had been founded on rock.
And everyone who hears these words of mine and does not
act on them will be like a foolish man who built his house on
sand. The rain fell, and the floods came, and the winds blew
and beat against that house, and it fell—and great was its fall!
(Matt. 7:24–27)

The "foolish" preaching of Jesus is wisdom. And the wisdom of
the world is folly. Both Jesus and Paul lay a foundation that is considered "weak" and "foolish" by the powers of this age. Ironically,
however, this destabilizing foundation is the one that endures.

The community built on this foundation is thus no less disruptive than the foundation itself. Just as the foundation laid by the
wise architect, Paul, interrupts the myths and rationalities and
conventions of the society, so the community built on that foundation will itself interrupt the culture around it. An unsettling building will be constructed on this foundation. The building that is the
Body of Christ will be a ridiculous, architectural monstrosity amid
all the glorious structures of Rome. Like the cross itself, the building constructed on this foundation will be an eyesore that interrupts the smooth and impressive architectural facades of empire.
Built on its odd foundation, the Body of Christ will disrupt the
body politic. The community built on the "weak" and "foolish"
foundation of Christ crucified will embody an alternative to the
hierarchies of high and low, insiders and outsiders, honored and
shamed that shape the surrounding culture. The powers of this age
may in fact bring out the bulldozers and seek to tear down this out-
of-place, culturally inappropriate structure—just as they crucified
Jesus.

3:12–15 *Construction Workers*

Continuing the building metaphor, Paul paints a comical picture
of church leaders—the construction workers—in verses 12–15.
Indeed, the image is slapstick, and the leaders are a bit like the

keystone cops.[8] All the laborers are dashing around, busily working on a building. They are grabbing all kinds of different materials.
Some are building with gold and silver and precious stones. Others
with wood and hay and straw. And they are all working on the same
building, which must appear rather odd constructed out of all these
different materials. The strangest thing of all, however, is that the
workers do not even know for sure what materials they are building
with. They are grabbing what they can, doing the best they can, but
with no assurance about the quality of their work.

Then someone yells, "FIRE!"—an all too common occurrence
in that day. All the laborers try to dash out of the building—running around, bumping into each other, trying to escape through the
flames. Only *after* the fire do they discover their building materials.
Some of the construction survives the fire, and those workers get
paid. Some does not survive, and those laborers are fined for shoddy
construction, though they themselves escape the destruction.[9]

That is Paul's image of church leaders. It is not that Paul does not
value church leaders—he does; they are important, called to build
up the church. But Paul will not let church leaders become the star
performers in the play. They are the lowly, often ridiculous, bit play-
ers in the drama—servants of God building on a foolish foundation.
Paul has seen the consequences of star performers in Corinth, so he
seeks to interrupt their assumptions and change the church's perspective. Paul's words were probably not received enthusiastically by
the self-important leaders in Corinth.

Christians are thus called to build an odd building, "God's temple," constructed on a destabilizing foundation. Even the construction work itself is unsettling; it is a journey in which the quality of
one's work cannot be known for certain until the day on which it is
finally revealed. Somewhat surprisingly, Paul provides no clear set of
instructions detailing exactly what or how to build on the foundation. Building is left to the discernment of the construction workers at the site. Some will build with imperishable materials, such as
gold, silver, or precious stones; others will construct with perishable

8. Welborn, *Paul, the Fool of Christ*, 238–42. My interpretation follows that of Welborn.
9. Hays argues convincingly that "wages" and "fines," like those given to a subcontractor, offer a
better interpretation than "rewards" and "punishments." See *First Corinthians*, 56.

resources, whether wood, hay, or straw. The quality of the work will not be known until it is disclosed and revealed on the Day of the Lord. Christian ministry, that is, lives in a liminal space between the new creation that has broken into the world and the fulfillment that is yet to come.

Paul suggests that all Christian ministry, like his own, is contextual and contingent. Just as Paul seeks a fitting word for the Corinthian congregation, so Christian ministers are always seeking fitting words and deeds that build faithfully on the foundation that has been laid in Jesus Christ. Beyond the foundation that has been laid, there is no master plan for every situation. No one set of blueprints fits every context. Interpretation, imagination, and improvisation are required.

As a result, the key gift for ministry, as with Christian faith itself, is discernment (see 2:14–16). In the liminal space between the old age and the new, leaders have to discern God's wisdom and power in the folly and weakness of the cross. Ministers have to discern the implications of this paradoxical gospel for the life of God's people. Ministry is a bold and risky adventure in which Christians build as faithfully as we can without fully knowing the quality of our work. Most of us wonder from time to time, "What if I'm wrong?" "What if I do the wrong thing or speak the wrong word?" It is an understandable question as one occupies the space between the ages with a "weak" and "foolish" gospel seeking to discern fitting words and deeds. Paul provides no clear assurances. Maybe we are building with silver and gold. Maybe we are building with hay or straw. All Paul offers is the proper foundation and trust in the Spirit. Ministry remains risky.

In this context, there can be no boasting in Christian leadership. The very uncertainty surrounding the quality of their building prevents ministers from proudly claiming *my* way as the *only* way. The need for discernment opens ministry up to the insights and faithfulness of others in the community. As well as interrupting the community with the gospel, ministers themselves must be open to interruptions by others, often others very different from themselves. Ministry in the unsettled liminal space between the ages creates the possibility for new forms of community and cooperation. In this space of discernment ministers become coworkers in *God's* field, co-laborers on *God's* building (3:9).

In the end, however, the quality of our work will be revealed. If what we have built endures, we will receive our pay. If our building perishes we will be fined for shoddy construction; our work will go up in smoke. Nevertheless, the builder who faithfully seeks to construct God's odd temple on the weak and foolish foundation of Christ will be saved. Those who do not build on the appropriate foundation, however, but rather foster the divisions and hierarchies of the old age will not simply be fined but will come to financial ruin.[10] Those who seek to destroy, rather than build, will themselves be destroyed by the holy God.

Paul concludes this section with disturbing images of violence and destruction (v. 15). These images, however, must themselves be destabilized; they cannot be taken at face value. Such images run counter to the very foundation Paul has laid— the foundation of the crucified Christ who in love resisted the violence and domination of the powers of this age. Paul's imagery here reflects more the way of the powers than the way of Jesus Christ. God will not work differently in the fulfillment of the new creation than God has worked in Jesus Christ's inauguration of that new age. Either Paul's warnings must be interpreted through the folly and weakness of the cross, or they must themselves be revealed as destructive, perishable preaching—mere wood, straw, and hay.

> We have never preached violence,
> except the violence of love,
> which left Christ nailed to a cross,
> the violence that we must each do to ourselves
> to overcome our selfishness and such cruel inequalities among us.
> The violence we preach is not the violence of the sword,
> the violence of hatred.
> It is the violence of love,
> of brotherhood,
> the violence that wills to beat weapons into sickles for work.
>
> Oscar Romero, *The Violence of Love* (Maryknoll, NY: Orbis Books, 2004), 12.

---

10. On *phtheirō* ("destroy") as including financial ruin, see *"phtheirō"* in Frederick W. Danker, Walter Bauer, and William F. Arndt, *A Greek-English Lexicon of the New Testament and Other Early Christian Literature*, 3rd ed. (Chicago: University of Chicago, 2000), 1054.

Again, we are left with paradoxes. The fire of God's crucified *love* reveals the quality of one's construction but nevertheless saves the builder. When the way of the cross is fully revealed as the wisdom and power of God, everyone's inadequate building will be exposed. Perishable work will be disclosed and burned away by a recognition of God's odd way of love—the same love that saves the builder despite his or her faulty work. Similarly, God's crucified *love* will paradoxically destroy the false "life" of those who have sought to destroy God's temple. Such love unmasks the person one has become in captivity to the powers of this age; it condemns the ways of domination and violence and death that have shaped a person's existence; it reveals the inauthentic lie on which one grounds his or her identity. The old "life" is destroyed, to be sure. It is painful, for that "life" may have brought a false sense of comfort and security. It is nevertheless the paradoxical destruction of love, the holy love embodied on the cross, the love that ultimately sets us free—even if it costs us our old "life." As Jesus stated the paradox, "For those who want to save their life will lose it, and those who lose their life for my sake, and for the sake of the gospel, will save it" (Mark 8:35).[11]

3:16–20
God's Temple of Fools

Paul then reminds the leaders what they are really building: God's temple. This temple, however, is not a physical structure but a people. In other words, Paul reconfigures the space in which God dwells. "Do you not know," he rhetorically asks the community, "that you are God's temple and that God's Spirit dwells in you?" (v. 16). Despite all the construction imagery, the temple is no longer a building or an institution. It is no longer confined to one physical location. Built on the foundation of the crucified Christ and formed by the power of the Spirit, this temple is a people, among whom God is moving to form and re-form the church.

Having affirmed indicatively that the community *is* God's temple

11. Walter Wink speaks of dying to the powers of death. See *Engaging the Powers: Discernment and Resistance in a World of Domination* (Minneapolis: Fortress Press, 1992), 157–64.

in whom the Spirit dwells, Paul turns to imperatives. He calls the community, once again, to be who they are. Even the imperatives consist of destabilizing pairs of opposites that set the community in the unsettled, liminal space between the ages: "Do not deceive yourselves. If you think that you are wise in this age, you should become fools so that you may become wise" (v. 18). In the midst of the old age, the wisdom of the Spirit appears foolish, at odds with the "spirit of the world" (2:12) that is creating divisions in the Corinthian church.

Paul is not speaking to individuals but to the community, to God's temple. He commands the church in its life together to embody an alternative to the powers of this age (2:8). Ironically, while using the structural image of the temple, Paul creates a liminal space that subverts hierarchical structures. He does not provide a rigid set of rules but creates the space where discernment and new community become possible, for it is in such liminal spaces that new forms of community may be born. As the anthropologist Victor Turner has noted, liminal spaces are precisely those where *communitas* —a new community of spontaneity and equality—happens.[12] The liminal space is one in which people are set free from the old structures and categories that divide them—wise and foolish, strong and weak—so new forms of relationship become possible. As Turner puts it, people are set free from the "structured, differentiated, and often hierarchical system of politico-legal-economic positions with many types of evaluation, separating [people] in terms of 'more' or 'less.'"[13] In this context, Paul summarizes a point he has made throughout this section: "Let no one boast about human leaders" (3:21). Such boasting is the

> The fool knows the truth because he is a social outcast, and spectators see most of the game. . . .
>
> Enid Welsford, *The Fool: His Social and Literary History* (Gloucester, MA: Peter Smith, 1966), 323.

---

12. See Victor Turner, *The Ritual Process: Structure and Anti-Structure* (New York: Aldine de Gruyter, 1995). Because the temple was the place of worship, Turner's work, which focuses on the liminality of ritual, is especially appropriate here. I will provide a more detailed account of *communitas* when Paul turns specifically to worship in chapter 11.
13. Ibid., 96.

antithesis of *communitas*. Humility, not arrogance, shapes the common life of God's temple.

In this liminal space, moreover, fools are actually critical figures; they play an important role in *communitas*. Figures like the court jester represent the poor, the marginalized, and the physically unusual—in Paul's terms, the "low and despised." As such, the jester symbolizes the moral values of *communitas* over against the coercive power of supreme political rulers—the powers of this age.[14] The one who is marginal, inferior—the outsider—becomes the agent of both liminality and community. Through the power of the Spirit, the foolish Christ, the foolish gospel, and the foolish preacher interrupt the old age for the sake of a new kind of community: God's temple, built on the foundation of the crucified Christ and formed and re-formed by the Spirit that "dwells in you" (v. 16).

3:21–4:7
Servant Leaders

Like a fool in the temple, Paul concludes this section by subverting the status of the leaders and the assumptions of the Corinthians. Whereas the Corinthians were claiming, "I *belong* to Apollos," "I *belong* to Cephas," "I *belong* to Paul" (1:12), the apostle now turns those claims upside down: the leaders belong to *you*, he declares. Ironically employing popular philosophy's claim that "the wise person possesses all things," Paul even hyperbolically declares that the Corinthians possess the world and life and death, the present and the future (vv. 21–23).[15] Through his exaggerated claims, Paul not only diminishes church leaders, but, like a good jester, he also sets up the "wise" and proud Corinthians for a final "devastating twist."[16] Just at the point where they are feeling high and lifted up—and not in a cruciform way!—Paul interrupts yet again: "and you belong to Christ, and Christ belongs to God" (v. 23). As he does throughout his opening theological vision, Paul proclaims that God is the central

14. Ibid., 109–10.
15. Hays, *First Corinthians*, 60–61.
16. Ibid., 61.

player; God is the primary actor on the stage—not the leaders, not the Corinthians, not even Paul himself. The wise in God's temple are not those who possess everything but those who recognize that they belong to Christ. All other claims are subordinate to this one. Belonging to Christ, belonging to God, the Corinthians and their leaders have no cause for boasting.

4:1–7 *The Steward*

Paul is not done, though. He continues to subvert the proud claims of Christian leaders by taking up the metaphor of the steward: "Think of us in this way, as servants of Christ and stewards of God's mysteries" (4:1). Having spoken of the church's servant leaders as farmers and construction workers, he takes things further and speaks of them, including himself, as stewards.

The personal context of Paul's words is important. If he seems a bit defensive, he has good reason. In the popular competitive sport of persuasive oratory, as has been noted, Paul wasn't even close to the medal stand. So, frustrated, Paul defends his ministry and his preaching over against the Corinthians. At one level, it is not a pretty sight. It is a very human moment. Paul sounds defensive and dismissive (vv. 2–5). But sometimes God may use even these human moments to speak to us. That is what happens here. In defending himself, Paul does something extraordinary. In fact, he offers a very odd, even foolish, defense of his ministry and preaching. "Think of us in this way," he says, "as servants of Christ and stewards of God's mysteries." The steward was the person responsible for the master's possessions. He had authority over other servants and slaves. As Paul makes clear, though, the steward was still just a servant, an underling, a subordinate. In fact, in the theater the steward was a minor, comic character depicted at times as a fool. He often pranced about with an exaggerated sense of his importance as the boss of other slaves, but he remained only a servant.[17]

Paul thus defends his ministry not by trying to "outdo" the other orators on their terms. He refuses to play the rhetorical game shaped

17. Welborn, *Paul, the Fool of Christ*, 242–47. My interpretation relies on Welborn.

by the powers of this age. He calls the church to stop playing that game as well. Instead, Paul defends his ministry by diminishing his status—almost poking fun at himself. He takes the role of the steward. Rather than trying to build himself up as another star performer, he takes the role of a laughable bit player in the drama. He is a mere servant of the crucified Christ, a mere steward of God's gospel. No self-respecting orator would have made that claim.

In verses 2–5, Paul steps into the role of the steward. *As that character*, Paul says, "It is a very small thing that I should be judged by you or by any human court. I do not even judge myself. . . . It is the Lord who judges me" (vv. 3–4). Paul speaks as the good steward, who knows that the Lord is the only one to whom he is accountable. That diminished role actually brings with it freedom. Freedom from having to be the star performer, the entertainer of the moment. Freedom from the temptations of human adoration as well as the threats of human judgment. Freedom to speak unpopular truths. Freedom to proclaim the foolish way of the cross because that is the mystery that God has entrusted to him. When Paul speaks as the steward, God remains at center stage; God is the only master who really matters. In the midst of a church pressuring him to be a star performer—as many preachers feel pressed to be today—Paul claims a role that brings freedom: the steward, whose only master and judge is God. Even if Paul at times struts around a bit, he confesses that he does so as the steward, the theatrical buffoon, who at times may have an overly grand sense of his own importance but always knows that he is a mere servant. Within this role, Paul can laugh at himself. This sense of humility before God frees Paul from burning out or selling out or having to be the star.

As serious as Paul is about his

I am not a master,
I am not a boss,
I am not an authority that
   imposes itself.
I want to be God's servant and
   yours.
. . . .
I have no ambition for power,
and so with complete freedom
I tell the powerful
   what is good and what is
   bad,
and I tell any political group
   what is good and what is
   bad.
That is my duty.

Romero, *Violence of Love*, 86, 205.

apostleship, by taking the role of the steward Paul suggests an orientation for ministry. This orientation is shaped by what the literary critic and philosopher Mikhail Bakhtin calls "open seriousness." According to Bakhtin, open seriousness is "purified seriousness."[18] This kind of seriousness is "always ready to submit to death and renewal. True open seriousness fears neither parody nor irony, nor any other form of reduced laughter, for it is aware of being part of an uncompleted whole."[19] Not surprisingly, open seriousness, for Bakhtin, is enacted in the communal embodiment of the fool—carnival—the quintessential liminal space in which society's hierarchies and divisions are broken down and new forms of community characterized by mutuality and equality become possible.[20]

Faithful ministry is characterized by this kind of seriousness. Moses himself learns this lesson when he encounters the living God at the burning bush. Moses' ministry begins with God's radically disruptive call. Possibly uneasy with this interruption, Moses tries to get control of God by asking God's name. In response, God gives Moses the divine name. But, ironically, God's name preserves God's freedom: "I AM WHO I AM" (Exod. 3:14). I will be who I will be. I will be with you as I will be with you. Divine laughter is implicit and almost audible in the name, "Yah[HA!]weh."

Paul, whose call was equally unsettling, understands the open seriousness of serving this free and living God. Because ministry has to do with God, it is serious. Because it has to do with God, ministry remains open. There is no controlling God. Indeed, the minister's ability to laugh at himself or herself—to take on the role of farmer or construction worker or steward or fool—is the only way to engage seriously with the living God. As Paul repeatedly affirms, God's Spirit continues to move in the liminal space between the ages, disrupting seriousness when it becomes closed, dogmatic, and idolatrous. The crucified and risen Christ continues to work through the Spirit, interrupting, fracturing, cracking up in order to move people toward the fulfillment of God's purposes. Consequently, Christian ministry

18. Mikhail Bakhtin, *Rabelais and His World*, trans. Helene Iswolsky (Bloomington: Indiana University Press, 1984), 122.
19. Ibid.
20. Ibid., 6–10.

remains open to the disruptive surprises of the Spirit. Faithful Christian ministers can laugh at themselves with open seriousness, welcoming life that is not complete but is always on the way, always lived in the dynamic and fluid movement between the old age that is dying and the new that continues to be born.

Moreover, Paul writes not simply about leaders but for the whole community of faith. "I have applied all this to Apollos and myself for your benefit" (v. 6). Faithful Christian community will also be shaped by open seriousness. In this community, there is no room for boasting because all the community has, as Paul has reminded the Corinthians from the beginning, is a gift from God (1:4–7; 4:7). Recognizing this reality, no believers can be "puffed up in favor of one against another" (4:6). Rather, the grateful stance of the gift recipient enables the members of the community to live together in the carnival Spirit of mutuality and equality.

4:8–13
Fools for the Sake of Christ

Reinforcing his point, Paul once again takes up the rhetoric and the role of the fool. He turns to sarcasm and hyperbole to interrupt the Corinthians once again by holding up a mirror to their claims and contrasting them with the life of apostles, including his own.[21] At the heart of this section is Paul's claim that he and his fellow apostles have become a spectacle to the world; they have become fools for the sake of Christ. They are foolish, weak, and held in disrepute, while the Corinthians consider themselves to be kings: wise, strong, and honored (vv. 9–10). In his challenge to the Corinthians, Paul again draws on the imagery of the Roman theater. As the theatrical fool, Paul interrupts the Corinthians in order to change their perception.

The Greek word translated "spectacle," placed parallel to "fools,"

---

21. As was noted earlier, the mirror is a common tool of the fool. In 1619 in a sermon preached at the funeral of Hans Miesko, the official fool at various courts of Stettin-Pomerania, pastor Philip Cradelius urged the congregation to use fools as mirrors for their own weaknesses. Enid Welsford, *The Fool: His Social and Literary History* (Gloucester, MA: Peter Smith, 1966), 147.

is *theatron*, which means a theater-act.[22] Paul thus declares that as an apostle he plays a role similar to the spectacle enacted by the fool in the Roman theater. As is the case in later theatrical forms through the centuries, in the Roman theater the fool was a lower-class buffoon, identified with the poor, who engaged in transgressive, disruptive behavior. He mocked the words and deeds of the serious and honorable characters, resisting privilege and authority and giving voice to what no one else dared to say. As a result of his disruptive behavior, the fool often suffered both verbal and physical abuse.[23]

It is precisely this role that Paul assumes, although for Paul it was not simply a temporary role but his life as an apostle. Paul should be imagined as a theatrical fool, dashing unexpectedly onto the stage and disrupting the entire play with his shocking words and antics. Like the theatrical fool, Paul engages in transgressive behavior; through the proclamation of the cross and his embodiment of the way of the cross, the apostle disrupts the world's understandings of power and wisdom. He interrupts all the elite characters on the world's stage: the rich, the kings, the wise, the strong, the honored (vv. 8–10). He says things that no one else dares to say. He proclaims and enacts his "coarse and vulgar joke" as the truth: the crucified Christ is the wisdom and power of God.

In an unsettling twist—counter not only to Paul's culture but also to much of the Old Testament tradition as well—foolishness becomes the very mark of discipleship and preaching; the fool becomes the one who is *closest* to God.[24] Dishonored fools are in fact

---

22. Welborn, *Paul, the Fool of Christ*, 50–51. See also *"theatron,"* in *Theological Dictionary of the New Testament*, vol. 3, ed. Gerhard Kittel, trans. Geoffrey W. Bromiley (Grand Rapids, MI: William. B. Eerdmans Publishing Co., 1965), 42–43. Welborn specifically locates the fool within the particular theatrical genre of the mime. Importantly, the mime was not a silent genre at that time but a form of coarse, realistic (mimic, mimetic) low comedy. See his discussion in *Fool of Christ*, 4, 5, and 36.
23. Welborn, *Fool of Christ*, 32, 36–37, 149. Welborn argues that all the abuses Paul lists were actually characteristic of the treatment of theatrical fools.
24. In much of the Old Testament, particularly the wisdom tradition, foolishness carries a thoroughly negative connotation, as Psalm 14:1 captures: "Fools say in their hearts, 'There is no God.' They are corrupt, they do abominable deeds; there is no one who does good." See Christine Roy Yoder, "Folly," *The New Interpreter's Dictionary of the Bible*, vol. 2, ed. Katharine Doob Sakenfeld et al. (Nashville: Abingdon Press, 2007), 471–72. Sometimes, however, wisdom in the Old Testament subverts the "common sense" of the world and is thus a kind of foolishness. See Alyce M. McKenzie, *Preaching Proverbs: Wisdom for the Pulpit* (Louisville, KY: Westminster John Knox Press, 1996), 41–58. In addition, the prophets did engage in foolish symbolic acts (Isaiah going naked in Isa. 20) and were called fools or "mad" (Hos. 9:7).

Christ's apostles. In the transgressive, topsy-turvy way of the fool, Paul declares again to the Corinthians that the myths and conventions and rationalities of the old age—the spirit of the world and the powers of this age—have been overthrown. The fool for the sake of Christ is the one who fools the world.

> To the rich and powerful in Corinth, Paul says: these fools at whom you laugh in the mime of life, whose weakness and poverty is a welcome reminder of what it is like to belong to the upper class, whose grotesque suffering is a source of amusement—these dishonored fools are the apostles of Christ!"
>
> Welborn, *Paul, the Fool of Christ*, 251.

In becoming a spectacle (*theatron*), Paul the fool again invites people to a new kind of discernment. *Theatron* is a cognate of the word *theaomai*, which means "to see, to look at, to behold."[25] *Theatron* involves a kind of attentive looking or beholding, as the English word "spectacle" actually suggests. As the foolish theater act, Paul invites an attentive looking, just as the audience in the theater must attend to the spectacle of the play. As he has done throughout the opening four chapters, Paul invites believers to discern in his folly the in-breaking of the new age. As a spectacle, that is, Paul the fool interrupts in order to facilitate a new and different perception—the bifocal vision required on the threshold of the old age and the new.

In this respect, Paul enacts one of the primary functions of fools through the ages. Fools are fundamentally agents of perspective. Indeed, some consider certain fools to be descended from inspired "seers," who have a kind of clairvoyance.[26] Fools see the world from an odd perspective that runs counter to dominant ways of perceiving. They seek to change the world by first changing our perception of the world. Don Quixote sees the enchanted golden helmet of

---

25. *"theaomai,"* in Frederick W. Danker, Walter Bauer, and William F. Arndt, *A Greek-English Lexicon of the New Testament and Other Early Christian Literature*, 3rd ed. (Chicago: University of Chicago, 2000), 445–46. See also *"theaomai," Theological Dictionary of the New Testament*, vol. 5, 317–18.
26. Welsford makes this argument, though not quite conclusively, with regard to court-fools. See *Fool*, 79. The famous German fool, Claus Narr, was considered to have a kind of "second sight" (Welsford, *Fool*, 145).

Mambrino where others see only a barber's brass basin.[27] Through
foolish Quixote, Miguel de Cervantes invites his readers to a new
perception of the world. Similarly, Paul sees wisdom and power on
the cross, where others see only the folly and weakness of a "coarse
and vulgar joke." Playing the fool, Paul interrupts "normal" perception and calls believers to new discernment.

Paul's words in this section need to be approached within the
framework of the theatrical fool he depicts in 4:9–10. Within this
context, Paul's contrast between the life of the foolish apostles and
the life of the Corinthians takes on a richer meaning: The Corinthians have become "kings," while the apostles are "last of all," sentenced to death.

> We are weak, but you are strong. You are held in honor, but we
> in disrepute. To the present hour we are hungry and thirsty,
> we are poorly clothed and beaten and homeless, and we grow
> weary from the work of our own hands. When reviled, we
> bless; when persecuted, we endure; when slandered, we speak
> kindly. We have become like the rubbish of the world, the
> dregs of all things, to this very day (vv. 10–13).

Paul hyperbolically depicts the contrast between the lowly fool
and the elite characters in the Roman theater, drawing out the parallels between the apostles and the Corinthians.[28] This sequence is
not simply an autobiographical account, although it probably does
depict elements of Paul's life. Rather, Paul is making a theological
statement, depicting the life of the fool for Christ.

The fool for Christ does not seek honor and standing in the world
but simply seeks to be faithful to the way of Jesus Christ. He or she
lives a scandalous life, at odds with the wisdom and power of the
world, a life that the world would never discern to be holy or sanctified or honorable. Even the response of the apostle to persecution
and slander is itself foolish and unsettling. When reviled, persecuted, or slandered, apostles bless, endure, and speak kindly (vv.

---

27. Miguel de Cervantes, *Don Quixote*, trans. Edith Grossman (New York: Harper Collins,
2003), 153–54. As Cervantes writes, "everything [Don Quixote] saw was very easily
accommodated to his chivalric nonsense and errant thoughts" (154).
28. Welborn argues that each characteristic Paul mentions actually describes the historical life of
the theatrical fools in Paul's day. See *Paul, the Fool of Christ*, 50–86.

12–13). Paul is not speaking generally of persecution or oppression. Throughout the letter he challenges the oppressive hierarchies in his culture. Rather, Paul speaks of the particular persecution of the apostles because they follow Christ. Like the fool's disruptive antics on the stage, the responses to persecution are not a form of passive subservience but a form of resistance.[29] The "foolish" responses of blessing, enduring, and speaking kindly serve to disrupt and expose the powers of this age for what they are—not the powers of life but the powers of death. Just as the cross unmasks the powers, so Christian discipleship unmasks these powers in foolish ways and invites people to discern the gospel of the new creation through discipleship that appears scandalous in the old age.

FURTHER REFLECTIONS
A Theological Tradition: Holy Fools

Paul's affirmation—"we are fools for the sake of Christ"—has inspired a long tradition of Christian holy fools who sought to enact Paul's words in their bizarre and remarkable lives. In so doing, they provide an embodied theological development of this passage, suggesting that abstract theological reflection is inadequate to engage Paul's words.

Holy fools are persons who, for the sake of the gospel, engage in bizarre, obscene, even insane activities, appearing to be lunatics, idiots, or buffoons.[30] This holy foolishness has taken a variety of forms. Some lived out their folly in monasteries, while others wandered the streets like madmen or madwomen. Others have appeared as antisocial eccentrics or as simpleminded; still others as jesters, both pleasant and very unpleasant.[31] Many of them went around unclean, even unclothed. Some wore chains or iron collars. They engaged in all kinds of bizarre and offensive behavior. Through such strange behavior, these figures disrupted both

29. Ibid., 84.
30. Wendy Wright, "Fools for Christ," *Weavings: A Journal of the Christian Spiritual Life* 9 (November/December 1994): 25.
31. Ibid.

religious and social conventions; they too "melted the solidity of the world,"[32] creating a liminal space in which new perspectives were possible but in which discernment was always invited and required.

In the West, St. Francis of Assisi is probably the most well-known holy fool. He gave up a wealthy, luxurious (and wild) life to become a poor wanderer and a pilgrim, roaming the cities and the countryside. He lived in absolute poverty, going barefoot and identifying with poor beggars. He kissed lepers, and he preached to the birds, who apparently listened better than some congregations. Though never canonized, Margery Kempe, an English woman from the fifteenth century, exemplified characteristics of a holy fool. An illiterate, she traveled—wandered—extensively, undertaking many pilgrimages. Everywhere she went, often at the most inopportune times, such as in the middle of sermons and even the mass itself, she would burst into tears and wail uncontrollably over the sins of the world and the suffering and mercy of Jesus Christ.

In the East, the Russian Orthodox saint Basil the Blessed has long been one of the most beloved holy fools. As tradition has it, for over seventy years in the fifteenth and sixteenth centuries Basil wandered the streets of Moscow year round—often stark naked—enacting, proclaiming, and embodying the gospel for the people of the city. Basil called sinners to conversion. He prophesied future events. He performed strange sign-acts, such as throwing rocks at the homes of those who made a public display of their almsgiving and kneeling to kiss the pavement before houses of notorious sinners. He took goods from shops and distributed them to the destitute, and he engaged in other ministries of kindness toward the poor. He is remembered in the colorful onion-domed cathedral on Red Square, St. Basil's Cathedral.[33]

The holy fools are like many of the characters in Flannery

32. Welsford, *Fool*, 223; Alexandra R. Brown, *The Cross and Human Transformation: Paul's Apocalyptic Word in 1 Corinthians* (Minneapolis: Fortress Press, 1995), 13.
33. For more on the holy fools, see John Saward, *Perfect Fools: Folly for Christ's Sake in Catholic and Orthodox Spirituality* (Oxford: Oxford University Press, 1980); Charles L. Campbell and Johan H. Cilliers, *Preaching Fools: The Gospel as a Rhetoric of Folly* (Waco, TX: Baylor University Press, 2012), 93–102; Charles L. Campbell, "Preacher as Ridiculous Person: Naked Street Preaching and Homiletical Foolishness," in Robert Stephen Reid, ed., *Slow of Speech and Unclean Lips: Contemporary Images of Preaching Identity* (Eugene, OR: Cascade Books, 2010), 89–108.

O'Connor's short stories. O'Connor's characters are often bizarre, even repulsive. When O'Connor, a Christian author, was asked why she wrote such strange stories with such grotesque characters, she replied that when you're writing for those who are "almost-blind, you draw large and startling figures."[34] To put that another way, "When you're engaging people whose imaginations have grown numb, you may have to draw with large and startling figures." The holy fools did just that: they sought to embody the foolishness of the gospel in big and shocking ways. In fact, they frequently appeared on the scene when the church was becoming compla-cent—numb—and needed to be startled back to its calling.[35]

The holy fools, like Paul, embody an unsettling reality of the gos-pel which many of us are tempted to ignore. That unsettling reality is this: scandal is an essential part of the message. The holiness and the folly are inseparable. The holy fools, like Paul, sought to make visible the image of God in its deeply scandalous form.[36]

As with Paul, the issue of discernment was central to the bizarre witness of the holy fools. In their one-man shows they staged the "problem of recognition."[37] They enacted a spectacle that was always intentionally susceptible to a double interpretation—just like Jesus' scandalous life, death, and resurrection.[38] Through their carnivalesque street theater, the holy fools, like Paul, created a space that provoked people to learn to "look." They enacted events that challenged people to discern the gospel within the scandal—the holiness within the folly. It was all carefully staged to provoke a kind of looking, a way of perceiving.

The holy fools quite intentionally created a crisis of recognition, a crisis of decision. Usually they were abused and ridiculed because most people never discerned the holiness within the madness. As Russian literary scholar Harriet Murav writes about the work of the holy fools: "The first step for the unrighteous, for those who are

---

34. Flannery O'Connor, *Mystery and Manners: Occasional Prose*, ed. Sally Fitzgerald and Robert Fitzgerald (New York: Farrar, Straus, and Giroux, 1957), 34.
35. Saward, *Perfect Fools*, 215.
36. Harriet Murav, *Holy Foolishness: Dostoevsky's Novels and the Poetics of Cultural Critique* (Stanford, CA: Stanford University Press, 1992), 49.
37. Ibid., 97. My discussion of the holy fools and perception is based on Murav.
38. Ibid., 96.

bored and do not know how to look,…is to be confounded." The righteous, however, did discern the gospel within the scandal, and they were converted or edified.[39] As Paul put it, "For the message about the cross is foolishness to those who are perishing, but to us who are being saved it is the power of God" (1:18).

The hagiographies of these holy fools, from which most of our information about them derives, followed a similar pattern.[40] In presenting the life of the fool, they too were inviting the reader to look; they were creating a crisis of recognition. At issue in the hagiographies is the reader's response. Were these people simply fools—or were they holy fools? Only those who knew how to "look" could discern the gospel within the scandal. As Murav writes,

> Holy foolishness is not a simple kind of sanctity but one that always foregrounds that which is problematic and confounds those who seek to categorize it. The hagiographer . . . represents the holy fool not as a simple innocent but as one who deliberately conceals his true nature from others by assuming a mask of folly. More specifically, the holy fool uses his secret knowledge to provoke and manipulate others.[41]

As these words suggest, things get even more confounding. Even when one learns to look, even when one recognizes the gospel within the scandal, there is still no separating the two.[42] The holiness and the foolishness remain intertwined. You can never somehow remove the kernel of the gospel from the husk of the scandal. As a result, there is no way to categorize the gospel or gain control of it. "The scandal is much more than a breach of decorum. It is that which cannot be mastered."[43] Perhaps that is why the holy fools would often mumble nonsensical speech as they engaged in their bizarre street theater; they were fracturing theology and reminding people of the limitations of words.

Moreover, central to the holy fools' bizarre antics was an attempt

39. Ibid.
40. The holy fools were in many ways literary creations of the hagiographies. While certainly real human beings existed behind these literary works, it is difficult to get at the actual history of these figures.
41. Murav, *Holy Foolishness*, 93.
42. Paul uses the Greek term *skandalon* when discussing the cross in 1 Corinthians 1:23.
43. Murav, *Holy Foolishness*, 96.

to conceal their sanctity.[44] They were diverting attention from their holiness by hiding it behind their indecent and disorderly behavior. The most dangerous temptation for the holy person is pride, so, even as many of the holy fools prayed all night in secret, they sought in public to avoid being praised for their sanctity. Consistent with Paul's emphasis in the letter to the Corinthians, holy folly was in a deep sense a practice of humility. The sanctity of the holy fools is intentionally hidden behind their scandalous antics. When holy fools perform a miracle or an act of clairvoyance, they often seek to divert attention from it and reinforce their foolishness. They conceal the sanctity their miracles reveal.

Consider one example from *The Life of Symeon the Fool*. When a tavern keeper discerns Symeon's holiness, Symeon goes to the man's sleeping wife and pretends to undress himself. She awakes and, thinking he is about to rape her, screams for her husband, whereupon the husband beats Symeon and tosses him out of the shop. From that time on the tavern-keeper thinks Symeon is beside himself—indeed, possessed.[45] Again and again, Symeon engages in such transgressive, deceptive acts in order to conceal his sanctity. Every time someone comes close to recognizing his holiness, he intentionally does something outrageous and scandalous to change the perspective on himself. By actively hiding his holiness, Symeon avoids the praise and acclaim that would come to him because of his holy life.[46] Paradoxically, his purpose is humility; he enacts a particular perspective on the scandalous, hidden holiness of the crucified Jesus.

With just a few words—"We are fools for the sake of Christ"— Paul inspired a long and rich tradition of *embodied theology*. In their scandalous behavior, the holy fools actually carried forward many of the central emphases of Paul's theology: interruption, scandal, discernment, humility. A full appreciation of Paul's theology will need to attend not simply to the doctrinal tradition of the church but also

---

44. On the tradition of concealed sanctity and its characteristics, see Derek Krueger, *Symeon the Holy Fool: Leontius's "Life" and the Late Antique City* (Berkeley: University of California Press, 1996), 66–71.
45. Ibid., 153.
46. Ibid., 51–52.

to the lives of the holy fools who, like Paul, fracture the theological
assumptions and cultural complacency of the church.

4:14–21
Imitate Me

Paul concludes this opening theological section with an admonishment to the Corinthians. He takes on the common—and comical—theatrical role of the anxious father who is dealing with unruly
children and needs to call on guardians (Timothy, after many others
have failed) to bring them under control (vv. 14–17).[47] The apparently odd reference to coming "with a stick" (v. 21), a common prop
of the theatrical fool, carries forward the theatrical metaphor.[48] Even
here, as he admonishes the Corinthians, Paul includes an ironic element; he is, in contemporary terms, like a frazzled parent trying
to herd cats. There is an element of self-deprecation even in Paul's
words of admonishment.

Paul's call for the Corinthians to imitate him is also both theatrical and foolish. Mimesis, imitation, was central in the theatrical
mimes, a genre of drama that mimicked and often parodied lower-
class life and in which fools were stock characters.[49] Now, playing on
this theatrical form, Paul invites the Corinthians to imitate him (v.
16). But he is inviting them to imitate the fool, to take up the role of
the fool for the sake of Christ.

Theologically and ethically, Paul's move is instructive. First, his
invitation to "imitate me" is paradoxical and ironic, just as the rest
of Paul's theological introduction has been. Paul has presented himself as an example of humility, rubbish, dregs for the sake of the gospel. Now he declares, "Imitate me," with apparent arrogance. But he
makes this claim as a fool for the sake of Christ. He calls the Corinthians to imitate him in his foolishness and weakness. It is an ironic
form of arrogance that undercuts itself. Like the accomplished orator, Paul holds up his character for imitation, but he simultaneously

47. Welborn, *Paul, the Fool of Christ*, 86–90. My interpretation relies on Welborn.
48. Ibid., 89.
49. On the mimes see ibid., 1–14.

subverts the traditional honor and stature of the orator. Paul invites the Corinthians to discern the kind of "concealed sanctity" that was embodied by the holy fools. Only those whom the Spirit has enabled to "look" would possibly seek to imitate him.

Second, what other choice does Paul have than to invite others to imitate him? There are no *Introduction to Christian Ethics* texts to which he could refer. Indeed, there is not yet even a New Testament. The gospel Paul proclaims is so scandalous that few are taking it seriously. What *does* discipleship look like? Paul is left pointing to himself because he really has nowhere else to turn. He is in the unsettling situation of embodying the character of the Christian life for others to imitate. The very character of that life militates against claiming honor—even the honor of faithfulness—for oneself. His call to "imitate me" is as unsettling as his calling from God and his proclamation of the gospel.

Paul's approach to ethics at this critical point in the letter is significant. As he seeks to build up the church, he does not set forth a list of rules or principles to follow. Rather, his approach is contextual. He points to the character of a particular life, even if it is his own. As faithfully as he can, he seeks to enact the life of discipleship in his specific situation. This is what such a life looks like in this time and place, he writes. The way to discern the shape of the Christian life is not through a set of abstract rules but by attending to the faithful discipleship of other believers in one's particular situation. Paul, that is, suggests a form of character ethics, whereby Christians grow as disciples by imitating those who are farther along on the way, just as a jazz musician initially learns to play his or her instrument by imitating one of the masters. Paul, in a sense, is improvising, seeking to live out the foolish gospel in the most faithful way he can. He invites the church not to follow an abstract set of rules but to join him in his improvisation. In theatrical terms, Paul invites believers not legalistically to follow a script but to learn from each other the improvisational habits and practices that constitute faithful Christian community.[50] For a contemporary church that has too often become captive to rigid and exclusive sets of moral rules (and has used 1

50. Samuel Wells, *Improvisation: The Drama of Christian Ethics* (Grand Rapids, MI: Brazos Press), 2004.

Corinthians to justify these rules!), Paul's approach offers a dynamic alternative. In the Christian community, in each particular context, believers are discerning together the character of discipleship; they are improvising on the gospel at the unsettled juncture between the old age and the new.

> The Bible is not so much a script that the church learns and performs as it is a training school that shapes the habits and practices of the community.
>
> Wells, *Improvisation*, 12.

The one thing that inhibits this kind of improvisation, Paul repeatedly asserts, is arrogance. So he returns to that concern as he prepares to address specific issues in the Corinthian community in the rest of the letter (vv. 18–19). His purpose is not simply to condemn arrogant individuals. Rather, his focus is the life of the community at the turn of the ages. Arrogance and Christian community simply cannot coexist.

The problem with arrogance is its certainty; it represents a kind of "closed seriousness" that has resolved the tensions of life at the turn of the ages and dismisses those who dare to differ. It represents captivity to the dominating spirit of this age, resisting the community-creating power of the Spirit (vv. 19–20). Arrogance is not open to the interruption of the gospel or the interruption of others; it inhibits the kind of dynamic *communitas* that Paul desires in the liminal space at the juncture of the ages.

Because the gospel is disruptive and unsettling, humility becomes a central virtue. This kind of humility does not wallow in self-denigration or refuse to resist domination, but it always remains open to interruptions by the gospel and by others in the community. Such humility is a form of "open seriousness" that recognizes the incomplete character of life at the turn of the ages, celebrates the liminal nature of Christian community, and lives in mutuality with others. This kind of humility is essential to the community that lives in the unsettled space between the old age and the new.

Paul frames his concluding words with both admonishment and love (vv. 14, 21). He thus suggests the character of the rest of the letter. On the one hand, he desires the spirit of gentleness that characterizes love; on the other, he adopts the necessary admonishment when correction is required. These two characteristics of Paul's engagement with the Corinthians are not contradictory. Admonishment can be a profound expression of love; being disciplined by a parent or friend may enable us to experience the deep concern and love of the other person. Similarly, expressions of love from those we have hurt or offended can often convict us of our failures in a way that harsh words of judgment do not. Here too Paul takes up the way of the cross, in which God convicts us through an act of love and loves us in an act of judgment. On the cross, these two aspects of God's work are held inextricably together in a tensive relationship. They cannot be taken apart, as if love does not involve admonishment or admonishment is a denial of love. This dynamic shapes the practical suggestions and directions that make up the remainder of the letter as Paul continues his efforts to build up the church.

5:1–13

Ecclesial Discipline

In chapter 5 Paul turns from the theological vision of chapters 1–4 to specific ecclesial practices that will occupy him throughout the remainder of the letter. Before moving to the details of these chapters, several emphases that shape my interpretation need to be highlighted. First, I approach Paul's discussion of ecclesial practices within the theological vision he develops in the opening four chapters. Paul's apocalyptic theological vision informs the rest of the letter, and one should not interpret the practical matters in isolation from it. One should not, for example, interpret Paul's ethical guidance as a set of rigid moralistic rules. Rather, Paul addresses a being-saved community that appears foolish to the surrounding culture. He does not write timeless ethical principles but rather seeks to speak a fitting word for a particular community living at the turn of the ages. To take Paul's unsettling, disruptive theological vision and transform it into universal moralisms would distort Paul's theology, isolating the ethical practice from the theological vision. Indeed, when Paul's practical directives become set in stone, they can—and have—become damaging to individual believers and the Christian community as a whole. They have, in fact, been used to perpetuate the very hierarchies and divisions Paul seeks to overcome. Surely, that would not be Paul's desired outcome in a letter proclaiming the unmanageable, foolish Word, the power of the Spirit, and the centrality of a community of love.

Second, the opening words of chapter 5 set the tone for what follows: "It is actually reported . . ." Paul is engaged in a dialogue, in which we are privy to one side only: we indirectly overhear the reports Paul mentions, and we read Paul's responses. Indeed, this letter itself is part of a larger, ongoing dialogue between Paul and the community. Paul states that he has written an earlier letter to the church addressing some of these issues (v. 9); in verse 10 and following he appears to be clarifying comments from the previous letter, probably in response to the Corinthians' concerns. This dialogical character of the letter is important. Paul is responding to issues raised and questions posed by the community itself. At points he is simply "doing the best he can," almost thinking out loud,[1] with no "command" from the Lord (e.g., 7:6, 25). Indeed, one wonders if Paul might have used this disclaimer even more often if he had known his letter would become Scripture for the future church.

Moreover, the dialogue does not end with this letter. The Corinthian community continued to push back, so that Paul had to write other letters to them. There is no final resolution through Paul's letters, but this fact is not something to fear. Rather, it is a helpful model for the Christian community. Ecclesiology is dialogical. Theological truth and ecclesial practice are never settled or final but reflect the dynamic of the being-saved community that is on the way at the turn of the ages. The letter to the Corinthians models the dialogical character of life in the church, where believers are always seeking to discern the gospel in the scandal as well as the foolish practices that move its life from captivity to the old age into the life of the new creation.

Finally, Paul's focus is the *community*. Paul seeks to discern "what the Spirit is saying to the church." Paul is concerned about ecclesial practices, and he should not be read within a Western, individualistic framework. Even when addressing the issue of the man living with his father's wife, Paul does not focus on the individual but on the responsibility of the community as a whole. He seeks to build up the church. He desires to form a distinctive community that embodies the life of the new creation in the midst of the powers of death.

---

1. New Testament scholar Frances Taylor Gench mentioned this possibility to me in a conversation.

5:1–8
Discipline and Redemption

In a counseling situation, one of the most important things a coun-selor does is to look beneath the "presenting issue" to the deeper issues that should be addressed for healing and growth. "Our child is not behaving in school" may be the presenting issue when a fam-ily comes for counseling, but the deeper issue that needs to be addressed is probably family dynamics. To focus narrowly on the child's behavior actually misses the most important issue at hand. In interpreting 1 Corinthians, it is important to avoid this error. In chapter 5, for example, *porneia* ("sexual immorality") should not be elevated from the presenting issue into the deeper, fundamental issue.[2] Even more, it should not be pressed into a moralistic treat-ment of sexuality, which would miss Paul's deeper ecclesiological concerns.

In chapter 5, the presenting issue is an extreme example of sex-ual immorality: a man is living with his father's wife. The example is so extreme that even the Gentiles or "pagans" would have been appalled at this behavior; there is nothing distinctively Christian about Paul's condemnation of the morality of this situation (v. 1). The issue is therefore probably not simply irresponsible notions of freedom in the Corinthian church, with some members asserting that sexual morality is irrelevant to the Christian life. Rather, the members of the Corinthian church probably agree with Paul about the morality of the behavior.[3] While the presenting issue is a person's sexual immorality, that is not the fundamental issue Paul addresses.

We do not know the specifics of the presenting situation, though we may discern a few important details. First, the woman is probably not the man's own mother but, rather, his "father's wife"—or stepmother—although we are not told the history of the father's relationships or marriages.[4] Second, the woman in this

2. *Porneia* can have a broad range of meanings. See Dale B. Martin, *The Corinthian Body* (New Haven, CT: Yale University Press, 1995), 169.
3. Ibid., 173.
4. The prohibition against living with one's "father's wife" appears in Deuteronomy 27:20 and Leviticus 18:8, 20:11. See Richard B. Hays, *First Corinthians*, Interpretation: A Bible Commentary for Teaching and Preaching (Louisville, KY: John Knox Press, 1997), 81.

case is probably not a member of the Christian community but an "outsider"; otherwise, Paul would not have simply addressed the immorality of the man but also the woman. Third, and most important, Paul understands the man's behavior to somehow be "polluting" the Corinthian community; just as unclean leaven changes the entire loaf of bread, so the continued presence of the man in the church makes the entire Body of Christ unclean. Thus, the man must be expelled from the church for the sake of the community's purity and holiness.[5]

This third point gets to the real issue beneath the presenting one. Paul's fundamental concern is the distinctiveness of the community of faith. His use of the Passover imagery of the paschal lamb highlights this emphasis; the blood on the doorposts of the Hebrew people sets them apart from the people of Egypt.[6] It is thus not surprising that Paul's first response to the sexual immorality of the man is not a condemnation of the man himself. Rather, Paul returns to a key critique addressed to members of the community at the end of chapter 4: arrogance (v. 2). Some in the community, most likely the elites, arrogantly claim that the presence of the man in the community is not a problem at all. Even though his actions are immoral, his presence does not pollute the entire Body of Christ; it does not affect the distinctiveness of the church. The actions of one person in the community do not have an impact on the church as a whole; one bad apple does not spoil the entire bunch.[7] For Paul, however, these believers' failure to discern their complicity in the church's pollution undermines their arrogant claims.

The conflict is ecclesiological; it goes to the very character of church. Paul assumes a dynamic, inseparable relationship between the individual parts of Christ's Body and the Body as a whole. In addition, he sees the church engaged in the ongoing battle between the new creation and the old age, a battle in which the new creation has interrupted the old age but in which the old age simultaneously

5. Hays notes the deep scriptural roots of this understanding of community made unclean by an immoral member; see *First Corinthians*, 82–83. Martin highlights understandings of disease that emphasize the polluting character of foreign agents and the need for boundaries in the Christian community; see *Corinthian Body*, 139–97.
6. Hays, *First Corinthians*, 83.
7. Martin, *Corinthian Body*, 163–64, 173–74.

continues to "infect" the new community. Interpreting this battle, Paul draws not only on the Passover metaphor of leaven but also on an invasive understanding of disease, according to which a body becomes sick because of invasive, outside elements. The man living with his father's wife is just such an infecting agent. As a consequence, Paul emphasizes the importance of protecting the boundaries between the church and the world, even as he recognizes the porous character of these boundaries in the life of the Corinthian church.[8] He stresses the importance of radical surgery in the body to remove the invasive cause of the illness.

Paul's understanding of the body is important, for the metaphor of the body runs throughout the letter. On the one hand, the Body of Christ clearly has female characteristics. The female body was understood at the time as more porous than the male body, more susceptible to invasion (or penetration) by outside agents.[9] By recognizing that outside agents can "invade" the Christian community and infect it, Paul actually develops a culturally female characteristic of Christ's Body. Indeed, later in the chapter, when he argues that Christians do not retreat from the world, Paul actually affirms these more porous boundaries between the church and the culture (vv. 9–13). Here, though, Paul argues that the Body of Christ should be more "male"—that is, it should have stronger boundaries to keep out the infecting agents and preserve the Body's overall health.[10] This male-female dynamic of the Body of Christ represents a fascinating dimension of Paul's ecclesiology in chapter 5.

Similarly, as has been noted, different understandings of disease color the ecclesiological conflict. The elite Christians in Corinth probably understood health and disease as a matter of balance; the various elements in the body and atmosphere had to be in proper balance in order for the body to be healthy. For these Christians, radical surgery to remove an infecting agent would not be required; rather, minor adjustments to restore the proper balance

---

8. As will become clear later, Paul does not call the church completely to retreat from the world. He presents what Martin calls a "modified sectarianism." Ibid., 170.

9. Ibid., 233.

10. Brittany E. Wilson, *Unmanly Men: Refigurations of Masculinity in Luke–Acts* (Oxford: Oxford University Press, 2015), 39–75.

were all that was called for.[11] For the lower class or weak people in the church, more popular understandings of disease—as the invasion of infecting agents or powers—probably prevailed. In his approach, Paul sides with the weak, as he will do in numerous instances throughout the letter. His primary concern is the divisive arrogance of the elites, who are unconcerned about the presence of the immoral man, rather than one specific instance of sexual morality.

Thus Paul, here as elsewhere, interrupts the assumptions and conventions of the elite Corinthians in order to build up the church as a distinctive community. There is no place for arrogance. Because of the immoral actions of one man and the community's failure to deal with him, the entire community is infected. No one is immune or above reproach. Arrogance simply serves to divide the community and prevent the Corinthians from engaging in the necessary discipline to restore the community's distinctiveness.

Paul's apocalyptic theological framework shapes his directives to the community about how to exercise the necessary discipline. The church is to "hand this man over to Satan for the destruction of *the* [not his, contra NRSV] flesh, so that *the* [not his] spirit may be saved in the day of the Lord" (v. 5). Paul is not suggesting the individual fleshy substance of the man be destroyed; he does not say "his flesh." Rather, the "flesh" (*sarx*), as noted earlier, refers to deathly existence in the old age. Satan represents the ruler of the old age, the driving force behind all the principalities and powers.[12] To hand the man over to Satan is to expel him from the community of the new creation back into the "world," the cosmos—the *sarx*— the powers of this age—which have already taken him captive. It is to hand him over to the powers of death, which already hold him in their grip.

Paul's purpose here is ecclesial discipline, not final judgment or vengeance. His purpose is redemptive: the destruction of the flesh so the spirit might be "saved in the day of the Lord" (v. 5). The goal is not simply the purity of the church but the liberation of the man

11. Martin, *Corinthian Body*, 163–64, 173–74.
12. Walter Wink, *Engaging the Powers: Discernment and Resistance in a World of Domination* (Minneapolis: Fortress Press, 1992), 59.

from the old-age realm of the flesh so he might live in the realm of the Spirit. This entire process takes place in the liminal, ongoing movement toward the new creation in which final redemption, as Paul noted at the beginning of the letter, occurs on the day of the Lord (1:8). Indeed, final judgment is left to the Lord; it does not belong to Paul or to the Corinthian community. Paul thus presents an apocalyptic form of church discipline, in which embodiments of the old age that invade and corrupt the community must be removed so that the purity of the community may be restored and the captive offender might be redeemed.

FURTHER REFLECTIONS
Liberation

Through his use of the Passover story as a metaphor for Jesus' death and the church's life, Paul signals that his purpose is not simply distinctiveness, but liberation. Although, as has been noted, Paul's allusions to the leaven and the paschal lamb do connote the distinctiveness of the church, they signify much more than that. The Corinthian church is captive to the powers of this age, and Paul seeks to liberate the community from the divisive old-age conventions that lead to arrogance. In the process, Paul offers a suggestive interpretation of Christ's sacrificial death.

Paul interprets Christ as the paschal lamb that has been sacrificed (v. 7). The christological implications of this move are significant. Through the lens of Passover, Christ's sacrifice is not a matter of the forgiveness of sins. Nor is it an act of vicarious atonement, in which Jesus endures the punishment and suffering deserved by human beings so that we might be saved. Nor is it an expression of a satisfaction theory of the atonement, according to which an angry God of justice demands satisfaction from sinful humans, which the death of Jesus provides. Nor does it represent a moral influence theory of the atonement, according to which we humans see the suffering love of Jesus on the cross and are moved to respond with our lives. None of these atonement theories applies here; another understanding of Christ's sacrifice is at work.

Through the lens of Passover, Christ's death enables liberation from captivity to the old age, just as the death of the paschal lamb enabled Israel's liberation from slavery in Egypt. The angel of death "passed over" Israel, whose doorposts were marked with the blood of the lamb. The blood did not forgive them or satisfy God's justice or ethically move them by God's suffering. Rather, the blood identified them as God's people and spared them from the powers of death so God could lead them out of Egypt toward the promised land. The people ate unleavened bread because there was no time for the leavening process; they were on the move (Exod. 12:39).

The Passover represents the new, liminal threshold space par excellence. God radically interrupts the powers of death in order to set free the Hebrew people. The Passover celebrated freedom even while the people were still in the midst of captivity; God was doing something new to liberate the captives. God was setting the Hebrews on the way. Passover marked God's liberating work on behalf of "low and despised" slaves who were considered weak and foolish in the world. The blood of the paschal lamb created the space between the old and the new within which the people of Israel now lived and moved. Significantly, the blood was on the doorposts, the literal *thresholds* through which the people would pass on their way out of Egypt. The blood of the lamb becomes a powerful metaphor for liminal, threshold life between the old age and the new creation.

Paul's interpretive use of the Passover, including the leaven and the paschal lamb, undergirds his disruptive, liminal theology. Viewing the Corinthian church through the lens of the Passover story, Paul invites the being-saved community into the threshold space in which the new creation has interrupted the old age and God is liberating the "low and despised" from the oppressive powers that be. This space is not a dour, narrow, moralistic space; it is a space in which to "celebrate the festival" (v. 8)—a space where the people anticipate and live into God's freedom. The "old yeast" is being left behind while the people journey toward the promised land of the new creation.

The old yeast, Paul declares, is characterized by "malice" and "evil." Paul again speaks to the character of the Christian community, not a specific "presenting issue." The church is not to be characterized by malice, even toward those who must be disciplined. Such malice, often the result of moral arrogance, does not contribute to genuine community and freedom. Nor is the community to be characterized by "evil." The church is not to pursue the ways of domination and death that characterize the powers of this age. Following this path, the community would lose its distinctiveness, its life in the new creation.

Rather, those who are being saved undertake their journey with the "unleavened bread of sincerity and truth" (v. 8), which are essential virtues for communal life that can be divided and destroyed by festering silence or malicious lies. There can be no genuine discernment in a community shaped by malice and evil but only in communities formed in sincerity and truthfulness. Sincerity calls for a purity of motive that is the opposite of malicious lies. Similarly, truthfulness breaks the silence and counters the deceit that the powers of this age use to further evil. These virtues interrupt the powers' efforts to keep people silent and encourage lies so their deceptive old-age "truth" will never be questioned. Sincerity and truthfulness unmask (apocalypse) the powers, bringing them out into the open and exposing them for what they are: not the agents of life but the powers of death.

In his brief summary at the end of this section, Paul does not turn to moralistic rules. Consistent with his concern for the deep issues of the Corinthian church, he highlights the virtues of sincerity and truthfulness that are critical to the ongoing life of the Christian community at the turn of the ages. Virtues are the dynamic qualities of character that enable persons and communities to negotiate the journey of life in particular ways. Paul here highlights two of the essential qualities for resisting the powers of death in the unsettled, tensive space between the old age and the new creation. Moralistic rules are simply inadequate in this space. The dynamic virtues of sincerity and truthfulness are required because they enable people to interrupt the silence and lies that are used by the powers of this age to maintain control.

5:9–13
In the World but Not of It

Having highlighted the distinctiveness and virtues of the Christian community, Paul proceeds to clarify the relationship between
members of the church and "immoral persons" *outside* the community. Paul makes clear that he has no interest in a narrowly
sectarian church or a rigid dualism that avoids contact with the
"world," a significant qualification of his emphasis on the church's
boundaries. Rather, Paul recognizes that rigid boundaries are not
possible; the community is porous, and believers inevitably interact with the world in multiple ways. Paul actually affirms the necessity of believers associating with the "immoral of this world"—the
"greedy and robbers, or idolaters." Otherwise, he writes, "you
would then need to go out of the world" (v. 10). Paul has no
interest in withdrawal from the world. There is no sense in which
Christians at this point live fully in the new creation. Rather, life
is pursued in the threshold space between the ages. Believers are
to live in the world but not of it. This kind of engagement with the
world will later shape Paul's discussion of other issues, such as eating meat offered to idols.

Although Paul does not stress this point, his recognition that
the Christian community associates with "outsiders" suggests that
the church itself might be interrupted in surprising ways by unbelievers. Because of his emphasis on communal boundaries and his
concern that the community not be polluted by immorality, Paul
may not expect too many of these interruptions. Such interruptions
are inevitable, however, as the church engages with those beyond
its boundaries. New challenges come, to which the church must
respond. Indeed, Paul's own life was interrupted as he encountered
those outside his religious community, whom he certainly considered immoral and unclean. Paul's very calling opens him to such
interruptions, to surprising ways in which the Spirit may be moving to form and re-form the Christian community. Paul's practical
reflections on several issues (e.g., eating meat offered to idols, marriage to unbelievers) are, in fact, responses to interruptions posed by
Christian life in the world.

Paul's apocalyptic interruptions, thus, are multiple. God in Christ has interrupted the old age with the new creation. The Christian community, as it resists the assumptions and conventions of the world, enacts in its life an interruption of the hierarchical arrangements and priorities of the larger culture. Finally, the church's engagement with the world may interrupt the community and invite the church's theology and discipleship to change and grow. New scientific findings about sexual orientation, for example, represent one contemporary interruption of the church, which calls for fresh discernment. Indeed, these findings challenge older categories of "moral" and "immoral." Similarly, the Spirit may use the church's engagement with other religions to interrupt and nurture the church's theology. The dynamic process of discernment moves not only within the community of faith but also at the intersection of the church and the world. The only way to avoid these kinds of interruptions is to isolate the church from any engagement with the world, which Paul refuses to do. Even in a section of the letter in which the apostle stresses the church's boundaries, the Body of Christ remains somewhat porous not only to the "pollution" of the world but also to possible interruptions of the Spirit through its engagement with the world.

Following his disclaimer regarding retreat from the world, Paul returns to the internal life and discipline of the community, which has been the focus of this chapter. Although believers may associate with immoral people outside the community, Paul rejects such association among brothers and sisters within the church. Emphasizing again the purity and distinctiveness of the church, Paul broadens the list of unacceptable behavior beyond sexual immorality to include the greedy, idolaters, revilers, drunkards, and robbers (v. 11). Paul's list is possibly a general catalog taken from the culture, which would suggest that condemnation of many of these activities was not distinctive to Paul; his list is not necessarily "countercultural." Or the list may reflect specific Deuteronomic prohibitions, suggesting that the Christian community continues the distinctiveness of the people of Israel.[13] Either way, the underlying theological focus is the same. As with the man who was sexually immoral, the church, following

---

13. Hays, *First Corinthians*, 87–88.

directions from the Hebrew Scripture, is to "drive out the wicked person from among you" (v. 13).[14] The Body is to expel those elements that are infecting and polluting it. Paul thus concludes this section with the same theological emphasis on discipline and distinctiveness with which he began, though now he has broadened it beyond the presenting case to include a range of other behaviors.

Here at the end of this section, Paul gives further specificity to his emphasis on the purity of the church: "Do not even eat with such a one," he writes (v. 11). Paul addresses the communal meals of the church, probably the Lord's Supper. Just as the Passover meal, to which Paul refers earlier, marked the distinctiveness of Israel, so the church's communal meal marks the distinctiveness of the Body of Christ. Table fellowship was an extremely intimate form of fellowship, and in the Lord's Supper that fellowship enacts the Body of Christ. The communal meals should thus be free of agents that pollute the Body.

Paul's command, however, raises a significant theological issue. The Lord Jesus Christ, whose power and spirit Paul claims (vv. 3–4), welcomed to table tax collectors, sinners, and unclean people. He not only shared a cup with a Samaritan woman but then spent two days with Samaritans, presumably eating at table in their homes (John 4:1–45). He shared the Last Supper itself with Judas, who would betray him; Peter, who would deny him; and others who would desert him. Jesus' meal practices were anything but pure in the eyes of the religious authorities. Paul himself even castigated Peter for refusing to eat with unclean Gentiles (Gal. 2:11–14). And later here in 1 Corinthians (11:17–34), even as he condemns the practice of the Lord's Supper in Corinth, he does not "drive out" those who are greedy from the community. Indeed, in light of Paul's long list of offensive behaviors, one wonders who could be pure enough to come to the Lord's table. Paul's emphasis on purity collides with the table hospitality and grace of Jesus the host.

The fragmentary character of Paul's letter comes clearly into view at this point. Paul speaks to a specific situation in Corinth where maintaining the church's distinctiveness has become a priority.

14. Deut. 13:5; 17:7; 22:21–24.

Writing to an extremely small, divided church, Paul emphasizes the importance of the church's peculiar identity as an interruption of the larger culture. Paul's underlying theological convictions, though, not simply his list of immoral persons, should shape the church's interpretation and appropriation of his words today. What does it mean for the church to live as a distinctive community in the context of widely different, contemporary cultures? Amid the dialogue of the various theological fragments of Scripture and guided by the Spirit of the Lord Jesus Christ (5:3–4), different communities of faith seek to discern the distinctive shape of their life together in their context. At the threshold of the ages, the life of the Christian community is never settled. The unruly, foolish gospel continues to interrupt our assumptions and conclusions. In the power of the Spirit, the community continually seeks to discern the ways in which Christ is forming and re-forming the church. Paul's lists of immoral actions and persons can never be isolated from this ongoing process of discernment. Such lists can never constrain the unsettling, disruptive freedom of the living God at the turn of the ages.

Paul himself returns to this emphasis at the end of the chapter. He began by declaring his own judgment of the man who was living with his father's wife. Here at the end, though, as he broadens his concerns beyond this extreme example, he declares that "you"—the Corinthian church—are to judge those who are "inside," while leaving to God the judgment of those "outside" (vv. 12–13). Paul places the process of judgment within the community of faith. Such judgment, Paul declares, requires the discernment of the church that is being formed and re-formed by the Spirit. Indeed, the Greek words for judgment (*krinō*) and discernment (*sunkrinō*) come from the same root. Paul has weighed in, but he concludes by turning matters over to the community as a whole. As he states elsewhere in the letter more than once, "Judge for yourselves" (10:15; 11:13). Indeed, the community's arrogant abdication of this responsibility to judge matters related to its life together lies at the heart of Paul's critique. Just as Paul began this section by stressing the role of the Spirit of the Lord Jesus Christ in his own word of judgment (vv. 3–4), so here at the end he trusts that same Spirit to guide the discernment of the community of faith.

6:1–20

Freedom

While continuing his emphasis on communal boundaries and discernment, Paul's underlying theological concern in chapter 6 is the character of Christian freedom. Beneath the presenting issues of going to court and fornication, freedom is Paul's focus. This emphasis becomes clear in the comments from some of the Corinthians to which the apostle is responding: "All things are lawful for me" (v. 12). This is the radical claim about freedom that Paul is addressing. And Paul replies, "but not all things are beneficial . . . I will not be dominated by anything" (v. 12). At the heart of this section, Paul signals the character of Christian freedom. It is not simply negative freedom—freedom *from*. Rather, it is freedom that takes into account power dynamics, the larger life of the community, and the *telos* or goal of the Christian life. In short, Christian freedom can never be simply freedom *from*; it is always freedom *for*—for others, for the community, for Christ.[1]

6:1–11
Power and the Courts

In his critique of going to court, Paul addresses issues of economic and social power among the elites in the Corinthian church, those who are probably claiming freedom for themselves. Simultaneously,

---

1. For a helpful discussion of different kinds of freedom, see William T. Cavanaugh, *Being Consumed: Economics and Christian Desire* (Grand Rapids, MI: Wm. B. Eerdmans Publishing Co., 2008), 1–32.

Paul challenges the social stratification in the Body of Christ. The judicial system in Corinth, as it is currently in the United States, was clearly weighted in favor of the wealthy and powerful. The elites took poorer people to court, and these elites could generally count on winning their cases. Because of the expense involved in taking someone to court, only the wealthy could afford it. Moreover, the judges in the court were from the upper classes and would inevitably rule in favor of their social peers. The socially prominent and powerful were able to use the legal system to their own advantage, seeking economic redress for offenses and defrauding the poor (v. 8).[2]

We get an interesting picture of this kind of judicial injustice in one of Jesus' sayings in the Sermon on the Mount. In Matthew 5:40, Jesus says, "If anyone wants to sue you and take your coat, give your cloak as well." Jesus here is speaking to lower status people who are the ones taken to court and sued. The situation is one in which the economic powers have so milked the poor that all they have left to be sued for are their garments. When their outer garment is claimed in court, Jesus counsels them to give the inner one also. That is, the victim of the economic system, who has no other recourse, takes off the inner garment and walks out of the court stark naked. In this way the victim exposes the system's essential cruelty and "burlesques its pretensions to justice, law, and order."[3] As the person walks out of court naked and people begin to ask what is going on, the economic system itself stands naked and is exposed for what it is—a system that treats the poor as "sponge[s] to be squeezed dry by the rich."[4] Jesus' lampooning of the justice system makes clear the use of the system by the powerful elites at the expense of the poor.

In Corinth, this systemic injustice has now infected the Christian community itself, as elite members of the community are taking poorer members to court. The social stratifications of power and privilege that exist in the culture have invaded the community and are creating divisions. The claim of freedom on the part of the elites in the community ("all things are lawful for me") ironically ignores

2. See Alan C. Mitchell, "Rich and Poor in the Courts of Corinth: Litigiousness and Status in 1 Corinthians 6:1–11," *New Testament Studies* 39 (Oct. 1993): 562–86.
3. Walter Wink, "Neither Passivity nor Violence: Jesus' Third Way," *Forum* 7 (March–June, 1991): 12.
4. Ibid.

their own captivity to the powers of this age embodied in the court system. The elites are not only oblivious to the dynamics of power oppressing the lower status members, but they also neglect the health of the Christian community. So Paul challenges the elites to resist the systemic injustice of the court system and to seek an alternative kind of arbitration within the church.

Paul's challenge is withering. First, Paul turns the hierarchical judicial system on its head, raising up the lower-status people within the Christian community, as he had done in the earlier chapters of the letter. Just as Jesus had been "raised up" on the cross as one of the "low and despised," now Paul "raises up" the "low and despised" in the community to the status of judges. Using rhetorical questions, to which the answers should be obvious, Paul highlights the lack of wisdom evident among the elites who take other members of the community to the courts. "Do you not know that the saints will judge the world?" (v. 2). Then, in an even more radical claim, "Do you not know that we are to judge angels?" (v. 3). The saints, of course, include everyone in the community; in that claim all the status markers are broken down, and the "low and despised" are raised up to the level of judges. Indeed, they are elevated far beyond the judges of local cases to the role of those who will judge not only the world, but angels. The hierarchical arrangements of Corinthian society, so evident in the judicial system, are overturned in the Christian community. Just as Paul elevates the "low and despised" in his opening theological vision, and just as he will challenge economic and social inequalities in later portions of the letter, so here Paul argues that the church should provide an alternative to the hierarchical arrangements of Roman society.

Second, Paul employs scathing irony and sarcasm to shame those in positions of power (v. 5). The social elites would have considered themselves wise. As has been noted, this does not mean they were proponents of a particular philosophical position or school. Rather, they were educated and had absorbed the popular philosophical wisdom of the culture, which included the cultural conventions about the hierarchical character of the body politic. Now Paul shames them, just as Paul had earlier affirmed that God has used what is "low and despised" to shame the wise (1:27). The worst possible experience for the elites, who seek to be honored, is that of shame. So Paul asks a sarcastic, ironic question: "Can it be that there is no one among you wise enough to decide between one believer and another?" (v. 5) Again, the issue is discernment, and Paul notes the irony of claiming to be wise, while having to go to outsiders to find those capable of deciding (*diakrinō*) legal cases. Contrary to the assumptions of the elite, true wisdom, in accord with the "foolish" wisdom of the cross, requires freedom *from* captivity to the hierarchical structures of the society and freedom *for* solidarity with those of lower-status position. It is better to be defrauded, Paul tells the elites in the church, than to participate in a system that wrongs and defrauds the poor (vv. 7–8). Just as Paul lowered himself socially for the sake of the "low and despised," so the elite Corinthian Christians are to do the same. The church, Paul proclaims, enacts a radical alternative to the surrounding culture. The Body of Christ operates differently from the body politic.

Paul reinforces his point by linking those elites who "wrong" (*adikeite*) believers in court to his list of "wrongdoers" (*adikoi*) who will "not inherit the kingdom of God" (v. 8–9). The list of wrongdoers ("fornicators, idolaters . . . ;" vv. 9–10) should not be lifted out of its context in Paul's argument.[5] Rather, it is hyperbolic rhetoric that seeks to interrupt and unmask the wrongdoing of those who oppress people through the judicial system. Paul initiates the list with a sarcastic rhetorical question, assuming agreement and challenging the wisdom of the elites: "Do you not know . . . ?" (v. 9). In addition, he frames the list with the twice-repeated claim that these "wrongdoers" will not inherit the kingdom of God (v. 9, 10).

There are internal inconsistencies in Paul's presentation, reinforcing the hyperbolic character of his claims. Paul's words sharply contradict his earlier comments regarding a similar list of "wrongdoers": "For what have I to do with judging those outside? . . . God will judge those outside" (5:12–13). Here, however, instead of leaving the judgment to God, Paul takes it upon himself to pronounce final judgment on the very people with whom he had earlier permitted believers to associate outside the community. In addition, Paul

---

5. The issue of male prostitutes (*malakoi*) and "sodomites" (*arsenokoitai*) will be treated later in this chapter.

disregards the process he has set out for dealing with the "yeast" in the community—a process that seeks the redemption of wrongdoers, not their destruction. He completely disregards the process of communal discernment and judgment that he has affirmed earlier—and that he is actually arguing for in this very section. Rather, contradicting most of what he has written, Paul simply dismisses categories of people as those who will not inherit the kingdom of God. Paul's language is not this dismissive or final even with regard to the man who was living with his father's wife.

Paul's comments cannot be lifted out of context and turned into a list of those whom God condemns, although the church has too often taken this approach. Even more, the church cannot pick and choose from this list, forgiving some of the "wrongdoers" (e.g., greedy, drunkards, revilers, adulterers) while strictly condemning other persons in the list, particularly those engaged in certain sexual activities. This approach is simply misguided; it takes the section out of context and too literally. Paul's list should rather be interpreted in light of its hyperbolic rhetorical purpose; he seeks to interrupt and unmask the elites in the community who wrongly take the poor to court. His words are a wake-up call to those who practice injustice. You too will not inherit the kingdom of God!

In addition to radicalizing the wrongdoing of those who unjustly take lower-status people to court, Paul's list also, more positively, reminds them that they have been changed in the waters of baptism: "But you were washed, you were sanctified, you were justified in the name of the Lord Jesus Christ and in the Spirit of our God" (v. 11). That is, Paul's comments not only expose the elites' ongoing captivity to the powers of this age but also envision the possibility of life in the new creation, into which they have already entered through the waters of baptism. They are washed and justified saints, baptized in the name of the Lord Jesus Christ and the Spirit of God. They have a new status—a foolish and weak one in the eyes of the culture, but a wise and strong one in the eyes of God. The indicative of baptism brings with it the imperative of a new life in the new age.

Paul affirms the social implications of baptism. Though many of us rush by the significance of being baptized "in the name of Jesus," it is an incredibly weighty phrase that sets believers free from the powers of this age. In the New Testament, "name" (*onoma*) can be a term for the principalities and powers (see, e.g., Eph. 1:21).[6] The name of someone or something can serve as a synecdoche for the entire system of deadly and dominating powers. For example, if one says the name, "Hitler," one is not simply referring to an individual but to an entire system of oppression. Similarly, the name of the emperor would include the entire imperial structure.

No one has captured this character of the "name" as a synecdoche for an entire system more clearly than Maria Alyokhina, a member of the Russian punk rock performance group Pussy Riot, in her closing statement following her trial for the group's disruptive performance in Moscow's Cathedral of Christ the Savior: "When we speak of Putin," she said, "we mean not so much Vladimir Vladimirovich Putin but the system he has created: a power vertical that requires the state to be managed personally at every level."[7] When Pussy Riot sang in the cathedral, "Virgin Mary, Take Putin Away," they were not simply speaking of an individual but of a system.

Similarly, when Christians speak the name "Lord Jesus Christ," we do not simply refer to an individual but to the new creation that Christ inaugurates. To be baptized in the name of Jesus is to be set free from the oppressive powers of this age and to be set within the new order that Jesus has inaugurated. In this new order, the dominating hierarchies of the old age are subverted by the new creation; the high-status people stand in solidarity with the "low and despised" and do not use their so-called freedom to oppress the poor. To be baptized in the name of Jesus is a radical, apocalyptic act that places one on the threshold between the old age and the new.

Being baptized in the name of Jesus also entails being baptized in the Spirit, for, as has been noted, the Spirit moves at the turn of the ages, giving the discernment necessary for life on the threshold. Having been freed from the powers of this age and incorporated into

---

6. See Walter Wink, *Naming the Powers: The Language of Power in the New Testament* (Philadelphia: Fortress Press, 1984), 21–22.
7. Quoted in Masha Gessen, *Words Will Break Cement: The Passion of Pussy Riot* (New York: Riverhead Books, 2014), 209.

the new social order of Jesus (the Body of Christ), believers are also given the Spirit to discern and live as saints between the ages. This is the apocalyptic character of being "washed, sanctified, and justified." It has radical social implications.

For Paul, Christian freedom is thus shaped by life in this new order. Christian freedom is not an abstract, individual freedom apart from a recognition of power dynamics that can make "some people more free than others." Rather, Christian freedom involves solidarity with the "low and despised" and mutuality with all the saints. Similarly, Christian freedom always includes consideration of the life of the Christian community. The "free" actions of the elites in Corinth brought divisive, old-age hierarchies into the Christian community. Genuine freedom, though, according to Paul, cannot simply entail the claim that "all things are lawful for me" but involves those of higher status lowering themselves for the sake of the community's life together, just as Paul did when he became an apostle, a "fool for the sake of Christ." Christian freedom is both freedom *from* the powers of death in the old age and freedom *for* life in the new creation. It is freedom within the space at the threshold of the ages created by the invasive action of Jesus and entered into through the waters of baptism. The "freedom" offered by the powers of this age is a lie; it is not the way of life but the way of death.

> **Freedom is not simply a negative freedom from but a freedom for, a capacity to achieve certain worthwhile goods.**
>
> Cavanaugh, *Being Consumed*, 7–8.

6:12–20
Freedom and the Body

In addition to addressing the claim that "all things are lawful for me," Paul also addresses a misguided understanding of freedom that neglects the embodiment of the Christian life. The elites, who had been nurtured in the philosophical assumptions and conventions of the day, could easily denigrate the body and emphasize the mind or spirit.[8] This denigration of the body is evident in the other quotation Paul cites from the Corinthians: "'Food is meant for the stomach and the stomach for food,' and God will destroy both one and the other" (v. 13). Counter to this claim, Paul asserts, "The body is meant not for fornication but for the Lord, and the Lord for the body. And God raised the Lord and will also raise us by his power" (vv. 13–14).[9]

While the presenting issue is fornication with a prostitute, Paul's deeper concern is an overemphasis on mind and spirit that neglects the body. The connection with Paul's treatment of going to court is interesting. Just as Paul has subverted the hierarchy in the body politic and inverted that hierarchy in the Body of Christ, now Paul similarly subverts the conventional hierarchy of the human body. In fact, in Paul's context, the hierarchy of the human body mirrored that of the social body. For example, the bodies of the male social elite were understood as beautiful and superior to the lesser bodies of women and persons of lower social status. In "raising up" the "low and despised"—including the body of one crucified—Paul is also subverting hierarchical understandings of bodily beauty and superiority. In addition, by emphasizing the importance of the body, Paul addresses philosophical "wisdom" that considers the flesh (*sarx*) inferior to the mind (*nous*) and the spirit (*pneuma*)—both of which were believed to be substances, but higher and more ethereal ones. Paul here subverts these assumptions, rejecting this hierarchical understanding of the human body in the same way he undercut the hierarchical arrangements in the Body of Christ.[10] Believers cannot dismiss the body by asserting the freedom of the mind and spirit because the Christian life is embodied in the world.

Similarly, just as Paul was concerned about the pollution of the Body of Christ in chapter 5, now he expresses similar concerns about the human body in chapter 6. The human body can become polluted by its life in the world just as the Body of Christ can be polluted by invasive agents from the world. The battle between the old age and the new creation takes place at the level of the human body

8. Dale B. Martin, *The Corinthian Body* (New Haven, CT: Yale University Press, 1995), 70, 175–76.
9. Richard B. Hays, *First Corinthians*, Interpretation: A Commentary for Teaching and Preaching (Louisville, KY: John Knox Press, 1997), 102.
10. Martin, *Corinthian Body*, 176.

as well as in the communal body.[11] The boundaries of the human body must be maintained and protected from pollution in a similar way as the boundaries of the Body of Christ.

Holding these two themes together—the Body of Christ and the human body of the believer—is Paul's christological interpretation of embodiment. First of all, Paul affirms the resurrection of the *body*, an extraordinarily disruptive, even foolish claim for an elitist philosophical culture that understood the body as inferior: God does not destroy the body but raises it (vv. 13–14). The crucified body of Jesus has become the resurrected body, subverting not only negative attitudes toward the human body but also social hierarchies of the beautiful, superior body. The human body is not "left behind" in the resurrection but is incorporated into the fulfillment of God's purposes. Consequently, it cannot be neglected or dismissed as insignificant by asserting a disembodied faith that purportedly "frees" believers from all constraints and restrictions. Such a spiritualizing of faith creates a misunderstanding of Christian freedom, which includes a concern for bodies. What believers do with their bodies matters.

Second, human embodiment matters because believers have been united with Christ; they are members of the Body of Christ, participating in his life even now in their physical day-to-day lives (v. 15). The Spirit dwells within believers, making their bodies a temple for the presence and holiness of God (vv. 19–20). Consequently, the living Christ through the Spirit is implicated in the character of Christian lives, including what we do with our bodies. Because believers have been incorporated into Christ, whose body has been raised, the life of the body has been elevated in importance.

The presenting case of prostitution is Paul's example. The body of the one who has sexual relations with a prostitute—as the Hebrew Scriptures put it, who becomes "one" with her—is polluted in this act (v. 16; Gen. 2:24). Contrary to cultural understandings in Paul's day, penetration is not simply a one way street, in which the male acts sexually on a passive recipient.[12] Rather, the male perpetrator's body is itself implicated. Ironically, Paul views the male body as

11. Ibid., 174–79.
12. Ibid., 177.

somewhat "porous" here, making it more receptive to pollution—but also moving it closer toward the female end of the spectrum of sex. In addition, Paul here makes the body of the prostitute an active agent (although, unfortunately, a negative, polluting one), rather than simply a passive recipient. The body of the male believer is thus polluted by the intercourse. And this polluted human body, because it participates in the Body of Christ, also corrupts Christ, something that is simply inconceivable to Paul (v. 17).

Theologically for Paul, intercourse is not simply between two individuals. Rather, in his apocalyptic framework, the intercourse is between the world—the powers of the old age—embodied by the prostitute, and the new creation within which the believer is supposed to live in the Body of Christ.[13] The struggle at the turn of the ages, that is, takes place not simply within the community of faith, but within the bodies of believers. As temples of the Spirit, Christians are called to embody in their lives the way of the new creation, rather than being dominated by the powers of this age. Freedom *from* the dominating old age entails life *for* the purposes of the new creation. Paul states this underlying theological emphasis clearly at the end of the chapter. Believers have been "bought with a price" (v. 20). They have been redeemed from captivity to the old age through Jesus' crucifixion and resurrection. Redemption is costly, calling for the new life of discipleship.

Embodied Christian freedom cannot simply be a negative freedom, freedom *from*. It has a *telos* or ultimate purpose that shapes it: "Glorify God in your body" (v. 20). Believers have been set free *from* the powers of this age and set free *for* lives that glorify God, both within the community of faith—the Body of Christ—and in embodied human lives. Ironically, this "weak and foolish" life is not a burden but the way of joy and fulfillment.

Moreover, within this larger

> Q: "What is the chief end of human beings?"
> A: "To glorify God and enjoy God forever."
>
> Westminster Shorter Catechism, in *The Constitution of the Presbyterian Church (U.S.A.)*, Part I, *Book of Confessions* (Louisville, KY: Office of the General Assembly, Presbyterian Church (U.S.A.), 2016), 7.001 (altered).

13. Ibid., 174–79.

framework of embodied Christian freedom, glorifying God with our bodies is far more encompassing than males refraining from intercourse with prostitutes, which is simply the presenting issue for Paul. Rather, glorifying God with our bodies includes positive acts of solidarity with the oppressed and resistance to all systemic injustices (like the judicial system Paul critiques) that destroy human bodies. Glorifying God with our bodies involves locating our bodies with and alongside those whose bodies are oppressed—just as Jesus placed his body in solidarity with the "low and despised" on the cross.

Glorifying God with our bodies involves sitting in our sanctuary pews and sharing our fellowship meals together with those whose bodies are considered "low and despised." Christians cannot glorify God in our bodies if our churches consist only of the economically privileged, the physically "abled," the well-fed and nicely clothed, the homogeneously light-skinned. Nor can Christians worship fully if only certain kinds of bodies—male bodies, heterosexual bodies, "abled" bodies—are permitted to preach from our pulpits or celebrate at our Eucharists. People are regularly privileged and oppressed because of their *bodies*. The Body of Christ, as Paul affirms, interrupts the hierarchies and privilege of the world and embodies a different kind of community that breaks down the boundaries between different kinds of bodies.

Glorifying God with our bodies also involves placing our bodies alongside those whose bodies are oppressed beyond the church walls. Years ago I was told to do just this: "Take your body out of your large home and warm bed," the leaders of a homeless ministry in Atlanta told me, "and place it on the streets for twenty-four hours. Sleep (or try to) on the cold concrete and wake up shivering. Look unsuccessfully for a toilet—and don't forget you can be arrested for relieving yourself elsewhere. Stand in line for hours for a meal, stomach growling. Walk the streets all day. Experience in your body, even if only for a brief time, the urgency and exhaustion of homeless people."

"Take your body into the Fulton County jail," they encouraged me. "Visit with inmates through a pane of glass, unable even to shake hands. Notice the lipstick marks on the glass, the residue of kisses which fell short of human lips—each one a cry for bodily contact with a husband or lover. And take your body to death row in Jackson, Georgia. Pass through a barred, electronic gate, a metal detector, another set of bars, and another, and another. Then, finally inside, hug death row inmates, and receive their hugs. Experience the isolation and humanity of people sentenced to die—in your body."[14]

These kinds of practices remind those of us who need reminding that the powers of this age oppress human bodies. Racism, mass incarceration, and homelessness all work on physical bodies. At a time when "spirituality" has been emphasized in Christian churches and seminaries, Paul reminds us that our spiritual lives are inseparable from what we do with our bodies. Paul's emphasis on embodied spirituality, in conjunction with his challenge to his culture's hierarchical arrangements, has significant implications for the church's life and ministry.

> The embodiment of the Easter story's pattern in our lives means . . . a new way of governing our bodies. That is how we are in touch with the story.
>
> Hans Frei, *The Identity of Jesus Christ: The Hermeneutical Bases of Dogmatic Theology* (Philadelphia: Fortress Press, 1975), 171.

FURTHER REFLECTIONS
Theological Trajectories

The trajectory of Paul's theology invites contemporary interpreters to reframe Paul's treatment of both prostitution and "sodomites," which remains captive to old-age hierarchical powers. In his treatment of prostitution, Paul's critique focuses on the male participant. His critique is developed within an oppressive, patriarchal framework; although the male is criticized, the female prostitute is the one who "pollutes" the Christian man. The woman is the polluting agent,

---

14. See Stanley P. Saunders and Charles L. Campbell, *The Word on the Street: Performing the Scriptures in the Urban Context* (Grand Rapids, MI: Wm. B. Eerdmans Publishing Co., 2000), 153–55.

reflecting the negative valuation of the feminine.[15] By upholding patriarchy, this approach actually contradicts Paul's theological claim that the hierarchical powers (*archai*) of the old age have been subverted and turned upside down. Consequently, the critique of prostitution needs to be reframed.

Within a framework that resists all oppressive hierarchies, the perspective on prostitution changes. No longer does the woman pollute the man and, through him, the Body of Christ. Rather, the problem is the man's bodily participation and privilege in a system that demeans women, makes them objects, and uses them for male pleasure. Just as the elites' participation in an unjust judicial system corrupts the community, so male participation in an unjust patriarchal system, here focused on prostitution, corrupts the Body of Christ. Paul's own theological perspective actually subverts the patriarchal assumptions in which his critique of prostitution is grounded. The trajectory of Paul's argument, which requires the discernment of the Spirit at the turn of the ages, moves the church to resist all forms of patriarchy, even though Paul himself remains captive to this old-age power and hasn't fully claimed the radical implications of his theology.

A similar trajectory moves the church in new directions with regard to those whom Paul calls "sodomites." Paul's comments on these persons are not directly relevant for the contemporary church; in fact, they have been destructive. First of all, as was noted earlier, this category of person is part of Paul's rhetoric that functions to emphasize his critique of privileged persons who benefit from an unjust judicial system. Paul's list of "wrongdoers" (vv. 9–10) should not be lifted out of that context and turned into some universal moral rule. Indeed, the function of this list in challenging an oppressive hierarchical system actually means that the list *cannot* be used to reinforce oppressive hierarchies, whatever form they may take. That would be contrary to Paul's purpose. Yet this kind of oppression is precisely what happens when Paul's condemnation of

15. Indeed, within Paul's culture, any intercourse with a woman implicated a man in the "feminine" and lessened the stature of the male. Paul's critique of prostitution is probably deeply rooted in the devaluation, indeed, the horror, of the feminine. Martin, *Corinthian Body*, 127.

"sodomites" leads to a system that privileges heterosexual persons and oppresses LGBTQ+ persons.

Second, Paul's understanding of "sodomites" is not directly relevant to contemporary understandings of sexual orientation. While Paul's condemnation of "male prostitutes" (*malakoi*) and "sodomites" (*arsenokoitai*) is unequivocal, what he means by these terms (and, indeed, how they are translated) is culturally contextual, generally unclear, and highly contested. Interpretations of these terms "as condemning modern homosexuality have been driven more by ideological interests in marginalizing gay and lesbian people than by general strictures of historical criticism."[16]

At least in part, Paul's position here is also probably embedded in a deeply patriarchal framework. The issue for Paul, at least with the term, "*malakoi*" is the "effeminate man" and is not related to sexual orientation. While the NRSV tries to give a negative "homosexual" moral dimension to *malakoi*, the word does not simply mean "male prostitutes." Rather, it means something like "soft," and it refers to "unmanly men" whose characteristics and behaviors were more toward the feminine end of the male-female spectrum. This spectrum, however, was not defined by sexual orientation.[17] Rather, the feminine represented the weaker, softer, more moist, porous end of the sexual spectrum:

> Women are weak, fearful, vulnerable, tender. They stay indoors and protect their soft skin and nature: their flesh is moister, more flaccid, and more porous than male flesh, which is why their bodies retain all that excess fluid that must be expelled every month. The female is quintessentially penetrable; their pores are looser than men's. One might even say that in the ancient male ideology women exist to be penetrated. It is their purpose (*telos*).[18]

Consequently, a "man could be branded as effeminate whether he had sex with men or with women. Effeminacy had no necessary

---

16. Dale B. Martin, "*Arsenokoitēs* and *Malakos*: Meanings and Consequences," in *Biblical Ethics and Homosexuality: Listening to Scripture*, ed. Robert L. Brawley (Louisville, KY: Westminster John Knox Press, 1996), 117. The category of homosexual as an abnormal orientation was not even invented until the nineteenth century.
17. Hays, *First Corinthians*, 97; Martin, "*Arsenokoitēs* and *Malakos*," 124–28.
18. Martin, "*Arsenokoitēs* and *Malakos*," 124.

relation to the sex of one's partner, but rather to a complex system of signals with a much wider reference code."[19]

These patriarchal assumptions, not contemporary understandings of homosexuality, lie behind Paul's use of *malakoi*. *Malakoi* is thus not a term focused on sexual immorality but reflects a broader patriarchal ideology that views the "feminine" as lower than the "masculine." The issue for Paul is the larger one of masculinity, the importance of preserving an appropriate male status and role. Paul's focus is not simply sexual activity, much less homosexual activity.[20] Consistent with the patriarchal assumptions of his culture, Paul, in short, condemns a very far-reaching understanding of effeminacy, which simply cannot be accepted as a *moral* category for contemporary Christians.[21]

Moreover, the term, *arsenokoitai*, inappropriately translated as "sodomites," suggests that Paul here is critiquing hierarchically oppressive relationships. While it is virtually impossible to know the exact meaning of the term, it does not refer in a general way to homosexual relationships. Rather, contextually understood, *arsenokoitai* points to relationships that are economically exploitive. Prostitution may certainly be such a relationship but not simply in a homosexual form. Denouncing such exploitive relationships is consistent with Paul's larger argument, in which he subverts the oppressive, exploitive hierarchical relationships within the judicial system. Turning *arsenokoitai* into a condemnation of homosexual activity in general represents an ideological distortion.[22]

Finally, one must consider the larger context of Paul's argument: his critique of claims to freedom from all constraints. The rhetorical function of his list is the critique of such claims to negative freedom—freedom *from*: "All things are lawful for me" (v. 12). Contemporary understandings of sexual orientation make it clear that it is not an individual choice; sexual orientation is biologically determined. LGBTQ+ persons, that is, are not exercising some excessive,

19. Ibid., 126.
20. This emphasis is confirmed by the fact that Paul says nothing here about homoerotic relationships among women.
21. For a lengthy list of actions that were considered "effeminate," see Martin, "*Arsenokoitēs* and *Malakos*," 128.
22. Ibid., 118–23.

individualistic negative freedom (freedom *from*), but are rather living into the persons God has created them to be. From this perspective, loving sexual relationships among LGBTQ+ persons participate in the *telos* of the Christian life; they glorify God, though these relationships, like all others, can also become exploitive and oppressive. LGBTQ+ relationships are thus theologically and ethically no different from heterosexual ones. The church's sexual ethic, including the privileges and responsibilities of marriage, should apply equally to persons of all sexual orientations.

Moreover, because Paul's own apocalyptic theology subverts oppressive hierarchies, the trajectory of his thought calls the church to resist all forms of hetero-archy—a hierarchical system privileging heterosexuals and oppressing LGBTQ+ persons. Christian participation in the systemic oppression of LGBTQ+ persons parallels the Corinthian elites' participation in the unjust judicial system, which Paul condemns. Indeed, Christian interpretations of this very text, driven by an ideological condemnation of homosexuality, are themselves captive to this very hetero-archy. Moving beyond a narrowly moralistic reading of Paul's list and attending to his theo-logic of the cross and resurrection, contemporary churches correctly challenge the oppression of LGBTQ+ persons.

Theological ethicist Nancy Duff has summarized the redemptive, indicative word at the heart of Paul's apocalyptic theology, as well as the overarching ethical implications of this indicative:

> Although we must be alert to the dangers of enthusiasm, we nevertheless live *now* in that new space created by the powerful invasion of Christ. Living within that new space we can no longer tolerate the Old Age distinctions in the social and political order which oppress and destroy. We refuse to allow the political order which has foundations in the Old Age to operate under the slogan "business as usual," because we do not recognize its legitimacy in God's world. It is in that new space created in Christ that the church is called into being and action.[23]

23. Nancy J. Duff, "The Significance of Pauline Apocalyptic for Theological Ethics," in *Apocalyptic and the New Testament: Essays in Honor of J. Louis Martyn*, ed. Joel Marcus and Marion Soards, *Journal for the Study of the New Testament Supplement Series* 24 (Sheffield, England: JSOT Press, 1989), 286–87. The "space" Jesus creates is a space of freedom from captivity to the powers (282–85). Duff is writing specifically about Galatians 3:28.

As Duff makes clear, the implications of Paul's theology encompass all unjust, hierarchical systems of the old order, whether it be an unjust judicial system or the oppressive systems of patriarchy and hetero-archy.

In Paul's apocalyptic theology, life at the turn of the ages calls for ever-new discernment by the Christian community in the power of the Spirit. Taking up the trajectory of Paul's underlying apocalyptic theology, rather than focusing narrowly on the presenting issues, the church resists all forms of systemic injustice and domination, even those, such as patriarchy and hetero-archy, that Paul himself has not sufficiently critiqued. Paul's own dynamic, Spirit-driven theology calls the church to this kind of ongoing movement and discernment, which seeks a fitting response for each new context. Indeed, Christian freedom *from* the powers of this age is inseparable from Christian freedom *for* social solidarity and communion with all who are oppressed. As it interrupts and resists all systems and structures that neglect or threaten human bodies, the church gives glory to the crucified and risen Christ.

7:1–40

Apocalyptic Adiaphora

Paul now presents an extraordinary riddle for the Christian Church and Christian theologians: When is the Word of the Lord *not* the Word of the Lord? The answer: in much of 1 Corinthians 7. Every Sunday countless preachers read Scripture and then declare, "This is the Word of the Lord," to which the congregation replies, "Thanks be to God." But throughout chapter 7, Paul repeatedly asserts that he is *not* speaking a word from the Lord (vv. 12, 25), and he refers to his advice as "my opinion" (v. 25) or "my rule" (v. 17) or "my judgment" (v. 40)—rather than the Lord's. So within the Scripture that the church claims to *be* the Word of the Lord there are sections that Paul declares are *not* the Word of the Lord. Paradoxically, trusting the Word of the Lord here involves reading Scripture as *not* the Word of the Lord. That is, we trust Paul's claim and read the appropriate sections as simply Paul's best, practical attempt to answer the Corinthians' conundrums.

Read in this way, the chapter confirms a central theological thread that runs throughout the letter and should shape interpretation by the contemporary church: an ongoing communal process of discernment lies at the heart of the church's life at the turn of the ages. Paul creates the space for this discernment in a variety of ways, as has been noted: through his tensive, unsettling language, his "destabilizing pairs of opposites," his dialogical engagement, and even his internal contradictions. In chapter 7 Paul takes this process a step further, explicitly locating himself in the middle of the discernment process. He claims no greater insight than anyone else but simply offers his best wisdom on the issues at hand. He leaves discernment and decisions on a variety of communal concerns up to the people involved; he trusts their gifts of the Spirit (v. 7).

Although he is an apostle, Paul lowers himself to the role of a participant in the community even as he gives advice for others. He does not set himself apart from or above the believers in the Corinthian church but engages with them in the process of discernment, trusting their role as well as his. Indeed, his concluding words at the end of the chapter highlight this theological emphasis: "And I think that I *too* have the Spirit of God" (v. 40). Possibly Paul is again being sarcastic and confrontational here: you all assume you have the Spirit; well, I do as well! On the other hand, consistent with his pragmatic, provisional tone, as well as his repeated disclaimers in the chapter, Paul appears rather to once again emphasize the role of the Spirit in the process of discernment. Remarkably, he simply claims that *he thinks* that *he too* has the Spirit. That is, he asserts that he should be listened to because he also has the Spirit and can be trusted. Implicit in the word, "too," however, is the affirmation that others in the community also have the Spirit. Paul's guidance is not authoritarian here—not the Word of the Lord—but one voice among all those who also exercise spiritual discernment. Paul here models a communal, dialogical, practical theology. Even with all their conflicts and disagreements, the members of the Corinthian church are invited into the Spirit-driven process of discernment. Similarly, the contemporary Christian community is invited to hear Paul's words, not as the Word of the Lord but simply as one voice in the larger process of continued communal discernment.

Paul also models theological humility—not a characteristic usually applied to Paul! He seeks to develop his theological vision in relation to practical and challenging issues facing the community—issues that members of the community have actually posed to him in writing. In this context, he recognizes that he simply speaks a human word, informed by the gospel and discerned through the Spirit, to be sure, but still a word that recognizes its limitations. Consequently, Paul leaves space for the Corinthians to wrestle with their own decisions, as well as space for the contemporary Christian community to interpret and develop his advice.

Paul here is dealing with matters that are theologically termed *adiaphora. Adiaphora* are matters that are not regarded as essential to the faith but are rather in the realm of the optional or permissible. The church has argued for centuries about which matters are *adiaphora* and which are essential. Repeatedly churches and denominations have divided over disagreements about what counts as *adiaphora*. Indeed, in some ways the Protestant Reformation was itself a disagreement over precisely these issues. All discussions about the true "marks of the church" involve decisions about what is *adiaphora* and what is not.

Although the church continues to debate and divide over these matters, in chapter 7 Paul makes one thing clear: for him a significant range of matters related to sexuality and marriage are *adiaphora*. With only one exception regarding divorce, which he immediately qualifies (vv. 10–11), Paul has no Word from the Lord on these matters. Paul's theological humility and his openness to a variety of marital relationships and arrangements should be a warning to the church. Questions about sexuality and marriage are matters for ongoing discernment and humility; they are not to be elevated to a defining or foundational characteristic of the church.

As one might expect in a section in which Paul deals with *adiaphora* and does not have a Word from the Lord, tensions and contradictions abound in chapter 7. These inconsistencies—and the humility that accompanies them—should not be viewed negatively. They are rather reminders of the contingency and particularity of all theological reflection. Paul's wrestling should both encourage and humble all pastors and theologians who dare to speak on difficult topics. Because *practical* theology wrestles with the life of Christian communities rather than engaging in abstract reflection divorced from real life, inconsistencies are inevitable. Such inconsistencies actually reflect faithful wrestling to develop theology in dialogue with profound human realities. The questions and struggles of Christian believers and communities are simply too complex to be plugged into rigid theological abstractions; messy, living theology is required.

Paul's theological reflection remains open to ever new interruptions and reconfigurations, often initiated by new dilemmas coming from the Christian community that lives in the midst of the old age "as though" living in the new (vv. 29–31). Paul's "as though" suggests the dynamic tensiveness and ongoing spiritual discernment of apocalyptic theology. On the move in this dynamic, liminal space, theology will repeatedly have its own captivity to the powers of the old age interrupted, even as it wrestles with the implications of the in-breaking new creation. In this context, inconsistencies are signs of the deep theological wrestling that takes place between the ages as well as the ongoing growth and change that theological reflection demands. A theology of interruption and theological humility belong together.

> The "particularity" of the Christian truth claim, therefore, is that Christians cannot claim the truth, and yet they are always already living in relation to it, in respect for the radical-hermeneutical tension of a narrative that both concerns and is interrupted by God.
>
> Lieven Boeve, *God Interrupts History: Theology in a Time of Upheaval* (New York: Continuum, 2007), 48.

Marital Relations

Paul's discussion of desire, sex, and marriage occurs within this apocalyptic theological framework. The apostle views marriage as one aspect of the ongoing struggle between the powers of this age and the new creation. Like Paul's earlier treatment of *porneia*, which concerns him now from a new angle, marriage is also part of a larger cosmic battle that is being waged at the turn of the ages. Paul's language signals this apocalyptic theological framework. Marriage is one way of resisting the temptations of *Satan*, the encompassing spirit and dynamic behind the powers of this age. Satan draws people into the old age through their sexual desires, and marital intercourse is one way of resisting Satan's lure (v. 5). Certainly, this is an interesting way to interpret the marriage bed: not as a positive fulfillment of human sexual passions but as an act of resistance to the cosmic powers of death. For Paul, desire, sex, and marriage at the turn of the ages are part of the cosmic battle.

At the same time that marital sex offers a means of resistance to Satan, marriage itself creates its own internal battle with the *cosmos*, the world under captivity to Satan and the powers of death (vv. 31–35). As was the case earlier, Paul's use of the term "cosmos" is not primarily a reference to God's good creation but rather to the old-age world in rebellion against God. Paul makes this clear when he calls Christians to deal with the world as though they had no dealings with it because "the present form of this world is passing away" (v. 31). The cosmos has been interrupted by the new creation and is being overcome. Marriage, unlike celibacy, places the marital partners right in the middle of this old-age battle. For both husband and wife, marriage creates anxieties about "the affairs of the world," rather than the "affairs of the Lord" (vv. 32–34). Indeed, the desire to please one's husband or wife competes with one's service to the Lord and can involve one in a kind of idolatrous "disordered love," which leads to captivity to the powers of this age.[1]

Paul's understanding of marriage is complex. On the one hand, marriage can be a means of resisting captivity to Satan and the powers of death. Paul, however, does not conceive this resistance in a positive light. He is not speaking of marriage as a constructive alternative to the powers of death. Rather, the resistance enacted in marriage is a kind of negative resistance; it is a way of avoiding captivity to the desires that indicate capitulation to the old age. Indeed, while marriage can be a form of resistance to Satan's temptations, it is already a concession to weakness in the face of these powers. For Paul, those who are "strong" and exercise self-control engage in the truest form of resistance.

On the other hand, marriage is not simply a form of resistance, but potentially a principality and power itself. In luring one into the "anxieties of this world," marriage can become an institution or "spiritual force" that holds people captive, diverts them from the life of the new creation, becomes a barrier to discipleship, and leads to a kind of death. Paul is more wary of marriage than celebratory of it. As theologian Bill Wylie-Kellermann reminds us, the family itself can become a power that holds people captive:

> To name it so [as a principality] means to recognize in the family a social reality with a life of its own, a God-given structure

---

1. In *The Confessions*, Augustine speaks of sin as disordered love. See, for example, book 4.

with a vocation to praise God and serve human life, indeed a creature accountable to judgement—to the sovereignty of the Word of God. It also means that we acknowledge the family as subject to the fall, as suffering a confusion and distortion of vocation, as regularly enslaving (instead of serving) human beings, capturing them in the bondage of death.[2]

Anyone who has been in a marriage shaped by a rigid patriarchal structure or by domestic abuse or by pressures to conform knows the reality of Wylie-Kellermann's words. Marriage itself can be the force that prevents life in the new creation; it can become a place of captivity, violence, and death.

While Wylie-Kellermann's words may be troubling for those who have made an idol of "traditional" marriage, Paul understands these dangers. In fact, Paul is much *less* positive about the possibilities of marriage than is Wylie-Kellermann, who claims a positive vocation for marriage and affirms ways in which the family might be a redemptive, constructive alternative to the powers of death. Indeed, he invites the church to explore these possibilities:

> How might the family in this our own imperial culture praise God and serve human life—serve all creation—as a circle of resistance? How can the unconditional love of long term commitments resist the market morality of consumption, resist the plague of materialistic individualism? How might new forms and ways of ordering family life and child-rearing seed a nonviolent future free of patriarchy and domination?[3]

Paul, however, does not propose a positive vocation for marriage. Rather, marriage is a "concession" (v. 6) for the weak, to help them resist "desire" (vv. 9, 36–38). For Paul, marriage brings all the dangers of an old-age power without the positive, redemptive possibilities. As a form of resistance, marriage is simply a kind of holding action that enables the weak to avoid "burning" while simultaneously embroiling them in the destructive powers of the world. Paul's

2. Bill Wylie-Kellermann, "Family: Icon and Principality," *The Witness* 77 (December, 1994): 17–18. For an extraordinary account of the family as a deadly "spiritual force," see the remarkable novel by Celeste Ng, *All the Things I Never Told You* (New York: Penguin Books, 2014).

3. Wylie-Kellermann, "Family: Icon and Principality," 23.

words—though, again, they are *not* a word from the Lord—do provide a sobering countercultural word for societies—and churches—that have elevated marriage and the family to the place of an idol.

Life in a World Passing Away

Paul's more general statements about the Christian life, including marriage, strikingly depict the liminal character of life at the turn of the ages:

> The appointed time has grown short; from now on, let even those who have wives be as though they had none, and those who mourn as though they were not mourning, and those who rejoice as though they were not rejoicing, and those who buy as though they had no possessions, and those who deal with the world as though they had no dealings with it. For the present form of this world is passing away. (vv. 29–31)

The Christian life is lived with a foot in both the new creation and the old age. There is marrying and mourning and rejoicing and possessing. Paul does not deny these realities; they are part of dealing with the cosmos that has been interrupted but not yet overcome. All these worldly dealings, however, including marriage, are "passing away" with the old age. The Christian life is an ongoing, rather paradoxical pursuit as believers seek to live now in the liminal space of the new creation while still engaging and experiencing the powers of this age.

Paul similarly captures this tension when he draws an analogy between marriage, circumcision, and slavery (vv. 17–24). In setting forth "my rule in all the churches" (not the Lord's) (v. 17) and advising Christians to "remain in the condition in which you were called" (v. 20), the deep theological issue for Paul is freedom—freedom from captivity to the powers and divisions of the old age. Here, too, obvious tensions remain in Paul's thought. On the one hand, he seems to reinforce the social hierarchies that oppress certain groups; he does not fully challenge the social structures of the old age. On the other hand, he breaks down boundaries between groups and subverts oppressive ideologies. The theological *trajectory* of his words invites resistance to all structures that oppress people and hold them captive.

"Circumcision," Paul declares, "is nothing, and uncircumcision is nothing" (v. 19). In Christ, Paul declares, "there is no longer Jew or Greek" (Gal. 3:28; cf. 1 Cor. 12:13). Here, most clearly, remaining "in whatever condition you were called" (v. 24) involves a kind of freedom. Christians have been set free *from* the divisions and victimization that come when religious identities and practices are given ultimate significance. Christians have been set free *for* obedience to God's commandments, which, Paul assumes, will guide us beyond such divisions.[4]

Paul's words also apply to Christian rituals, including baptism and Eucharist. These practices have created divisions and oppression; far from setting people free, they have been means through which the church has "circled the wagons" in rigid and exclusive ways. Arguments surrounding the Eucharist, for example, contributed to the development of apartheid in South Africa,[5] and for centuries the table has been an exclusive and oppressive space for women, who have not been allowed to serve as celebrants. Similarly, the Eucharist has been a time not of communion but exclusion for many LGBTQ+ persons. Baptismal practices (e.g., immersion *versus* sprinkling) have also divided churches almost from the beginning. Christian practices have furthered racism and, in a grotesque reversal of Paul's words about circumcision, anti-Semitism.

Earlier in the letter, as was noted, Paul downplayed baptism because it was causing divisions in the community (1:13–17). Later he will critique the community's practice of the Lord's Supper because it is reinforcing economic and status hierarchies (11:17–31). Paul thus invites the church to look deeply into its religious practices to discern the ways in which they have been divisive and even oppressive. Only in freedom from these divisions can genuine Christian *communitas* exist in the church. Indeed, there is probably a confessional dimension to Paul's comments about circumcision

4. It is not exactly clear what Paul means by "commandments." Circumcision, after all, was commanded. Paul is possibly speaking more broadly about the commandment to love. At the least, he assumes the core of God's commandments will not lead to divisions or oppression.
5. Johan Cilliers, "The Role of the Eucharist in Human Dignity: A South African Story," in *Religion and Human Rights: Global Challenges from Intercultural Perspectives*, eds. Wilhelm Gräb and Lars Charbonnier (Berlin: Walter de Gruyter, 2015), 201–20.

because he himself had persecuted the uncircumcised earlier in his life. When Christian practices reinforce the hierarchies and divisions of the old age, they have become captive to the powers of death. Circumcision is *adiaphora* for Paul. And throughout his letter, Paul points to a similar understanding of Christian rituals and practices, even the sacraments.

Paul's treatment of slavery is more complex, though he explicitly emphasizes Christian freedom (vv. 21–24). Paul does not affirm a general system of slavery, much less the kind of slavery that was practiced in the United States. Slavery is an aspect of the old age that is passing away. Paul actually encourages slaves to take the opportunity for freedom if it comes: "Were you a slave when you were called? Do not let that trouble you; but if a chance of liberty should come, take it" (v. 21, NEB).[6]

In addition, Paul subverts the hierarchies of slave and free within the church. Employing destabilizing, paradoxical rhetoric, Paul interrupts and jumbles the hierarchical categories that shaped the social order. He creates a space for new forms of community. "For whoever was called in the Lord as a slave is a freed person belonging to the Lord, just as whoever was free when called is a slave of Christ" (v. 22). The slave is free in Christ; the free person is a slave of Christ. Even if he counsels slaves to "make use of your present condition now more than ever" (v. 21), Paul issues a radical command: "You were bought with a price; do not become slaves of human masters" (v. 23). Here Paul doesn't simply declare that in Christ there is no longer slave or free (Gal. 3:28; 1 Cor. 12:13), but he actually reverses the hierarchy: the slave is free, the free person a slave. He affirms the work of Christ as a subversion of human slavery. Indeed, because crucifixion was a punishment especially applied to slaves who overstepped their bounds, the crucifixion of Christ (the "price" for which believers were bought, v. 23) directly challenges the hierarchical system of slavery. On the cross, the "low and despised" one is "lifted up," no longer a slave, but the Lord. Any slave who is in

6. This translation (which follows those of the RSV, NIV, JB, and the NRSV footnote) is more accurate than that of the NRSV, which reads, "Were you a slave when called? Do not be concerned about it. Even if you can gain your freedom, make use of your present condition now more than ever." See Richard B. Hays, *First Corinthians*, Interpretation: A Commentary for Teaching and Preaching (Louisville, KY: John Knox Press, 1997), 125.

Christ has similarly been "lifted up" in the Lord. And all who consider themselves "high" are now slaves in the crucified Christ. The
paradoxical, destabilizing theo-logic of the crucifixion subverts the
human system of slavery. Bought with this price, identified with this
paradoxical, crucified Lord, no one should become a slave to human
masters. The Christian community, the Body of Christ, is called to
enact this new reality in its life together.

Significant tensions remain in Paul's treatment of slavery. Despite
his subversions and reversals of the hierarchy of slavery, in his closing summary statement Paul still counsels slaves, along with others,
to "remain with God" in "whatever condition you were called" (v.
24). Paul does not directly denounce slavery, although his rejection
is implicit in his understanding of slavery as part of the world that is
passing away. Here too Paul's theology remains tensive at the turn
of the ages; the Christian lives in the world "as though" in the new
creation. The danger, which has been enacted throughout history, is
that the freedom Paul proclaims will be spiritualized with no societal implications. Or the church will lose the subversive dimensions
of Paul's theology and reify systems of slavery in a way that would
surely be horrifying to the apostle. Neither of these options is viable
with Paul's theology.

Paul never understands the Christian community as simply a
spiritual reality. Rather, the Spirit takes form in the Body of Christ.
Paul's claims about the freedom of the slave in Christ, as well as his
command not to become slaves of human masters, are to be enacted
concretely in the life of the Christian community. The church is
to embody these new relationships in the midst of the world. The
church as a whole, that is, lives now "as though" slavery has passed
away. The church enacts a different kind of body politic, a different kind of social ethic. In its life
together the church interrupts the
system of slavery, even as slaves are
encouraged to remain in the condition to which they were called.
Even while Paul does not directly
challenge the system of slavery, his
words do undercut the ideology

> The church does not have a
> social ethic; the church is a
> social ethic.
>
> Stanley Hauerwas, *The Peaceable King-
> dom: A Primer in Christian Ethics* (Notre
> Dame, IN: University of Notre Dame
> Press, 1991), 99.

underpinning it. By destabilizing the categories of slave and free, Paul interrupts the ideology and creates the space for new perception. While there is no denying the tensions in Paul's theological position, there is also no way to spiritualize his affirmations or dismiss their radical social implications. The trajectory of Paul's theology points to a radical resistance to all forms of human slavery.

Just as Paul's apocalyptic theology creates the tensions in his position on slavery, one specific aspect of that theology, here emphasized for the first time, informs his counsel to remain in the condition in which one is called: the world is passing away and *"the appointed time has grown short"* (v. 29). Soon the old age will be overcome and the new will be fulfilled. The cosmos is "passing away," and not just sometime in the distant future (v. 31). The moment calls for urgent and "unhindered devotion to the Lord" rather than anxieties about the world (vv. 32–35). Indeed, the primary reason Paul counsels people to remain in their current condition is because the structures of the old age are *quickly* passing away: marriage is passing away, slavery is passing away, possessions are passing away. With the time so short, believers do not need to concern themselves about the world's "domination system." It has been interrupted and will soon be overcome by the Lord. Ironically, Paul's advice to remain in the condition to which you were called contains within it the ultimate critique of these conditions: the Lord is moving to bring an end to these structures—and soon will. That is the arc of Christ's work, whether the time is short or extended. For the

> The arc of the moral universe is long, but it bends toward justice.
>
> attributed to
> Martin Luther King Jr.

contemporary church, which no longer understands the time to be short, serving the Lord now involves resisting these hierarchical structures rather than simply accepting, reifying, or idolizing them.

Glimpses of the New Creation

The tensions in Paul's theology become especially pronounced in his discussion of men and women. Paul actually accepts and works within the overarching male-dominated hierarchy of his culture.

Although he seems to affirm that "in Christ there is no longer Jew or Greek, no longer slave or free," Paul does not assert that "there is no longer male and female" (compare Gal. 3:28 and 1 Cor. 12:13). The presenting question, posed by the Corinthians, probably by the elites, assumes that the woman is the source of pollution, much as Paul had assumed earlier: "It is well for a man not to touch a woman" (v. 1). Within the hierarchical understanding of male and female in that culture, sexual intercourse weakens the stronger male, drawing him toward the female end of the male-female continuum. This understanding reflected widespread assumptions of the elites in the culture and need not be attributed to a distinctively Christian spiritual asceticism that opposed the human body.[7]

In addressing this concern, Paul never rejects the fundamental assumption. His theology is deeply shaped by patriarchal conventions about the strong and the weak. Throughout chapter 7 Paul clearly prefers celibacy to marriage. He permits marriage as a concession to the weak, as a guard against *porneia* (vv. 2, 6), through which, as was seen earlier, the male is polluted by the body of the woman, which also pollutes the Body of Christ. Paul's preference for celibacy is clear. Marriage is a concession, and Paul wishes "that all were as I myself am;" "it is well for them to remain unmarried as I am" (vv. 7–8). He even establishes a hierarchy toward the end of the chapter: It is "no sin" to marry, he writes. "But if someone stands firm in his resolve, being under no necessity but having his own desire under control, and has determined in his own mind to keep her as his fiancée, he will do well" (v. 36–37). The one who marries *does not sin*; the one who refrains, *does well*. Then, as if reevaluating his earlier comment, Paul adjusts his view of marriage while still maintaining the hierarchy: "So then, he who marries his fiancée *does well*; and he who refrains from marriage *will do better*" (v. 38). Writing to men, Paul sets up two comparisons, both of which give higher value to the self-control of the strong: It is "no sin" to marry, but the one who exercises self-control does well. He who marries does well; he who refrains from marriage does better.

---

7. Martin, *Corinthian Body*, 207.

As Paul makes clear, the deeper issue is not simply sexual intercourse or *porneia* but *desire* itself.[8] Like many elites in his culture, Paul apparently viewed desire as a physiological condition, an illness—a literal burning or heating up of the body (v. 9). As such, it weakened the body—again moving the male body, in particular, "down" closer toward the female in the continuum of sex. The highest value, consequently, is self-control, a "strong" life that has transcended desire (vv. 9, 37). Marriage becomes both a concession to and control for desire: "For it is better to marry than to be aflame with passion" (v. 9). Marriage is *not* a relationship in which desire may be celebrated and fulfilled in intimate intercourse. There is nothing positive about desire, even within marriage. Rather, desire remains negative, and self-control is the highest value. Indeed, Paul may have even understood sexual relations within marriage to be free of desire, though that is difficult for contemporary persons to imagine.[9] At both the level of sexual intercourse and the deeper level of desire, Paul develops his thought within the male dominated hierarchy of the strong over the weak, with the weak being more closely related to the female end of the male-female continuum. Patriarchal assumptions shape his theology here as elsewhere in the letter.

Throughout this chapter, however, there are repeated interruptions within this overarching framework. Possibly the most significant interruption is Paul's own recognition that he has no "command from the Lord" on these matters. Paul at least recognizes that he may be operating within assumptions that run counter to the Lord's purposes and will need revising as the Spirit continues to move between the ages. Paul does not "melt the solidity" of the cosmos here but in many ways reinforces it; so he does not claim to offer any divine commands. Rather, he is negotiating the space between the ages as faithfully as he can.

Throughout his negotiation, there are some rather remarkable interruptions of the patriarchal arrangements of the cosmos. Within marriage, for example, Paul commands remarkable mutuality in sexual relations—something unheard of in his culture:

8. My discussion of desire draws on Martin, *Corinthian Body*, 212–17.
9. Martin, *Corinthian Body*, 216.

> The husband should give to his wife her conjugal rights, and
> likewise the wife to her husband. For the wife does not have
> authority over her own body, but the husband does; likewise
> the husband does not have authority over his own body, but
> the wife does. (vv. 3–4)

"Likewise." The mutuality inherent in that word represents a striking interruption of the hierarchy of marriage. Marriage can be an alternative to the patriarchal assumptions of the old age. Sexuality is no longer depicted in terms of the active male and passive female, or as the prerogative of the man but not the woman. Rather, both the husband and wife deserve their conjugal rights, and each has authority over the body of the other. Here Paul provides a glimpse of something new, a glimpse that interrupts the *status quo*, including the "solidity" of his own theological framework. While there is no affirmation of "desire" here—the relationship is spoken of rather passionlessly in terms of "rights" and "authority"—the mutuality is clear. "Likewise."

Another interruption occurs, remarkably at the one place where Paul does speak a command from the Lord (vv. 10–11). Paul forbids divorce.[10] He begins with a word to the wife: she "should not separate from her husband" (v. 10). Possibly he begins here because women were resisting the hierarchical arrangements of marriage in light of the disruptive new age that had appeared in Christ.[11] The interruption, however, occurs immediately. Despite a word from the Lord, Paul makes an extraordinary exception: "but if she does separate, let her remain unmarried or else be reconciled to her husband" (v. 11). With a word from the Lord, Paul does permit the woman to separate from her husband as long as she doesn't marry someone else. Within the Christian community, Paul offers women a way to be faithful and valued outside the requirements of marriage. No longer is the woman simply defined by or dependent upon her husband. Singleness and celibacy for women are valued as highly as for men.[12] Paul here echoes Jesus' words to the Sadducees who posed

10. Paul possibly knows Jesus' prohibition against divorce. See Matt. 5:31–32; 10:11–13; Mark 10:1–11; Luke 16:18.
11. Jouette M. Bassler, "1 Corinthians," in *The Women's Bible Commentary*, Carol A. Newsom and Sharon H. Ringe, eds. (Louisville, KY: Westminster John Knox Press, 1992), 324.
12. Bassler, "1 Corinthians," 324.

to him a question about marriage: "For when they rise from the dead, they neither marry nor are given in marriage" (Mark 12: 25). Jesus declares that in the age to come, women will no longer simply belong to or be defined by men. Paul gives us a glimpse of that "age to come" that has now broken into the cosmos.

One final example actually interrupts Paul's underlying assumption that the woman's body is a source of pollution. In his discussion of marriage to an "unbeliever," Paul affirms that the relationship can actually produce holiness: "For the unbelieving husband is made holy through his wife, and the unbelieving wife is made holy through her husband. Otherwise, your children would be unclean, but as it is, they are holy" (v. 14). Because of his reference to children, Paul is clearly speaking of sexual intercourse here; and it does not pollute but actually can make the unbeliever holy. It is not only the husband who makes an unbelieving wife holy but also the wife who makes an unbelieving husband holy. Within Christian marriage, the body of the woman not only does not pollute, but it can, like the man's, be a vessel of holiness. Not only does Paul welcome unbelievers by accepting these kinds of relationships; he also interrupts the assumptions about pollution that shape his culture's (and his own) perception of women's bodies. The interruption of the new creation into the old age appears yet again in Paul's theology.

Chapter 7 is thus an extraordinary example of adiaphoristic theology at the turn of the ages. On the one hand, interpreters should not simply turn Paul into some kind of "progressive." He clearly functions within a fundamentally male-dominated hierarchy of the weak and the strong. His own theology remains to some degree captive to the old age "cosmos." On the other hand, one should not interpret Paul's words in a static, moralistic way in order to reify any hierarchical status quo. Interruptions and tensions abound, even within Paul's assumptions about the male-female hierarchy. In the midst of the old age, Paul gives us glimpses of the new creation. The old age nevertheless continues to exercise its influence, and even Paul remains captive to some of its perspectives and priorities. Paul's own concession that he is often not speaking a command from the Lord, as well as the disruptive qualifications that punctuate his argument, highlight his own recognition of the dynamic, contextual character of theology between the ages. At the turn of the ages, as we seek to do theology in the Spirit, we celebrate the glimpses of the new, even as we remain humble about the ways in which theology itself may remain captive to the old. We keep moving and struggling to resist the old-age hierarchies that are passing away.

8:1–13
Theology in the Key of Love

Once again, Paul addresses a concern posed to him by the Corinthians: "Now concerning food sacrificed to idols . . ." (v. 1a). The presenting issue is not one that is compelling for the contemporary church in North America, but it was obviously important for the Corinthians, as evidenced by the fact that Paul responds with an extremely lengthy and complex argument that comprises chapters 8–10. Paul once again engages in practical theology, seeking to address a concern in the liminal space at the threshold of the ages. He explores the territory at the intersection of the church and the world (*kosmos*), and he seeks to discern the character of the Christian life in this space. In doing so, Paul immediately takes us beneath the presenting issue to the central theological claims that guide spiritual discernment. The result, in part, is a fascinating theological reflection on the character of theology itself.

Theological Reflection on Theology

After posing the presenting issue, Paul cites the words of the Corinthians: "all of us possess knowledge" (v. 1b). This claim reveals that Paul is not dealing with some kind of gnostic knowledge available to a select few. The knowledge cited here, the questioners assume, belongs to *all* in the community. Moreover, this knowledge, despite the use of the term *gnōsis*, is actually theologically sound monotheism, rooted in claims from the Hebrew Scripture; it is not an esoteric knowledge based in philosophical speculation. "No idol in the world really exists," the Corinthians write, "there is no God but one" (v. 4), which is surely a reference to the Shema: "The LORD is our God, the LORD alone" (Deut. 6:4). No wonder Paul affirms the comments of the Corinthians: "We know" these things, he responds (vv. 1, 4). Unlike at other points in the letter, the issue here is not *bad* theology but *good* theology—theology that sets one free from captivity to the countless "so-called" gods and idols (v. 5) that imposed themselves on the Corinthians' daily lives. Yet, ironically, it is this sound, potentially liberating theology that is creating divisions and complications within the Christian community. The seemingly liberated "strong" feel free to participate in the various banquets and events at which meat sacrificed to idols is served. The "weak," however, who also "know" there is only one God, come to a different conclusion; they view the eating of meat offered to idols as a betrayal of the Christian faith.

Paul's theological response is immediate. He lifts up the primary character of life in the Spirit at the turn of the ages: love.

> Knowledge puffs up,
> *but* love builds up.
> Anyone who claims to know something
> does not yet have the necessary knowledge;
> *but* anyone who loves God is known by him.
>   (vs 1–3)

With two disruptive "buts," Paul stresses that knowledge is in the service of love; love is the key in which theology must be pursued. Theology itself, Paul proclaims, can be unloving; it can be so set in its own certainty that it does not contribute to the love of God and neighbor. Theology can forget that it too is on the way at the turn of the ages, as the "not yet" in Paul's comment emphasizes (v. 2). Here again Paul returns to an earlier emphasis captured in the Presbyterian Church's Historic Principles: "Truth is in order to goodness, and the great touchstone of truth is its tendency to promote holiness."[1] Now, however, Paul sharpens this affirmation: "Knowledge is in order to love, and the great touchstone of knowledge is its tendency to promote love." Apart from this ordering, knowledge,

---

1. *The Constitution of the Presbyterian Church (U.S.A.)*, Part II, *Book of Order* (Louisville, KY: Office of the General Assembly, 2015), F-3.0104.

including theological knowledge, simply "puffs up"; it divides people, creating a sense of superiority in those who claim to know. Paul emphasizes in a distinctive way the twofold commandment: love of God and neighbor (Mark 12:30–31 and par.). "Love builds up," he declares, returning to his emphasis on *oikodomein* (see chap. 3), although now with a more specific focus on love. Whereas some of the Corinthians had simply emphasized knowledge of God, Paul shifts their perspective to the community; knowledge of God cannot be isolated from love for brothers and sisters in the church. Love for neighbor, not simply knowledge of God, builds up the church. Love is the dynamic movement of the Spirit among those who are being saved in the liminal space between the ages.

This love, however, is not simply for the brothers and sisters. It is ultimately love for God: "anyone who loves God is known by him" (v. 3). Paul here possibly reminds the Corinthians of the second part of the Shema, which cannot be isolated from the first: "Hear, O Israel: The Lord is our God, the Lord alone. You shall love the Lord your God with all your heart, and with all your soul, and with all your might" (Deut. 6:4–5). Knowledge that there is only one God is insufficient. The first and second parts of the Shema cannot be separated. Here Paul thoroughly subverts the "puffed up" claims of theologians. Love for God is the source of theological humility. Paul does not say, "anyone who loves God knows God." Rather, he takes the initiative out of human hands and places it squarely with God, as he has done earlier in emphasizing God's call: "anyone who loves God *is known by God*." The only true "knower" is God, and being known by God is not some abstract, academic exercise. Such knowing involves a deep, intimate, loving relationship initiated by God. So necessary is love for theology that claiming to know something ourselves means that we do not have the necessary knowledge. Knowledge apart from the love of God and neighbor is simply not the knowledge Paul affirms.

Paul further clarifies this theological knowledge in his parallel statements about God and Jesus Christ:

> For us there is one God,
> the Father,

from whom are all things
and for whom we exist,
And one Lord,
Jesus Christ,
through whom are all things
and through whom we exist.
(v. 6)[2]

In a remarkable theological claim, with important Trinitarian
implications, Paul affirms monotheism while also making parallel
claims for both Jesus Christ and God "the Father." Like God, Jesus
Christ is both the source and goal—the alpha and the omega—of
the Christian life. Knowing God, Paul proclaims, is inseparable from
knowing Jesus Christ. There can be no abstract, academic knowledge of "radical monotheism" apart from the particularity of Jesus,
who enacts God's "foolish" and "weak" way of love in the world.
Paul, that is, "fleshes out" the knowledge of God with the love of
God in Jesus Christ. These two are inseparable, and the character of
Jesus' love shapes the life of the Christian community.

Paul thus offers a profound theological reflection on theology
itself. Theology, even good theology, can become divisive and damaging apart from love for God and neighbor. St. Augustine's words
about biblical interpretation also apply to theology: "Whoever,
therefore, thinks that he understands the divine Scriptures or any
part of them so that it does not build the double love of God and
of our neighbor does not understand it at all."[3] Indeed, Paul's words
provide an Augustinian hermeneutical lens for reading his letter to
the Corinthians. Interpretations that claim "knowledge" apart from
the love of God and neighbor do "not yet have the necessary knowledge" (v. 2). Love becomes the key hermeneutical consideration for

2. Richard Hays notes that a better translation is "And one Lord, Jesus Christ, through whom are
   all things and we through him [go to God]." This translation best captures the parallel with the
   affirmation about God and highlights Jesus as both the agent of creation and eschatological
   redemption. See Richard B. Hays, *First Corinthians,* Interpretation: A Bible Commentary for
   Teaching and Preaching (Louisville: John Knox Press, 1997), 139–40. Hays also notes the
   connections to the Shema.
3. Augustine, *On Christian Doctrine,* 1.35.40. Quoted in Dale B. Martin, "*Arsenokoitēs* and
   Malakos: Meanings and Consequences," in *Biblical Ethics and Homosexuality: Listening to
   Scripture,* ed. Robert L. Brawley (Louisville, KY: Westminster John Knox Press, 1996), 130.

the Christian life and the Christian community at the turn of the ages.

"What is the loving thing to do?" That is the theological question Paul asks. He frames his discussion of meat offered to idols as a dialogue about Christian love. This approach is not simplistic. There are no easy answers, as is evident by the tensions and disclaimers throughout his letter. As a gift of the Spirit, love is inseparable from the other primary work of the Spirit: discernment. Here at the middle of the letter, Paul thus brings the character of life at the turn of the ages into sharper focus. This life is characterized not primarily by knowledge, even sound theological knowledge, but by the love of God and neighbor.

Freedom and Love

Through his theological reflections, Paul also further develops his approach to Christian freedom. He affirms Christian freedom from dietary restrictions, again citing words from the Corinthians: "Food will not bring us close to God" (v. 8). Paul agrees, making a claim that in many ways parallels his assertion that both circumcision and uncircumcision are nothing (7:19): "We are no worse off if we do not eat, and no better off if we do" (8:8). Paul here stands with the strong. Food offered to idols is another adiaphoron. "But," Paul continues, "take care that this liberty of yours does not somehow become a stumbling block to the weak" (v. 9).[4] Christian freedom, again, is never simply a negative freedom—a freedom *from*, even if freedom from idols is grounded in good theology. Christian freedom always has a positive dimension; it is freedom *for*, now clarified by Paul as freedom *for love*. It is the freedom to build up the Christian community in love, not simply to assert one's own liberty.

This freedom for love is especially important in relation to idols. For idolatry is the central desire of the powers of this age. Instead of serving God's will and sustaining human life in society, the powers of

---

4. There is possibly some irony in Paul's statement here. Earlier he has described the cross as a "stumbling block" (*skandalon*) to those who are wise and strong (1:23). Now, it is the "strong," living counter to the way of the cross, who themselves become a "stumbling block" (*proskomma*) to the weak. Because they have stumbled over the cross, they are causing the weak to stumble. Although the terminology is different, the imagery is similar.

this age make idols of themselves and place their own desires above
God's purposes for humanity and creation. In their rebellion, they
crucified Jesus (2:6–8), and they actually seek to separate us from
the love of God (Rom. 8:37–39). The powers claim the ultimate and
complete loyalty of human beings, as if the meaning and value of life
itself is grounded in serving their ends. They do everything in their
power to create the illusion that they, not God, are the divine regents
in the world. The Beast in the book of Revelation first and foremost
seeks to receive *worship*.[5] Idolatry is the fundamental desire of the
powers of this age.

> The principality, insinuating itself in the place of God, deceives humans into
> thinking and acting as if the moral worth or justification of human beings is
> defined and determined by commitment or surrender—literally, sacrifice—of
> human life to the survival interest, grandeur, and vanity of the principality.
>
> William Stringfellow, *An Ethic for Christians and Other Aliens in a Strange Land* (Waco, TX: Word,
> 1973; repr. Eugene, OR: Wipf and Stock, 2004), 81.

Paul understands the subtle and all-encompassing ways the powers seduce human beings and hold them in idolatry. "Since some
have become so accustomed to idols until now," he writes, "they still
think of the food they eat as food offered to an idol" (v. 7). Idolatry
simply becomes common sense; people become so "accustomed to
idols" that the world, shaped by the powers of this age, becomes the
air they breathe without even noticing it.[6] Captive to the "power of
the air" (Eph. 2:1–2), people cannot even imagine any alternative.

In Corinth idols were pervasive; they were part of the all-
encompassing "power of the air." So Paul is realistic about the captivity of the weak to these powers. It is almost like a physical captivity,
and the impossibility of simply extricating oneself from this "air"
must be taken with absolute seriousness.[7] Because the influence of

5. See, for example, Revelation 13:4, 12, 15.
6. Walter Wink, *Naming the Powers: The Language of Power in the New Testament* (Philadelphia:
Fortress Press, 1984), 84.
7. According to Dale Martin, "conscience" (*syneidēsis*; v. 7) should not be understood in a
contemporary, individualistic way, but is virtually synonymous with the "body." Weakness
here is a physical condition that holds one captive. Dale B. Martin, *The Corinthian Body* (New
Haven, CT: Yale University Press, 1995), 179–82.

idols runs so deep, it is not simply a matter of teaching the weak or providing more knowledge. Rather, the weak need to be loved into freedom. That is the way of Christ, who *died* for the weak—to set them free (v. 11). So Paul tells the strong to give up publicly eating meat sacrificed to idols, lest they be seen by their weak brothers and sisters, who will be confirmed in their captivity to these idolatrous powers (v. 10–11). In so demonstrating their love for the weak, they will enact the way of Christ.

Paul thus does not tell the strong to argue or to teach the weak, but to love them, as Christ loved them. Through this approach, Paul also offers an important theological insight not only to the church in Corinth, but to all churches in the midst of division and conflict— an insight that many churches have discovered in painful ways. More knowledge, more argument about the fine points of theology, rarely moves people to freedom from captivity to the powers. Rather, the "weak" way of love is more powerful in setting people free.

Moreover, for Paul, this kind of love involves social solidarity. The issue is not simply a personal or religious one related to meat offered to idols. His words to the strong have significant implications for social status. Paul once again challenges the social hierarchies of his day. Meals in that culture were means through which social status was recognized and maintained. Only those of high status attended meals at the temples where meat was served; lower-status people did not have the means to eat meat or the connections to be invited to these banquets. In addition, attendance at these meals was an impor- tant way of maintaining one's high-status position. Participating in these public performances of the social hierarchy was a crucial com- ponent of honor and status.[8]

In telling the strong to refrain from eating meat offered to idols, Paul actually challenges the strong themselves to live free from cap- tivity to social status by lowering themselves in solidarity with those who are more marginal in the society. Ironically, the strong may have been just as captive to the conventions surrounding their social status as the weak were to the conventions about idols. Social hierarchies can also become part of the "air" created by the powers of this age,

8. Ibid., 75.

part of the "spirit of the cosmos" that becomes the water in which we swim without even noticing our own captivity. Indeed, claims of "freedom," including theological claims, can actually become means of justifying participation in a social order that brings rewards to those of high status. Theological justifications for actions that are captive to the powers of death are pervasive and persistent—from the Crusades to slavery to the death penalty to economic inequality to homophobia to genocide. In the wilderness, after all, Jesus was tempted by Satan, who effortlessly quoted Scripture for his own purposes (Matt. 4:5–6).

Perhaps the theological arguments of the strong are just that—good theology taken captive to the social order for the benefit of those in power: "Idols don't exist, so we can participate in the prestigious temple banquets, eat meat offered to idols, and maintain our social status and honor." That is, "We can continue to enjoy and perform our status and privilege in the hierarchy without regard for those who are weak—those on the margins. The one and only God frees us for these activities." Even good theology can be used by the powers of this age; even good theology can be taken captive and used as a tool to maintain unjust social hierarchies. The strong in this sense may have been just as captive to the "power of the air" as the weak.

Consequently, Paul speaks a sharp word to the strong. "When you thus *sin* against members of your family, and wound their conscience when it is weak, you *sin* against Christ" (v. 12). Sin, for Paul, is not simply an individual action understood in personal terms. Rather, sin is a power that holds people captive. It involves being a "slave," not to Christ or the Spirit, but to the spirit of the world, including the hierarchies and forms of domination that characterize the *kosmos*. Sin, for Paul, is captivity to the powers of death that crucified Christ and continue their destructive path in the world; it is captivity to the power of death—the "last enemy" that must be overcome (15:26). Sin is thus not a small, individual action but an enormous force from which humans must be set free. Sin against the weak is inseparable from sin against Christ, for sin is captivity to the powers of death that crucified Christ as one of the weak.

Once again there is profound irony in Paul's words. Despite

claiming their freedom from the idols of this world, the strong are themselves captive to the power of sin. By employing a theology of freedom—even a "good" theology—as a justification for their place in the social hierarchy, the strong themselves remain captive to the very powers of this age from which they claim liberty. Social status itself has become an idol they serve. In their adamant defense of "one Lord," they actually deny their own affirmation by subordinating God to their own social status.

"Knowledge puffs up, but love builds up" (v. 1). Love, not knowledge, is the shape of freedom from the powers of this age; love is the character of freedom *for*. Love, as Paul will explore more fully in chapter 13, forms a being-saved community whose life together is becoming-free from the priorities of the violent, dominating, deadly powers of this age. As Paul develops it here, love resists systems of domination that subordinate some groups of people to others. That is why love is a priority for the strong; it sets them free from captivity to the powers of death that crucified Christ. Love liberates them from the "power of the air" that they fail to perceive.

Building Up in Love

The English word "up" in its dual use here (puff *up*, build *up*) is theologically significant, particularly in Paul's context, in which "high" and "low" were such important status markers. Indeed, "puffed up" (*physioi*) indicates a conceited, self-important claim of high status; it is inherently self-referential and hierarchical.[9] Knowledge, Paul proclaims, including theological knowledge, all too often "puffs up." It too often participates in systems in which those who consider themselves to have knowledge place themselves above those who apparently do not. Just ask any theological student who has been "put *down*" by a professor or a condescending peer for expressing an unacceptable theological position. Such "puffed-up" knowledge also participates in systems that elevate some forms of knowing above others—an Ivy League education over technical college training or

---

9. "*physioō*," in Frederick W. Danker, Walter Bauer, and William F. Arndt, *A Greek-English Lexicon of the New Testament and Other Early Christian Literature,* 3rd ed. (Chicago: University of Chicago, 2000),1069.

a homeless person's street smarts. As in Paul's context, such knowledge is captive to social hierarchies, in which certain forms of knowledge, accessible only to high-status elites, are elevated above other ways of knowing. Knowledge too easily leads some to look *down* on others who do not have the requisite education or understanding, as the strong were looking *down* on the weak in Corinth. Knowledge, in this sense, is not other-directed but becomes divisive, "puffing up" the one who possesses it.

The image of "building *up*" (*oikodomein*), however, is different. Love that "builds up" is other-directed, focused not on one's own superior status but on the needs and well-being of the larger community. "Building up," moreover, requires starting at the lowest point, the foundation, and working up. *Oikodomein*, as was noted earlier, is the task not of the high-status elite but of construction workers; it necessarily involves giving up status for the sake of the community. Building up in love is an ongoing process in which the hierarchies are broken down for the sake of the *communitas* of the Body of Christ. This is the work of love, Paul states. Love doesn't "stand over" but "builds up." Although even love can be distorted, it is the way that *resists* the systems of domination, subverts hierarchies, and builds up community.

Within this context it is important to note that Paul is speaking to the strong, to those in danger of "puffing up" themselves because of their knowledge and status. Love calls the strong to lower themselves and stand in solidarity with the weak for the sake of building up the community. Paul does not speak to the weak. He does not address those on the margins who are the victims of domination. He does not warn them against being "puffed up;" that is not their problem. Paul's words are contextually specific and cannot be taken as a blanket Christian condemnation of the sin of pride.

"We are all guilty of the sin of pride," preachers often say. But that is simply not true, as feminist theologians, in particular, have reminded us. For those who are "low and despised" pride is not the issue. Rather, their captivity to the powers of this age may involve internalizing a low view of themselves that neglects the way in which Christ himself has lifted them up with himself into a new status. Their captivity to the powers of death results in their *not* claiming the fullness of the persons whom Christ declares them to be. When the young African American girl, Pecola, in Toni Morrison's novel, *The Bluest Eye*, prays to God every night for blue eyes so that she will be beautiful, her captivity to the domination system of race—a system historically justified by theology—is complete. Even the divine has become subordinate to that racist system. Pecola's problem is not being "puffed up"; it is having her spirit crushed. Those who are privileged in this system, and especially those who use knowledge to justify it, are the ones to whom Paul speaks; he does not demand humility of Pecola.[10]

Paul's call to the strong to lower themselves in solidarity with the weak is thus not a universal statement. He does not call everyone to lower themselves before others because of the sin of pride. Such a call for humility can itself be oppressive and reinforce systems of domination. Rather, Paul calls for solidarity that subverts the hierarchies and theologies that create the Pecolas of the world. He calls for *communitas*, for an other-directed mutuality and equality in the liminal space at the turn of the ages. Such *communitas* involves the lifting up of the low and despised, not a call for them to be subject. Paul thus calls for new forms of identity, shaped not by the domination systems of the old age but by the Spirit of love embodied in Jesus Christ. Knowledge alone cannot create such a community. For "knowledge puffs up, but love builds up."

In the concluding verse of this chapter (v. 13), Paul shifts to first person. He does not demand of anyone else what he is not prepared to do himself—a helpful guideline for all theologians and ministers! Paul enacts and embodies the words he has been speaking; he makes the word flesh. "Therefore, if food is a cause of their falling, I will never eat meat, so that I may not cause one of them to fall."[11] Paul lowers himself; he gives up the social and religious privileges and status that come with eating meat. Not because it is theologically necessary—idols, after all, do not exist—but because it is the loving thing to do. Standing in solidarity with the weak, Paul also participates in Christ's work of resistance to the powers; Paul claims his

10. Toni Morrison, *The Bluest Eye* (New York: Vintage International, 2007), 46.
11. Here Paul does use the term *skandalizō* ("fall"), linking his commitment to Christ's scandalous work on the cross.

freedom from the system of domination that elevates some and subordinates others. It is not unlike a "white" person refusing to participate in the privileges that come in a system shaped by hierarchies of race. Or a wealthy person giving up his or her status in a hierarchical system based on economic power. Or a professor no longer standing above his or her students, puffed up with knowledge, but rather standing with them so the classroom might be built up through the wisdom and love that *all* have to share.

Paul thus fleshes out his earlier comments to the strong in Corinth: "We are fools for the sake of Christ, but you are wise in Christ. We are weak, but you are strong. You are held in honor, but we in disrepute" (4:10). These comments do not simply describe the sad state of Paul's personal affairs. They instead describe Paul's active resistance to the domination system of his day—a system based on knowledge and honor and strength. They describe Paul's active solidarity with those on the margins, those considered foolish and weak and shamed. Paul participates in the work of Christ, who resisted the domination, violence, and death of the powers of this age. By living out the "scandal" (*skandalon*, 1:23) of the cross, which is a "stumbling block" to the wise and the strong, Paul refuses to cause the weak to "fall" (*skandalizō*; 8:13). The hierarchies of high and low, weak and strong, are themselves scandalized, subverted. Paul's refusal to eat meat is thus not simply a personal, private matter. It is a public subversion of the hierarchies and conventions of the old age that hold people captive, including some in the Corinthian church. It is a public act of love that seeks to build up the community of faith.

9:1-27
Enacted Theology

In this chapter Paul continues to address the issue of eating meat offered to idols, although he does so indirectly by responding to questions about his own apostleship.[1] Building on his final claim in chapter 8 that he will never eat meat so as not to cause the weak to fall, Paul continues to use his own life as an example, demonstrating that the decision not to eat meat is consistent with his character and calling as an apostle. Paul's words should thus not be read as an isolated discussion of pastoral remuneration. Rather, Paul's argument serves his larger discussion of eating meat offered to idols in chapters 8-10.

The issues in this chapter, as well as their personal character, are sharply stated in the opening rhetorical questions: "Am I not free? Am I not an apostle?" (v. 1) The character of freedom continues to inform the letter, and Paul again stresses that Christian freedom is not simply a negative freedom *from* but rather freedom *for* the loving way of Christ that builds up the community. Paul, that is, points to his apostleship as an embodiment (v. 27) of his statement at the beginning of chapter 8: "Knowledge puffs up, but love builds up." Indeed, the structure of the chapter mirrors this earlier claim. In verses 1-14, Paul presents in great detail what should be "common knowledge" in the community. Implicit in his extended use of rhetorical questions is the assumption that "we know" these things (echoing his assertion in 8:1, 4); it is obvious that the laborer deserves to be paid, and Paul marshals a wide variety of evidence to support his assertion.

1. Richard Hays, *First Corinthians,* Interpretation: A Bible Commentary for Teaching and Preaching (Louisville, KY: John Knox Press, 1997), 146.

In verse 15, however, Paul interrupts this line of argument (as in 8:1, 3) with a striking "but": "But I have made no use of any of these rights." Indeed, Paul foreshadows this "but" with a brief, abrupt, twofold interruption of his argument in verse 12: "*Nevertheless*, we have not made use of this right, *but* we endure anything rather than put an obstacle in the way of the gospel of Christ." Through these disruptive "buts," Paul shifts from knowledge that puffs up and asserts "rights" to love that builds up. His own rejection of his "rights" becomes an example of love that seeks to build up the community of faith, paralleling his refusal to eat meat in order to stand in solidarity with the weak.

In the second half of the chapter (vv. 15–27) Paul demonstrates the ways in which, as an apostle of Christ, he seeks to build up the community of faith in love. In discussing his distinctive freedom as an apostle, Paul thus addresses criticism that he is unfit for the apostolic office because of his refusal to accept pay from the church and his low status as a manual laborer. This lack of fitness is actually the shape of love that seeks to build up the church. Simultaneously, by noting the character of his life as an apostle, Paul theologically reinforces his decision to give up eating meat in solidarity with the weak, and he reiterates his call to the strong to love in the same way.

In the course of his argument, Paul presents his apostleship as a form of resistance to the dominating, hierarchical powers of this age, similar to that of the crucified Jesus. In addition, he develops an important theology of ministry. While many other aspects of Paul's theological reflection in this chapter could be discussed, I will focus on these two.

Apostleship as Resistance

At the heart of this chapter is Paul's emphasis on his "rights," as the NRSV translates the Greek, particularly his "right" to be paid as an apostle and his refusal to take advantage of these "rights" (vv. 5, 6, 12, 15). The danger with this "rights" language in the modern context is that it can be viewed individualistically; it can be isolated from its connection both to the powers of this age and to the community of faith, which provide the framework for Paul's thought. In the context of the powers of this age, Paul's giving up of "rights" should be seen as an act of resistance to the priorities and tactics of the powers. In the context of the community of faith, Paul's discussion of "rights" is inseparable from his theology of the preacher in service to the community.

The Greek term translated "rights" is a loaded one: *exousia*. Elsewhere in the New Testament *exousia* refers to the powers of this age. In the well-known phrase, "principalities and powers," for example, the word translated "powers" in the King James Version is *exousia* in various plural forms (see, e.g., Eph. 1:21; 2:2; 3:10; 6:12; Col 1:16; 2:10, 15), although the NRSV translates the phrase rather inadequately as "rulers and authorities."[2] In 1 Corinthians 15:24, *exousia* is used in precisely this way, as Paul links *exousia* with the other major terms for the powers—*archē* and *dynamis*—in a threefold assertion that Christ will overcome *all* the powers of this age: "Then comes the end, when he hands over the kingdom to God the Father, after he has destroyed every ruler [*archēn*] and every authority [*exousian*] and power [*dynamin*].[3] The theological implications of *exousia* are much more significant and encompassing than a modern understanding of rights.

The sense of Paul's words to the Corinthians sounds quite different if this aspect of *exousia* is taken into account. Consider an alternative translation:

> Do we not have the *powerful authority* [*exousia*] to receive our food and drink? Do we not have the *powerful authority* [*exousia*] to be accompanied by a believing wife . . . ? Or is it only Barnabas and I who have no *powerful authority* [*exousia*] to refrain from working for a living? [vv. 4–6]. . . . Nevertheless, we have not made use of this *powerful authority* [*exousia*], but we endure anything rather than put an obstacle in the way of the gospel of Christ. [v. 12]

2. "Rulers and authorities" carry connotations of individual persons and fail to capture the scope of the New Testament usage.
3. The King James Version here translates *exousia* as "authority," reserving the word "power" for *dynamis*. Elsewhere in 1 Corinthians Paul uses the word *archōn*, making his use of *exousia* in this context significant (see 2:6, 8; see also Rom. 8: 38, where *archē* and *dynamis* are used with the same meaning; also Rom. 13:1–3, which employs *exousia* (KJV, "powers") with a similar, though more complicated, sense.

Paul's words sound quite different when the full force of *exousia* is taken into account, rather than having the term translated into contemporary "rights" language.

Although limited, the NRSV translation of *exousia*—authority—does highlight a critical dimension of the term. As Walter Wink has noted in his extensive examination of *exousia*, the word points to the claims the powers make to exercise their authority over others. In particular, the term points to the powers' use of justifications, legitimations, and sanctions to reinforce their domination over human beings.[4] Justifications refer to the claims the powers make concerning the rightness, appropriateness, or necessity of their actions. The United States, for example, justified its invasion of Iraq on the basis of the (false) claim that Iraq possessed weapons of mass destruction. Corporations similarly justify their actions based on the necessity of making a profit and maintaining growth. Even tyrannical regimes will justify their dominating power as necessary to maintain order and security.

Legitimations are more formal than justifications. They refer to such things as laws, contracts, and judicial decisions that give legitimacy to the powers' activities. Before engaging in the war on terror, for example, the United States received the approval of the U.S. House and Senate—both on the same day, September 14, 2001. In addition, sandwiched between the votes of the House and Senate, the National Prayer service gave the blessing of the religious community to the war on terror—even turning the pulpit over to President Bush. Both legislative and religious legitimacy were garnered in support of the war on terror. Such extensive legitimacy was necessary for such an open-ended, far-reaching war. Similarly, even tyrannical regimes will hold elections to legitimate their power, with the ruling party often receiving around 99% of the votes. Although the election is a sham, it is a means of producing legitimacy.

Sanctions refer to the means at the powers' disposal to enforce compliance to their will. The military, the police, public shaming, peer pressure, excommunication, job dismissal—all can be used as a means of sanctioning the powers' activities. The ultimate sanction is

4. See Walter Wink, *Naming the Powers: The Language of Power in the New Testament* (Philadelphia: Fortress Press, 1984), 15–17.

death. The powers will simply put to death those who refuse to recognize their justifications and legitimacy—just as they put to death Jesus himself. Not surprisingly, at the end of his letter, where Paul speaks of Christ overcoming all the powers, he declares that the last enemy is "death" (15:26). For death is the ultimate *exousia* of the powers. Such sanctions, culminating in death, are a critical dimension of *exousia* wielded by the powers to maintain order and control in order to ensure their own survival and dominate human beings.

Paul's use of the term *exousia* is deeply rooted in these dynamics of the powers of this age. Indeed, a look at his arguments in verses 1–14 reveals that he is, in fact, delineating the justifications and legitimations of his "powerful authority" to receive pay as an apostle. He pulls out all the stops. He begins with justifications, citing the "powerful authority" enjoyed by the other apostles (vv. 4–6). Then he draws analogies to other lines of work—military service, planters of vineyards, tenders of flocks—where the common sense assumption is that, of course, these people are paid (v. 7). Am I not also, he suggests through his rhetorical questions, justified in claiming pay for my service?

Paul then turns to legitimations—indeed, *religious* legitimations—to support his claims. Scripture itself—God, in fact— legitimates his "powerful authority." Like the oxen who are not muzzled while treading out the grain (Deut. 25:4), so one who sows spiritual goods should reap material benefits (vv. 8–12a). Then he continues, drawing more indirectly on Scripture: those employed in the temple get their food from the temple, as do those who sacrifice at the altar (v. 13; see Lev. 7:28–36). He concludes with the strongest justification and legitimation of all: a direct command from the Lord: "those who proclaim the gospel should get their living by the gospel" (v. 14).

Paul thus engages in the rhetoric of the *exousia* in the first half of the chapter, justifying and legitimating, almost ad nauseam, his claims upon the Corinthians. He delineates his "powerful authority" as an apostle over the Corinthians. What is missing in his detailed argument is any mention of sanctions. Paul offers no means by which he intends to enforce his claims or punish the Corinthians for disobedience. On the one hand, this omission makes sense because there is really no need to enforce his claims; the strong Corinthians are apparently criticizing him for *not* being paid, for *not* making use of his elevated position. Indeed, Paul's refusal to accept payment is viewed as a sign of weakness and low status.

On the other hand, however, Paul does not bring sanctions to bear because in the remainder of the chapter he rejects all his justifications and legitimations for the sake of building up the community in love. He makes no use of any of these *exousiai* (v. 12). Indeed, he proclaims, through a rhetorical question, that he has the *exousia not* to work for a living (v. 6), ironically subverting the hierarchical assumptions of an apostle's "powerful authority." In a striking theological move, Paul even declares that he would rather die than exercise this authority (v. 15). Just as Christ died, rather than take up the means employed by the powers of this age, so Paul would rather die—he would rather take the way of Christ—than to employ the means of domination used by the powers. Moreover, he knows that resisting these powers can lead to death, for death is the final sanction employed by the powers. Rather than sanctioning his own authority, Paul resists the ways of the powers, preferring to suffer the sanction of death rather than to claim his own *exousia*. The love that builds up from below simply cannot participate in the power enforced from above. To play that game is to be captive to the spirit of this age rather than moved by the odd, alternative power of God's Spirit.

As this brief excursion into the character of *exousia* suggests, Paul's rejection of the "powerful authority" that he could exercise over the Corinthian community is in fact an act of resistance to the powers of this age. Paul does not lord his claims over the community in the way of the powers. Rather, he seeks to live in the Spirit, who moves with a "foolish" and "weak" power to build up the community in love. In the remainder of the chapter Paul develops more fully the character of this apostleship.

Weak Ministry

Paul's presentation of his alternative ministry is quite personal and poignant. While Paul's words could be read as defensive and even sarcastic, they may also be heard as deeply rooted in the anguished heart of the apostle. Paul's apostleship has been challenged, and there is pathos in his defense: "Are you not my work in the Lord?" Paul asks the Corinthians. "If I am not an apostle to others, at least I am to you; for you are the seal of my apostleship in the Lord" (1b–2). It is hard to miss the pain and pleading in those words. It is important for pastors and preachers to hear. Ministry, for Paul, is no impersonal, managerial undertaking. His apostleship is his very life. Paul is no aloof, detached apostle; he is vulnerable, deeply engaged, and open with the community he loves. Here too Paul embodies the way of Christ, who did not exercise power over others but in vulnerability risked rejection—and crucifixion—at the hands of those he loved and came to save.

Paul here reminds pastors of the vulnerability of preaching. The preacher proclaims a "weak" and "foolish" Word, with no control over what will happen after it is spoken; he or she can only trust that through God's Spirit the Word will not return empty (Isa. 55:11). In this sense, preaching—and the Word itself—represent an alternative to the domination and violence of the powers of this age. It is not just the content of preaching that is "weak" and "foolish," but the practice of preaching itself. As Jacques Ellul has argued, the very character of the Word as "word" represents an alternative precisely to the dominating, violent means of the powers of this age. The Word allows humans the freedom of decision, choice, and expression. The Word requires mutuality, the participation of the one speaking and the one listening; it refuses to make others into objects or commodities to be used or ruled over. Rather, in always inviting response, the Word makes persons conscious of their opportunity—and responsibility—to become subjects rather than objects.[5]

The Word, that is, does not coerce or control its outcome. It is a very fragile agent for pursuing truth in the world; it "evaporates as soon as it has been said," and the speaker cannot control the results.[6] Transform the world with nothing but a word? How foolish is that! How long will it take? How much faithfulness, and even suffering, will it require? One does have to be a bit foolish to bet one's life and

---

5. Jacques Ellul, *The Humiliation of the Word*, trans. Joyce Main Hanks (Grand Rapids, MI: William B. Eerdmans Publishing Co., 1985), 63–67, 38, 45.
6. Ibid., 40–41.

ministry on a word. Nevertheless, God promises to work through the Word and not through domination and control.[7]

The vulnerability of the Word is reflected in Paul's anguish. For the only visible fruit of preaching is the community that hears the Word and lives it. As preachers know, the Word is spoken, and the preacher gives up control. Indeed, the great majority of sermons preached through the centuries—including Paul's—are completely lost to us. There is no record of them. The only visible evidence for these sermons is the churches that were built up through their ephemeral words. There is an important reminder in this fact, which is being lost as many sermons now are recorded, digitized, and appear online. The visible fruit of the Word proclaimed is not a polished manuscript or a widely viewed digital performance. Rather, the visible fruit is the congregation that hears and lives the Word.

Paul thus declares, "you are the seal of my apostleship in the Lord" (v. 2). The "seal" (*sphragis*) represents the official recognition of something; it marks something visibly and certifies its authenticity. Other than having seen the risen Lord (v. 1), which no one can validate but Paul himself, the only concrete, visible "seal" or authentication of Paul's apostleship is the congregations that are the fruit of his preaching. The Corinthian church is divided and conflicted, arguing with Paul and even criticizing his apostleship. Participating deeply in the life of the congregation, Paul speaks with an anguish that characterizes the faithful pastor or preacher who seeks to build up the community in love. Paul's implicit theology of preaching places front and center the vulnerable character of the Word, the preacher's participatory love for the church, and the anguish of living in this tension.

In describing his work as an apostle, Paul develops a theology of cruciform ministry characterized by resistance to the *exousia* of the powers. The character of the love that seeks to build up, rather than lord over, shapes Paul's theology of ministry. At the heart of this ministry is Paul's solidarity with the weak through his tent-making work in a low-status position. This labor is the source of some of the criticism leveled at Paul by the strong in Corinth; no honored and

---

7. Ibid., 68. See Isaiah 2:1–4, where the word goes forth from Jerusalem and leads to the beating of swords into plowshares and spears into pruning hooks.

respectable leader or orator would earn a living through an occupation reserved for the weak. Just as Christ embodied solidarity with the shamed and low and weak on the cross, so Paul stands with the "low and despised" through his daily labor. Earlier in the letter, Paul had spoken metaphorically of apostles as mere construction workers, field hands, and stewards (3:5–15). Now Paul embodies this position literally through his work in a low-status job. Foolishness and weakness characterize Paul as he subverts the normal ethos and honor of the orator.

Ironically—even foolishly!—Paul claims that he occupies this low-status position so he can boast. Paul, that is, boasts in his low-status work, which enables him to preach the gospel free of charge. He boasts in his solidarity with the weak and dishonored. Paul again unsettles the assumptions of the powers of this age as well as the conventions of the strong in Corinth. Paul's argument sheds further light on his theology of ministry. Paul does *not* boast because of his proclamation of the gospel. Theologically, that is impossible because the proclamation of the gospel is an *obligation* laid upon him: "If I proclaim the gospel, this gives me no ground for boasting, for an obligation is laid on me, and woe to me if I do not proclaim the gospel" (v. 16). Preaching is "not of my own will" but is the consequence of being "entrusted with a commission" (v. 17). There can thus be no reward for proclaiming the gospel (v. 17).

Preaching is not something people choose to do. The frequent advice of pastors to those considering a call to ministry is apt here: "If you can do anything else, do it." That is not a derogatory comment about ministry or a subtle encouragement to avoid it if you can. Rather, it is a reminder that ministry is a calling, an obligation laid upon the person. Jarena Lee, a nineteenth-century African American woman, understood Paul's words; she knew about the intense obligation to preach that comes even to one considered "low and despised" in her day:

> Between four and five years after my sanctification, on a certain time, an impressive silence fell upon me, and I stood as if someone was about to speak to me, yet I had no such thought in my heart. But to my utter surprise there seemed to sound a voice which I thought I distinctly heard, and most certainly

understood, which said to me, "Go preach the gospel!" I immediately replied aloud, "No one will believe me." Again I listened, and again the same voice seemed to say, "Preach the gospel; I will put words in your mouth, and will turn your enemies to become your friends."[8]

From that point on, the call to preach was, according to Lee, "a fire shut up in my bones."[9] Like Paul, she pursued that obligation even in resistance to ecclesial powers that rejected her credentials to preach because she was a woman. A similar sense of frustrated calling has been experienced by countless other women through history. Indeed, as with Paul, those who sense most deeply and poignantly their obligation to preach may be precisely those whose credentials are questioned by the church. The obligation laid upon these women led Lee and others to argue for the right of women to preach. The calling of God continues to interrupt the conventions and hierarchies of the powers of this age.

There is no worse oppression than to press the word of the Lord within, and hinder those from speaking that long to speak, that their minds may be refreshed.

Eleanor Knight, quoted in Catherine A. Brekus, *Strangers and Pilgrims: Female Preaching in America, 1740–1845* (Chapel Hill: University of North Carolina Press, 1998), 193.

Paul's emphasis on the divine commission to preach (vv. 16–17) theologically creates space for *anyone* to proclaim the gospel when God has laid an obligation on them. Ironically, Paul might be considered the patron saint of all those whose calling to preach has been challenged by the church. After all, Paul's own preaching credentials were themselves being challenged by the Corinthians—and he defends himself, like women have done throughout history, on the basis of his calling. Like many women, Paul, too, poignantly and personally experienced the anguish of this commission. Like them,

8. Jarena Lee, "My Call to Preach the Gospel," in *The Company of Preachers: Wisdom on Preaching, Augustine to the Present*, ed. Richard Lischer (Grand Rapids, MI: William B. Eerdmans Publishing Co., 2002), 76.
9. Ibid., 78. See Jeremiah 20:9.

Paul, in pursuit of his calling, had to resist the hierarchical structures—the *exousia*—of the powers of this age. Paul's own theology of preaching opens the doors to all whom God has called. He stands in solidarity with them. Who, after all, can stifle God's obligation and commission?

Paul thus cannot boast that he preaches the gospel; he has no choice. So his only boast is that he offers the gospel "free of charge." "What then is my reward? Just this: that in my proclamation I may make the gospel free of charge, so as not to make full use of my *exousia* in the gospel" (v. 18). Again, Paul boasts in his weakness. He boasts in the very low-status occupation that is the focus of the strong Corinthians' challenge. This work enables him to offer the gospel to everyone with no obstacles. His "low and despised" labor paradoxically sets him free to be "a slave to all, so that I might win more of them" (v. 19).

This paradox is itself grounded in the foolish proclamation of the cross that is at the center of Paul's preaching. Christ, after all, gave himself free of charge for the salvation of the world. Paul's ministry thus becomes a "living paradigm of the gospel itself. His renunciation of rights [*exousia*] allows him to share in the pattern of Christ's own sacrificial action and thereby paradoxically share in the life-giving blessings of God."[10] Just as Christ's crucifixion embodied the weak power of God, so Paul's solidarity with the weak embodies an alternative power to that of the *exousia* of this age: the power of love.

This cruciform character of Paul's ministry is the shape of love in the service of the gospel for the building up of the church. This love is a form of resistance to knowledge that puffs up and hierarchies that reinforce status. Paul here does not affirm sacrifice for the sake of sacrifice. He does not celebrate suffering for the sake of suffering. He does not equate the cross with enduring abuse or oppression. Rather, the sacrifice and suffering Paul endures are specifically in the service of the gospel and the church; they are not an end in themselves but the consequence of his resistance to the *exousia* of domination. Paul speaks of the "slavery" that comes from his solidarity with the "low and despised" (v. 19). In the odd new creation this

10. Hays, *First Corinthians*, 153.

slavery to the gospel is the shape of freedom. Just as Jesus' crucifixion was not a celebration of suffering for the sake of suffering, but rather the sacrifice that resulted from his resistance to the powers of death, so Paul's cruciform ministry is fundamentally an act of resistance and only secondarily sacrificial. Such is the character of life between the ages. Because the new creation has interrupted the old, Paul lives by the Spirit in the love that builds up. Because the old age continues its deadly work, this love continues to take the shape of resistance and often leads to sacrifice.

Moreover, as Paul suggests in vv. 20–23, in this in-between space the apostle's ministry takes the shape not only of the disruptive fool but also the trickster. The most quintessentially disruptive, liminal figure among all the fools is the trickster. An essential characteristic among most trickster figures is their boundary-crossing character. Their space is the threshold (*limen*), the in-between. Indeed, they have been called the "lords of in-between."[11] They are most often found on the road, which runs from one village (the space of structure and order) to another but belongs to neither.[12] They are almost always on the move, walking along, dealing with one random encounter after another. Not surprisingly, Hermes became the patron of travelers. And the "herm," a stone pillar erected for Hermes, was often found in doorways, gates to the city, or on the road—specifically at crossroads; it served as "an altar to the forces that govern these spaces of heightened uncertainty, and to the intelligence needed to negotiate them."[13] Moreover, tricksters are frequently on the road—on the move—during dusk or twilight, the threshold time between daylight and darkness. The trickster, in short, is "the god of the threshold in all its forms."[14] Theologically, it is thus not surprising that such a figure might appear in the apocalyptic, liminal space at the turn of the ages!

In their liminality, tricksters are figures of paradox and marginality. They are ambivalent and thoroughly unsettling, interrupting and confusing social categories and order—sacred and profane, moral

11. Lewis Hyde, *Trickster Makes This World: Mischief, Myth, and Art* (New York: North Point Press, 1998), 6.
12. Ibid.
13. Ibid.
14. Ibid., 6, 8.

and amoral, clean and unclean, divine and human, heaven and earth, male and female, life and death. They are shape-shifters, fluid and in flux, never to be mastered, not even by contemporary categories of interpretation. Returning from the theft of his brother Apollo's cattle, for example, Hermes becomes a mist and slips through the keyhole of his cave, so he can later defend himself by saying he did not step over the threshold of the cave.[15] The male Winnebago trickster suddenly transforms himself into a woman and bears children.[16] A trickster will die and then suddenly return to life; go to the underworld then return to the living. Tricksters live and function at the boundaries, regularly unmasking, crossing, and redefining those boundaries. They are figures on the margin, belonging to the periphery, not the center. As such, they are transgressive, disruptive figures. They dispel "the belief that any given social order is absolute and objective."[17]

Paul's theological description of his ministry in vv. 19–23 suggests his role as a kind of trickster, crossing boundaries, shifting shapes, serving in the liminal space where the old categories are dying and the new is being born—all for the sake of the gospel. It is an unsettled, fluid, often paradoxical ministry that Paul describes:

> For though I am free with respect to all, I have made myself a slave to all, so that I might win more of them. To the Jews I became as a Jew, in order to win Jews. To those under the law I became as one under the law (though I myself am not under the law) so that I might win those under the law. To those outside the law I became as one outside the law (though I am not free from God's law but am under Christ's law) so that I might win those outside the law. To the weak I became weak, so that I might win the weak. I have become all things to all people, that I might by all means save some. I do it all for the sake of the gospel, so that I may share in its blessings. (vv. 19–23)

15. For an English translation of the Homeric Hymn to Hermes, see ibid., "Appendix I: The Homeric Hymn to Hermes," 313–31.
16. For the Winnebago Trickster Cycle, see Paul Radin, *The Trickster: A Study in American Indian Mythology* (New York: Schocken: 1956, repr. 1972).
17. Mary Douglas, quoted in William J. Hynes and William G. Doty, "Historical Overview," in William J. Hynes and William G. Doty, eds., *Mythical Trickster Figures: Contours, Contexts, and Criticisms* (Tuscaloosa: University of Alabama Press, 1993), 21.

Paul's words are dizzying in places, befitting the odd space between the ages. He is one under the law, though not under the law; he is one outside the law, though not free from Christ's law. On one level, Paul sounds rather wishy-washy, like a chameleon who will gladly change colors depending on whom he is addressing: "I have become all things to all people." Most of us have seen so many politicians engage in this tactic that we are rightly suspicious of it. On another level, however, this is not what Paul is up to at all. Rather, Paul is crossing boundaries and disrupting categories to bring the gospel to diverse people. He identifies with others so that he can proclaim the gospel in a way that can be heard. Becoming "a slave to all" is simply a means to the end of trying to "save some" (vv. 19, 22).

There is poignancy in Paul's passionate humility here. He will do whatever it takes—in order to "save *some*." Even just a few. This is the calling of the preacher—the "obligation" laid upon those who would proclaim gospel. The goal of preaching is not to speak an abstract word divorced from the context of the people. Rather, as Pope Francis, that contemporary "holy fool," has noted so powerfully, the gospel is always "inculturated" for those to whom the preacher speaks.[18] Paul reminds all preachers that sharing the blessings of the gospel involves serving others where they are.

At the deepest level, Paul's trickster-like activity embodies the disruptive gospel itself. By crossing these various boundaries and unsettling these social categories Paul enacts the in-breaking new

---

Once the Gospel has been inculturated in a people, in their process of transmitting their culture they also transmit the faith in ever new forms; hence the importance of understanding evangelization as inculturation. Each portion of the people of God, by translating the gift of God into its own life and in accordance with its own genius, bears witness to the faith it has received and enriches it with new and eloquent expressions.

Pope Francis, *Evangelii gaudium.*

---

18. See Pope Francis's apostolic exhortation, *Evangelii gaudium: On the Proclamation of the Gospel,* in which he repeatedly emphasizes the importance of inculturation for preaching, https://w2.vatican.va/content/francesco/en/apost_exhortations/documents /papa-francesco_esortazione-ap_20131124_evangelii-gaudium.html.

creation. Through Paul's ministry the Spirit is moving to form a new community in the liminal space between the ages. The very character of the gospel, Paul suggests, compels this kind of boundary-crossing witness. Paul simply lives out a gospel that does not stand on religious or ethnic superiority but rather is free in Christ to cross all boundaries to serve others. As Richard Hays notes, "Paul represents himself as a conciliator, seeking to overcome cultural and ethnic divisions in order to bring people of all sorts into the one community of faith."[19] As Paul suggests, it is only through such a trickster-like ministry that he himself can share in the gospel's blessings (v. 23). The word he proclaims is enacted in his service. His preaching and his life become one.

Paul's final image of the race should be considered in this context (vv. 24–27). He is not speaking of an individualistic spiritual asceticism. Rather, he is talking about a race in the service of the community of faith—a race that crosses one boundary after another in order to embody and proclaim the gospel. The race certainly involves discipline and self-control. The image of the race, though, also reminds the Corinthians of the ongoing movement of Christian discipleship. Christians are being saved, on the way to a prize that far exceeds the wilting wreaths bestowed on the best athletes. The race is not for oneself but for others, so "some" might be saved. The imperishable wreath of victory belongs to the one whose freedom in Christ empowers service to others. That is the race Paul runs and the race he calls the church to run.

19. Hays, *First Corinthians*, 153.

10:1–11:1
Hermeneutical Theology

In chapter 10 Paul concludes his treatment of eating meat offered to idols with sharp warnings against idolatry. In doing so he employs a hermeneutical theology shaped by figural imagination to give a sharper narrative identity both to the one God and to the church. Through his use of typological or figural interpretation of Scripture, Paul incorporates the church into the story of Israel and points the strong in Corinth beyond a static monotheism ("there is no God but one," 8:4). He reminds the Corinthians that the God of the *Shema*, affirmed earlier, is also the God who accompanied Israel in the wilderness and judged them for their idolatry.

Figural Imagination

The centrality of figural or typological interpretation is twice signaled by Paul in chapter 10. Paul declares that the things that happened to Israel in the wilderness occurred as "examples" for the church. The NRSV translation, "examples," is inadequate. The Greek word is *typos*, and it refers to the wilderness events as "types" for the church. (v. 6, *typoi*, and v. 11, *typikōs*).[1] The purpose, for Paul, is not simply a moralistic example or warning. Rather, Paul is incorporating the church into the story of Israel, as he signals at the beginning of the chapter by referring to Israel as "our ancestors" (v. 1), even though he is writing primarily to Gentiles.

---

1. *"typos,"* in Frederick W. Danker, Walter Bauer, and William F. Arndt, *A Greek-English Lexicon of the New Testament and Other Early Christian Literature*, 3rd ed. (Chicago: University of Chicago, 2000), 1019–20.

Figural interpretation is a form of hermeneutical theology. This approach to Scripture highlights the *patterns* that connect various events, people, and institutions in the story. While respecting the particularity and integrity of the various events, people, and institutions, figural interpretation discerns the narrative connections among them. More importantly in this context, figural interpretation incorporates the contemporary world, particularly the contemporary people of God (in Paul's case, the church in Corinth), into that story; it is not only a way of reading Scripture but also a way of reading the world. Through figural interpretation the world of the contemporary people of God is seen and described in terms of the patterns and connections discerned in the biblical narrative. The opposite of "translation," typology is one of the primary means of intratextual interpretation, which incorporates contemporary experience and reality into the "storied world of the Bible." It is a means of carrying forward the biblical story into the present and the future.[2]

This twofold function of figural interpretation is evident throughout Scripture. A good example is the exodus, which serves as a narrative pattern both for connecting various key events in the biblical story and for repeatedly incorporating the people of God into that story. The exodus narrative provides the pattern for describing the Israelites' escape from Egyptian captivity and entry into the promised land. Later that same event figures their return from exile (see Isa. 40:3–5; 42:16–21). The Gospels then locate the coming of Jesus within this same story and interpret his death and resurrection as a continuation of this story (see Mark 1:1–3 and par. Luke 9:31).[3] In chapter 10 Paul draws on the same exodus figures to interpret the life of the Corinthian church, including the liturgical actions of baptism and the Lord's Supper. All these figural moves connect events, people, and institutions within the biblical narrative and also incorporate God's people (at many times and places) into God's ongoing story.

Such figural interpretation can be used in radical and challenging

---

2. See Charles L. Campbell, *Preaching Jesus: New Directions for Homiletics in Hans Frei's Postliberal Theology* (Grand Rapids, MI: Wm. B. Eerdmans Publishing Co., 1997), 250–57.
3. In Luke 9:31, Jesus' death and resurrection is described as an *exodon* (NRSV, "departure").

ways to create a distinctive identity and build up community. Martin Luther King Jr., for example, drawing on a long tradition in African American preaching, used this approach to "figure" the civil rights movement through the lens of Exodus and the journey to the promised land. The depth of this figure is captured in the extraordinary trilogy about King and the civil rights movement by Taylor Branch. The titles of the three volumes are *Parting the Waters, Pillar of Fire,* and *At Canaan's Edge.* King's figuration was a particularly challenging use of the exodus-wilderness-promised land pattern. The pilgrims to America had also figured their journey as an exodus, with America as the promised land. King, however, refigures America from an African American perspective, proclaiming that a *new* exodus is necessary *within* the United States. For African Americans, the United States is more like Egypt, and a new journey through the wilderness is needed for America to become the land of promise. Indeed, in the process, as can be seen in his final address in Memphis, King himself becomes a Moses figure who leads the people through the wilderness, who "has seen the Promised Land," but who "may not get there with you."[4] King's life ends, like that of Moses, "at Canaan's edge," and, as racism persists in the United States, we remain at that edge.

This kind of interpretation is precisely what Paul does in chapter 10. He interprets the church in Corinth through the figural lens of Israel in the wilderness. Something much more dynamic than mere "examples" is at work. Figural interpretation, as Richard Hays notes, is *metaphorical,* holding together two dissimilar situations—in this case the experience of Israel in the wilderness and the situation of the church in Corinth—in order to create a space in which something new might be discerned. Such interpretation is not a matter of technique or method but imagination. "It is questionable . . . whether typology should be considered a method of interpretation; it is, rather, a framework of literary-historical sensibility that creates the hermeneutical conditions necessary for the metaphorical linkage of scriptural text and contemporary situation."[5]

4. Martin Luther King Jr., "I've Been to the Mountaintop," http://www.americanrhetoric.com /speeches/mlkivebeentothemountaintop.htm.
5. Richard B. Hays, *Echoes of Scripture in the Letters of Paul* (New Haven, CT: Yale University Press, 1989), 161.

Requiring and engendering imagination that broadens and enriches reality, Paul's figures function with the paradoxical supposition that something can at the same time both be and not be. All the Israelites were *"baptized* into Moses in the cloud and in the sea" (v. 2), but baptism here is metaphorical, not narrowly historical or literal; it "figures" Christian baptism in dynamic relation to the Exodus narrative of Israel. The "rock" in the desert is, for Paul, Christ— but only metaphorically so; the rock is not meant to be identified literally with Christ but "figures" the church's life as a journey with Christ through the wilderness (v. 4). These examples highlight the both-and character of figural interpretation; it respects the original events, institutions, and persons but figures contemporary situations through them.

The Liminal Wilderness

Paul's use of the wilderness figure is significant. Paul could have chosen any number of warnings against idolatry from the Hebrew Scriptures, but he chose the wilderness, the paradigmatic liminal space of Israel's journey from the old to the new. At the beginning of his treatment of eating meat offered to idols, Paul echoed the Shema (8:4; Deut 6:4–9), which Moses speaks when the people of Israel are on the verge of the promised land but have not yet fully entered it. In the wilderness stories Paul uses throughout chapter 10, he draws on Israel's liminal experience as a figure for the church living at "the ends of the ages" (v. 11). The wilderness figure highlights the character of the church's life between the ages, which is an ongoing journey, a movement of being saved.

In that liminal space, the great temptation is to seek the false security of idols. The great dangers are to resist the ongoing movement, to complain about an unsettled life (vv. 9–10), and even to long for the old captivity (see Num. 14:1–4; Exod. 16:2–3). In unsettled, liminal spaces, people are tempted to build and worship manageable golden calves (Exod. 32:1–6). Rather than continuing to journey with the living God, people create gods out of something more stable but something far less than God. The temptation is to settle into complicity with the powers of this age rather than living in the space of the new creation. Paul's use of the wilderness figure further highlights the character and temptations of life at the turn of the ages.

In this liminal, wilderness space, Paul moves beyond a static, monotheistic theology, which can itself become a kind of idolatry, and he narrates the dynamic character of the living God, who is a jealous God, suffering no rivals. "The Lord is one" is good, sound theology (8:4). By itself, though, that confession does not reflect the active God of the wilderness, who is the same God who is moving at the juncture of the ages. In this liminal space, the dynamic is conflictual, a battle between God and the demonic powers of this age rather than a complacent confidence that idols do not exist because there is only one God. The powers of this age are continually active, and more than anything they desire human worship.

In their rebellious opposition to God, the powers of this age become "demons" (v. 20); they are forces that take human beings captive and demand their loyalty; they are not to be toyed with. In the face of these powers, God actively opposes and judges all forms of idolatry, as Paul attests in his delineation of the various acts of judgment in the wilderness (vv. 7–14). Incorporated into this story, the Corinthians—and the contemporary church—stand warned of the dangers of replacing the living God with any seemingly secure idol, including the hierarchical arrangements of status and knowledge that can hold persons captive.[6] As Paul frames this section: "Do not become idolaters" (v. 7). "Therefore, my dear friends, flee from the worship of idols" (v. 14).

The God of the wilderness, Paul recognizes, is not just the judging God but also the faithful God (v. 13). God's purpose is not simply vengeance but redemption; God seeks to set people free from captivity, as God did in the Exodus, and to create a faithful community, as God sought to do in the wilderness. Life in the wilderness—at the juncture of the ages—is a time of conflict and testing, but God will not "let you be tested beyond your strength, but with the testing he

---

6. The eating, drinking, and playing of v. 7 is probably a reference to the activity of the people following the construction of the golden calf (see Exod. 32:1–6); sexual immorality was also often associated with idolatry. For a more thorough exploration of the many Old Testament allusions in 1 Corinthians 10, see Richard B. Hays, *First Corinthians*, Interpretation: A Commentary for Teaching and Preaching (Louisville, KY: John Knox Press, 1997), 159–71.

will also provide the way out so that you may be able to endure it" (v. 13).

Paul's affirmation of God's faithfulness comes as an abrupt interruption of his depiction of the jealous God in the surrounding verses. Just as the new creation interrupts the old age, the faithfulness of God interrupts the temptations of the demonic powers and God's acts of judgment. God's faithfulness promises a "way out" as believers are being saved on the way to the new creation. Paul thus affirms God's twofold disruption of the powers—both through judgment and through deliverance. The tensiveness of life at the turn of the ages is reflected in the activity of God, who judges human captivity to the powers but also faithfully continues to work for redemption. Indeed, God may be viewed as a trickster who makes "a way out of no way" for those struggling against the clutches of idolatry.[7] As Paul affirms at the very beginning of the letter, in the liminal space between the ages the Lord "will also strengthen you to the end, so that you may be blameless on the day of our Lord Jesus Christ. God is faithful; by him you were called into the fellowship of his Son, Jesus Christ our Lord" (1:8–9).

Paul's wilderness figure, however, does not simply highlight the community's journey with the living God amidst the demonic powers that vie for the Christian community. Paul simultaneously reminds the community of its own identity. Figured as an Exodus people on the way in the wilderness, the Christian church is again identified with the "low and despised"; it is identified with slaves who have been liberated from captivity. As he does throughout the letter, Paul turns the hierarchical structures of the world on their heads, reminding the Corinthians that God chose slaves in Egypt, just as in Corinth God "chose what is foolish in the world to shame the wise; God chose what is weak in the world to shame the strong; God chose what is low and despised in the world, things that are not, to reduce to nothing things that are, so that no one might boast in the presence of God" (1:27–29). As liberated slaves, the Corinthians cannot boast in their own social status or superior knowledge,

---

7. The phrase, "way out of no way," comes from Zora Neal Hurston's discussion of the slave trickster figure, High John the Conqueror. See Zora Neale Hurston, "High John de Conquer," *The American Mercury* 57 (October 1943): 452.

but, like Israel, are dependent on the calling and activity of the living God. Inappropriate boasting becomes a sign that the church remains captive to the old-age hierarchies perpetuated by the powers of this age. Paul's wilderness figure thus serves as a multi-faceted theological and ethical lens for interpreting the church.

Liminal Liturgical Time

In this chapter another dimension of the church's life between the ages also comes to the fore: *ritual*. Through his figural imagination, Paul merges the wilderness, ritual, and the "ends of the ages." Ritual is a paradigmatic liminal space; it is the locus of the church's liminal existence par excellence. When the people of God cross the threshold into worship, they enter, as ritual theorists have repeatedly noted, an in-between, liminal space and time. Ritual enacts "'a moment in and out of time,' and in and out of secular social structures."[8] As in the wilderness, one goal of liturgy is the formation of a new community with a new identity, one shaped not by the hierarchical old-age social structures but by the new creation. In this liminal, ritual space *communitas*, Paul's goal for the Corinthian community becomes possible. Ritual thus enacts wilderness time and space; it is the paradigm of the church's life at the threshold of the ages. Not surprisingly, in the coming chapters Paul will turn to a detailed exploration of the church's worship and the new forms of community it invites.

In chapter 10 Paul figures Christian worship—particularly baptism and the Lord's Supper—through the story of the exodus and the wilderness journey, a framework that should be kept in mind in the chapters that follow. Through his hermeneutical theology, Paul depicts the liminal character of Christian worship between the ages. He first figures baptism as an exodus into the wilderness, echoing not only the story of Israel but also the story of Jesus, whose baptism sent him immediately into the wilderness to be tempted by Satan. "I do not want you to be unaware, brothers and sisters," Paul writes,

8. Victor W. Turner, *The Ritual Process: Structure and Anti-Structure* (New York: Aldine de Gruyter, 1995), 96.

> *Communitas* breaks in through the interstices of structure, in liminality;
> at the edges of structure, in marginality; and from beneath structure,
> in inferiority. It is almost everywhere held to be sacred or holy, possibly
> because it transgresses or dissolves the norms that govern structured
> and institutionalized relationships and is accompanied by experiences of
> unprecedented potency.
>
> Victor Turner, *The Ritual Process*, 128.

"that our ancestors were all under the cloud, and all passed through the sea, and all were baptized into Moses in the cloud and in the sea" (vv. 1–2).

Baptism inaugurates Christian life between the ages, just as through the waters and the cloud the people of Israel began their journey through the wilderness. Baptism, that is, moves Christians into the unsettled space in which the old structures that held them captive have been interrupted, but the new has not yet fully arrived. Baptism inaugurates Christians into the being-saved community, in which the old-age hierarchies have been interrupted by God's foolish wisdom and weak power. The conventional, binary structures of weak and strong, high and low, honored and shamed, wise and foolish, us and them are all unsettled in this space. For the one into whom Christians are baptized is the one who is high and lifted up— on a cross.

In this time and space, as in the wilderness, a new kind of community—*communitas*—becomes possible, one not structured by the powers of the old age. In this space, as was the case for Israel, a new and distinctive communal identity can be formed, although the process continues until the new creation has fully come. In worship, the paradigmatic liminal space, the old divisions and hierarchies that hold the Corinthians captive may be transcended in the diverse unity of the Body of Christ. The liturgical life of the church, Paul suggests, provides the time and space where this new communal identity is enacted, even if only momentarily—and even though liturgy itself can become captive to the old age powers, as will become clear in the following chapters (e.g., 11:17–31).

In liturgy at the turn of the ages, as in the wilderness, the great temptation is to substitute safe and secure idols for the jealous, living God who draws believers into the unsettled journey of being saved. The great danger is that worship does not become a "time in and out of social structures" but a practice that is captive to and complicit with the demonic powers of this age. The danger is that people become complacent, the old-age structures are re-enacted, and worship simply reinforces the status quo. When this happens, worshipers have forgotten they are dealing with the living God of the wilderness, and no real *communitas* ensues. Paul's figural linking of Exodus, wilderness, and baptism reminds—and warns—Christians of their unsettled journey with God, a journey inaugurated through the waters of baptism.

> **The churches are children playing on the floor with their chemistry sets, mixing up a batch of TNT to kill a Sunday morning. It is madness to wear ladies' straw hats and velvet hats to church; we should all be wearing crash helmets. Ushers should issue life preservers and signal flares; they should lash us to our pews. For the sleeping god may wake someday and take offense, or the waking god may draw us to where we can never return.**
>
> Annie Dillard, *Teaching a Stone to Talk: Expeditions and Encounters* (New York: Harper & Row, 1982), 40–41.

Similarly, the community's liturgical meals are reframed by the wilderness figure. They too are part of the journey. Just as the people of Israel in the wilderness "*all* ate the same spiritual food, and *all* drank the same spiritual drink," so the members of the church *all* share in the body and blood of Christ at the Lord's Supper (vv. 3–4). This common participation in the Body of Christ is repeatedly emphasized by Paul through his repetition of the words *koinōnia* and *koinōnos*, an emphasis not fully captured in the NRSV, which uses the words "sharing" (*koinōnia*; v. 16) and "partners" (*koinōnos*; v. 18, 20) as translations. *Koinōnia and koinōnos* reflect the profoundly intimate community embodied in meal practices, especially in the Lord's Supper.[9]

9. *Koinōnia* represents the sharing; *koinōnos* those who are doing the sharing. In what follows I will use the familiar *koinōnia* to discuss the communal character of the meal, though I will note where *koinōnos* is used.

Paul emphasizes two sides of *koinōnia* in order to present two aspects of the Corinthians' participation in the Body of Christ. Both emphases support the rich use of the term "Communion" for the Lord's Supper in numerous Christian traditions. In verse 16, *koinōnia* is an intimate participation in Christ himself: "The cup of blessing that we bless, is it not a *koinōnia* in the blood of Christ? The bread that we break, is it not a *koinōnia* in the Body of Christ?" Paul's rhetorical questions reflect the polemical edge of his argument: "You know this! So you also know that you cannot simultaneously share this meal with Christ and participate in meals that make you partners (*koinōnous*) with demons" (paraphrase of vv. 20–22). In verses 17–18, Paul emphasizes the other dimension of *koinōnia*; he reminds the Corinthians that their *koinōnia* is not simply with Christ but with *each other* in the Body of Christ: "Because there is one bread, we who are many are one body, for we all partake of the one bread. Consider the people of Israel; are not those who eat the sacrifices partners [*koinōnoi*] at the altar?" *Koinōnia* with Christ at the table brings with it *koinōnia* with the entire community of faith. The liturgical meal is, theologically, the place where the church enacts the *communitas* Paul seeks.

This *koinōnia* actually becomes an act of resistance to the powers of this age, who seek to shape the community in their own image. Rather than perpetuating the hierarchical power arrangements of the culture, the meal interrupts them. For the meal is a participation in the foolish wisdom and weak power of the crucified Christ. And the meal is a *koinōnia* among the "low and despised" whom Christ has called into his body. In this communion, there is no room for high and low, honored and shamed, weak and strong. The old categories and statuses are subverted and a new community—the community of the new creation—is called into being. To become "partners" (*koinōnoi*) with demons thus involves not only worshiping a power other than Christ but also participating in the hierarchies of the old age, rather than entering into the *communitas* of the new creation.[10]

From the perspective of the wilderness journey, the practice of

---

10. Paul confirms this understanding of the Lord's Supper and directly addresses the danger of the meal becoming captive to the hierarchical social structures in 11:17–31.

baptism, and the *koinōnia* of the meal, Paul reframes and reinforces the challenges to the strong in Corinth that shape his treatment of eating meat offered to idols: "'All things are lawful,' but not all things are beneficial. 'All things are lawful,' but not all things build up. Do not seek your own advantage, but that of the other" (vv. 23–24). As the liberated slaves of the exodus and as the wilderness people of baptism and Communion, members of the Body of Christ do not rely on the knowledge that puffs up but rather seek to live out the love that builds up (8:1). Serving others in the community is central to the life of those who are being saved at the turn of the ages; it is an expression of our participation in the foolish wisdom and weak power of the Body of Christ.

Improvisational Discipleship

Having refigured the character of Christian community and the issue of eating meat offered to idols, Paul concludes with practical guidance for Christian participation in the cultural practices of the day. He highlights the improvisational character of Christian life in the world. Throughout chapters 8–10, Paul has provided some fundamental "scales and chords" to guide the Corinthians, but, like a good jazz musician, he is keenly aware that life in the world requires improvisation in the moment, guided by the inspiration of the Spirit. In setting forth his practical guidance, Paul himself improvises on the scales and chords he has offered the Corinthians, demonstrating ways for them to live in the complex situations in which they may find themselves.[11]

His emphasis again reflects his concern for the weaker brothers and sisters in the community. He addresses three situations. First, the Corinthians can eat whatever is sold in the marketplace, even if the meat has been sacrificed to idols (vv. 25–26). For, as Paul has affirmed earlier, the idols do not really exist; there is one Lord, and "the earth and its fullness are the Lord's" (v. 26). Second, if one is invited to a meal, the believer may go and eat whatever is served (v. 27). Even if the meat has been offered to idols, there is not a problem. Third, however, if

---

11. For a theatrical account of the Christian life as improvisation, see Samuel Wells, *Improvisation: The Drama of Christian Ethics* (Grand Rapids, MI: Brazos Press, 2004).

another believer notes that the meat has been offered to idols and is troubled by this fact, one should not eat out of concern for the brother or sister (vv. 28–29). Paul is thus no reactionary sectarian urging withdrawal from the world. Rather, he seeks a middle way that recognizes no other gods but also values the concerns of brothers and sisters. At the threshold between the ages, this kind of nuanced discernment and improvisational discipleship is essential as believers negotiate the tensions between the old age and the new creation.

Finally, Paul summarizes the twofold lens that guides this discernment; he names the primary scales and chords on which the Corinthians should improvise. First, "whatever you do, do everything for the glory of God" (v. 31). Paul here echoes the first question and answer of the Westminster Shorter Catechism: "Q. 1. What is the chief end of human beings?" "A. To glorify God, and enjoy God forever."[12] This is the *telos* of the Christian life, which guides believers along the way of being saved. However, because this God is the one who was crucified for the sake of the world, a second lens follows: in everything, Paul says, do not be a stumbling block to others; like Paul himself, do not seek your own advantage, but that of others, so they may be saved (vv. 32–33). Again, having reframed and deepened his argument, Paul returns to and recaps the guidance with which he began this section in chapter 8. As participants in the Body of Christ, love God and love each other (8:1–4). Let those scales and chords shape your improvisation.

As a concluding example of this improvisation, Paul offers himself as an experienced performer to whom the Corinthians may apprentice themselves. "Be imitators [*mimētai*] of me," he writes, "as I am of Christ" (11:1; see also 4:16). Paul's invitation is rich and complex, consistent with his emphasis on improvisation. As he did earlier in the letter (4:14–21) the apostle recognizes that rules and guidelines alone are inadequate for learning the art of discipleship. As with other arts and crafts, a mentor-apprentice model is necessary. Budding young jazz musicians, for example, will often apprentice themselves to an experienced player, imitating that musician in order to

---

12. Westminster Shorter Catechism, in *The Constitution of the Presbyterian Church (U.S.A.)*, Part 1, *Book of Confessions* (Louisville, KY: Office of the General Assembly, Presbyterian Church (U.S.A.), 2016), 7.001 (altered).

grow into the art of improvisation. Then, over time, the apprentice claims his or her own style and voice. The same process occurs in other arts and crafts, from bricklaying to furniture making to metal working to painting. Even preaching is often best learned this way, as the emphasis on mentors and apprentices in African American traditions attests. In inviting the Corinthians to imitate him, Paul is recognizing the dynamic, improvisational character of discipleship, which cannot be pursued by simply memorizing abstract guidelines.

Moreover, Paul's call for the Corinthians to imitate him is, as it was earlier, complex because of the irony and the humility in his invitation. The invitation is ironic because Paul himself is being criticized by many of the Corinthians. Believers are questioning his authority and his "weak" and "foolish" character. When Paul says "be imitators of me," his words must have sounded not only bold, but possibly comical to many of the Corinthians. At the very point at which he is being criticized, Paul says "imitate me." Paul's invitation itself is a form of interruption that unsettles the Corinthians' notions of discipleship and calls them to discernment.

Along with this deep irony, there is also genuine humility in Paul's words. He adds a phrase to his appeal in 4:16: "Be imitators of me, *as I am of Christ*" (11:1; italics mine). On one level he seems to be saying imitate me *because* I imitate Christ. Paul's invitation, however, may have another, deeper sense. He may also be saying "imitate me *to the degree that* I imitate Christ." In this interpretation, Paul not only speaks with humility, but he invites the Corinthians to ongoing discernment. Paul's life does offer a model for living out the way of Christ in the contemporary context. Discerning that life, though, requires not simply imitating Paul in any narrow or mechanical fashion but always looking to Christ and seeking to follow him. Even as Christians necessarily learn from the mentors—the saints—with whom we serve as apprentices, we follow those mentors only to the degree that they imitate Christ. In this reading, Paul even opens himself up to critique, recognizing that he himself may fall short of imitating Christ. He recognizes that he too is on the way, being saved. In the liminal space of wilderness and worship, there is no cause for boasting in oneself but only in Christ.

11:2–34
Word and Sacrament: Communitas and Order in Worship

In chapter 11 Paul addresses issues related to worship raised by the Corinthian church. Specifically, he speaks to the two liturgical components that have provided the fundamental structure of Christian worship through the centuries: Word and sacrament. He begins by addressing conflicts surrounding prophecy and prayer in the church (vv. 2–16). Then he turns to address problems related to the Lord's Supper (vv. 17–31). In the process of addressing these liturgical matters, Paul wrestles with the dialectic between *communitas* and order that will occupy him through chapter 14. Theologically, he wrestles with the tensions between the old-age structures and the new-creation community that collide in the liminal space at the turn of the ages.

11:2–16
Word: Public Prophecy and Prayer

Paul's wrestling becomes immediately apparent in his discussion of women praying and prophesying in verses 2–16, which has been recognized as one of the most tortured, contradictory, and confusing sections in all of Paul's letters.[1] It should not be surprising, however, that this contorted section occurs precisely at the point at which Paul turns to worship. Ritual, as I have noted, is the

1. For an excellent discussion of this text see Frances Taylor Gench, *Encountering God in Tyrannical Texts: Reflections on Paul, Women, and the Authority of Scripture* (Louisville, KY: Westminster John Knox Press, 2016), 37–81. Gench's essay provides an excellent overview of the issues in this text and the various approaches to them, which I will not rehearse here. My discussion is indebted to Gench's essay.

prototypical liminal space and time of the church. It is the time in which the church enters into the new age that has broken into the world; it is the space in which the congregation seeks to embody the community of the new creation in its fullness. As ritual theorists have argued, liturgy enacts the in-between space and time in which the rigid hierarchies and structures of a culture are relativized and *communitas* becomes possible.[2] It is the place that subverts "the structured, differentiated, and often hierarchical system of politico-legal-economic positions with many types of evaluation, separating [people] in terms of 'more' or 'less.'"[3]

The space of worship is thus a tensive space, an in-between space at the turn of the ages. There is a dialectic between *communitas* and order, for ritual is a "moment in and out of secular social structure";[4] it is "betwixt and between the positions assigned by law, custom, convention, and ceremonial."[5] Consequently, for those "concerned with the maintenance of 'structure,' all sustained manifestations of *communitas* must appear as dangerous and anarchical, and have to be hedged around with prescriptions, prohibitions, and conditions."[6] This dialectic creates the tensions inherent in worship. While liturgical order is important, the danger always exists that the radical *communitas* of the new creation will accommodate to the powers of the old age and simply replicate their structures and hierarchies. Worship can become distorted into a false order that becomes a repressive prison.[7] Christian worship is the prototypical space that focuses the tensions between the powers of the old age and the Spirit of the new creation.

It is thus not surprising that the church today speaks of "worship wars" and regularly argues about enculturation in Christian worship. At times enculturation is celebrated, as when a particular culture makes Christian worship its own, drawing on its own music and art and symbols. At times enculturation, often in destructive

2. Victor Turner, *The Ritual Process: Structure and Anti-Structure* (New York: Aldine de Gruyter, 1995), 95.
3. Ibid., 96.
4. Ibid.
5. Ibid., 95.
6. Ibid., 109.
7. Gordon W. Lathrop, "*Ordo* and Coyote: Further Reflections on Order, Disorder and Meaning in Christian Worship," *Worship* 80 (2006): 202, 208.

forms, goes unnoticed or is denied, as when Western colonial practices, including evangelical hymns, European liturgical forms, and
"classic" sermon styles are imposed on other cultures and equated
with pure, traditional Christian faith. And at times enculturation
becomes directly oppressive, denying the equality and mutuality of
communitas, as when cultural attitudes toward women or LGBTQ+
persons, often with biblical underpinnings, limit leadership in worship or exclude such participation altogether. The liminal tensions
between the new age and the old continue in contemporary worship wars. Because of the character of ritual, it is not surprising that
struggles often focus on Christian worship as the church pursues its
liminal journey within and toward the new creation.

Paul steps right into this liminal liturgical context in chapter 11.
He wrestles with the tension between the radical *communitas* of the
new creation breaking in through the Spirit and the need for order
in Christian worship. He engages the tension between the *ordo* of liturgy and the disruptive folly of the cross. This tension between *ordo*
and interruption has been highlighted by liturgical scholar Gordon
Lathrop:

> A liturgy that seeks to enable the inviting and beautiful cen-
> trality of bath, word, prayers, and table, should also seek to go
> the way of the four gospels, the way of the Spirit, and seek to
> let its order be constantly broken open to matters that are far
> beyond its ordering ability. Such a liturgy means to reorient
> local practice and local perceptions of the world so as to invite
> us again and again to walk in this world in the way of faith, not
> control. Indeed, such a liturgy invites us to the active criticism
> of both the religion and politics of control.[8]

In the midst of this liturgical space, Paul seeks to address questions raised by the community concerning the proper attire of
women who prophesy and pray in Christian worship. He is literally
all over the map trying to address the situation. His deep struggle at
the intersection of *communitas* and order becomes clear in his opening words: "I commend you. . . . But . . ." (vv. 2–3). Here, significantly,

---

8. Lathrop, "*Ordo* and Coyote," 212. As the title of Lathrop's article suggests, the trickster figure
is symbolic of liturgical disruption.

the disruptive "but," unlike at other points in the letter, does not represent the interruption of the gospel but rather the interruption of "prescriptions and prohibitions" shaped by larger cultural conventions. Rather than the new creation interrupting the old age, here, with respect to women, the process is reversed: the old age exerts force on the new creation. Paul seeks in a contorted way to maintain "gender differentiation during worship through appropriate management of female heads."[9] While Paul repeatedly disrupts the hierarchies that elevate the strong over the weak, and while he lifts up people of low economic status in the church (as will be seen in vv. 17–31), Paul has more difficulties extricating himself from the "hierarchy implicit in the subordination of women."[10]

Importantly, Paul is *only* dealing with the clothing or hairstyle required *when* women prophesy and pray, which the apostle *assumes they will do*. Paul is not discussing *whether* women should prophesy, and he is certainly not presenting a general theory of gender relations. He is simply responding to a particular, practical issue of women's hairstyle and/or head coverings when they speak in worship. Moreover, although he is definitely concerned about women's bodies and sexuality, Paul is not, as much later Christian tradition has done, requiring that women dress or speak like men in order to prophesy. They will prophesy as *women*, though with a certain (male-defined!) sartorial modesty. Taking Paul's words about the relationship between men and women in this section as a universal rule is misguided and inappropriate, even if he were saying something crystal clear, which he is not. Paul simply develops a range of arguments—several of them contradictory—to address the conflict concerning a woman's attire *when* she is prophesying and praying. Although this text has been used to oppress and subordinate women through the centuries, such a use of this text is not only at odds with Paul's underlying theology of the new creation, but with the specific focus of his argument here.

Paul's arguments, in fact, run the gamut; it is as if Paul is throwing

---

9. Gench, *Encountering God*, 46.
10. Dale B. Martin, *The Corinthian Body* (New Haven, CT: Yale University Press, 1995), 232–33. Although Martin does not emphasize this point, Paul does at times recognize that this hierarchy is theologically problematic.

in everything but the kitchen sink trying to find some traction to address a challenging situation. Along the way, however, he interrupts and subverts his own positions. Indeed, one scholar has even suggested that Paul is presenting various sides of the issue so the Corinthians can work through them toward some kind of reconciliation.[11]

The tensions and contradictions begin immediately. Paul begins by commending the community (v. 2), possibly because they have indeed grasped his emphasis on Christian freedom and the mutuality within the Body of Christ. Indeed, women may in fact be claiming this very gospel freedom in Christian worship by refusing to submit to head coverings (or to having their hair up) when they prophesy and pray in Christian worship.[12] They may even be living into the liminal, baptismal space proclaimed by Paul in Galatians: "As many of you as were baptized into Christ have clothed yourselves with Christ. There is no longer Jew or Greek, there is no longer slave or free; there is no longer male and female; for all of you are one in Christ Jesus" (3:27–28).[13] Having been "clothed in Christ" at baptism, the women may now be rejecting the imposition of additional clothing requirements. In worship the women are possibly living with élan into the *communitas* of the new creation.

Having commended the Corinthians, however, Paul immediately interrupts himself with a "but." He begins to develop "prescriptions and prohibitions"; he seeks order. "But I want you to understand . . ." (v. 3). Paul backtracks, as if the Corinthians are taking his traditions a bit *too* seriously. He offers a confusing theological argument, drawing metaphorically on the term "head," which will occupy him throughout the text: "Christ is the head of every man, and the husband is the head of his wife, and God is the head of Christ" (v. 3). Paul may be using "head" in a hierarchical way to mean "rule over" or as a term for "source" (to flow from, as the head of a river). Either

---

11. Margaret Mitchell, cited in Gench, *Encountering God*, 48–49, 51.
12. At times Paul seems to be speaking of head coverings (e.g., vv. 5–6, 10, 13). At other times he seems to refer to hair styles, wearing hair up rather than down (e.g., v. 15).
13. See Richard B. Hays, *First Corinthians*, Interpretation: A Bible Commentary for Teaching and Preaching (Louisville, KY: John Knox Press, 1997), 182–83. The concluding "male *and* female" is a reference to the creation narrative in Genesis 1:27, the "no longer" interrupting the old creation with the new. In 12:13, Paul will make a similar reference to baptism, although he strikingly omits the reference to male and female.

use, however, implies a subordination of women to men.[14] Moreover, the consequences Paul draws from these theological claims involve a huge leap. Because of these theological assertions about headship, women's heads should be covered when they pray or prophesy, while men's should not (vv. 4–5). A man's *literally covered* head disgraces his metaphorical head (presumably Christ), while a woman's *literally unveiled* head disgraces her metaphorical head (presumably her husband). It is not at all clear why Paul's rather ambiguous theological claims necessitate these contradictory practical conclusions.

Moreover, Paul's purportedly theological arguments are in fact shaped by cultural conventions about women's hair. Even here Paul's arguments become contradictory. On the one hand, Paul asserts, for a woman to pray or prophesy with unveiled head is the *same* as having her head shaved, which is disgraceful (v. 5). On the other hand, Paul says if a woman will not veil herself, she *should* cut off her hair—that would apparently solve the problem of praying or prophesying with inappropriately long hair (v. 6). Again, though, that is not an option because a woman with a shaved head is disgraceful. Therefore women should wear veils when they speak in worship. This argument is not only logically contorted but pure cultural convention, unrelated to the theological points Paul has been making.[15]

Sensing that he hasn't really made his case, Paul continues with a problematic biblical argument based on the creation story from Genesis (vv. 7–9). Interpreting Genesis for his own practical purposes, Paul asserts that only man was created in the image of God, a contradiction of the clear statement in Genesis 1:27: "So God created humankind in [God's] image, in the image of God [God] created them; male and female [God] created them." Having argued from Genesis 1, Paul then adds a reference to Genesis 2 about God

14. Paul also appears to subordinate Christ to God, which has significant problems within Trinitarian theology as later developed by the church. A Trinitarian theology, which emphasizes the mutuality and equality of the persons of the Trinity, invites a rethinking of headship in this framework. See Hays, *First Corinthians*, 192; Gench, *Encountering God*, 61–62.

15. The sense that female sexuality undermines social order also underlies Paul's arguments. Martin, *Corinthian Body*, 245. This argument has continued in relation to women preaching; often one reason women were not allowed in the pulpit is because they might sexually arouse the men in the congregation. And, of course, issues related to female sexuality continue to shape approaches to women's dress in the pulpit.

creating woman *from* and *for* man, not man *from* or *for* woman (vv. 8–9). Here too Paul's interpretation ignores the mutuality between male and female that the Genesis story depicts.[16] Paul's use of these biblical passages to argue that a man should not cover his head when speaking in worship, while a woman should, is a *non sequitur*. There is simply no necessary reason that his problematic assertions about Genesis should lead to the conclusions he draws. And he apparently recognizes that members of the Corinthian community will not be satisfied with this argument.

So Paul continues with his strangest point of all—a supernatural argument about the angels (v. 10). Paul's argument may have something to do with the sexuality of women's bodies and their vulnerability to corruption by sexually predatory angels,[17] but no one really understands what Paul is saying here. We can only peer dimly into cultural assumptions and conventions we do not yet understand.

Paul thus offers a range of arguments to encourage women to cover their heads when they prophesy or pray in public worship. Then suddenly and unexpectedly, in verses 11–12, an interruption occurs, as we have been led to expect in 1 Corinthians. Paul "fractures" his own arguments, almost as if he is presenting the counter argument: "*Nevertheless,* in the Lord woman is not independent of man or man independent of woman. For just as woman came from man, so man comes through woman; but all things come from God." Once again *the Lord* interrupts: *In the Lord* there is neither hierarchy nor subordination between men and women, but mutual interdependence. *In the Lord,* possibly Paul's strongest and most central theological affirmation, one must reframe the arguments Paul has made up to this point. *In the Lord* the new creation has broken in and one must affirm *communitas* in the Body of Christ. Paul thus "seems

16. As interpreters have recognized, the creation story depicts a covenant relationship between man and woman, not the subordination of woman to man. See Walter Brueggemann, *Genesis,* Interpretation: A Bible Commentary for Teaching and Preaching (Louisville, KY: John Knox Press, 1982), 47. Also Gench, *Encountering God,* 46–47.

17. The different interpretations here are complex and too involved to discuss. See Gench, 47–49. This argument is possibly related to understandings of female bodies as being more porous and open to invasion than male bodies as well as to understandings that "the moment of prophecy was the moment of invasion," the moment when people were most vulnerable and endangered because "open to the forces of prophetic inspiration." See Martin, *Corinthian Body,* 241, 229–49.

to be condoning, indeed encouraging, the subordination of women
(vv. 3–10) while simultaneously acknowledging the equality of men
and women, at least in the Lord."[18] *"Paul lets social roles 'in the world'
and social roles 'in the Lord' clash right in the setting of worship."*[19]

Paul doesn't stop there. He has apparently made up his mind
about head coverings, so he proceeds, but he now abandons theological argument altogether; it is as if he has recognized that *theologically* he has just undermined his own position. So he simply—and
oddly—falls back on cultural expectations: "Does not nature itself
teach you that if a man wears long hair, it is degrading to him, but if
a woman has long hair, it is her glory? For her hair is given to her for
a covering" (vv. 14–15).[20] Here long hair is a glory and given for a
"covering," so one wonders why it should be veiled or worn up. Paul
then concludes with a statement that has echoed through the church
for centuries: "Besides, we've never done it this way before"—"we
have no such custom" (vv. 16a). He brings to bear the weight of the
larger church, the other churches that may take exception to or be
offended by what the Corinthian women are doing (v. 16b). For
an apostle whose theology is grounded in the folly of the crucified
Christ, this turn to "nature" and convention is shocking. Indeed, in
the section that follows on the Lord's Supper Paul takes the opposite
approach; he rejects the cultural conventions around meal practices
for a radical communion in the Body of Christ. For whatever reason, Paul simply remains captive to conventions regarding the subordination of women, symbolized, ironically, in the very veiling that
enables them to prophesy and pray in worship.[21]

My purpose here is not to make Paul look ridiculous or misogy-
nist. It is to recognize that he is a theologian who at times struggles
with his own captivity to the powers of this age. He simply does the
best he can. Indeed, Paul himself will later humbly recognize his
own and the church's limitations: "For we know only in part, and we

---

18. Martin, *Corinthian Body*, 229.
19. Judith Gundry, quoted in Gench, *Encountering God*, 50.
20. By "nature" Paul is actually referring to cultural conventions. See Gench, *Encountering God*,
    51–52. Here the issue seems to be hairstyle rather than head covering.
21. As Martin notes, the veil does give women authority to pray and prophesy but at the same
    time symbolizes the inferiority of the female body and the subordination of women to men.
    Martin, *Corinthian Body*, 246.

prophesy only in part; but when the complete comes, the partial will come to an end. . . . For now we see in a mirror, dimly, but then we will see face to face. Now I know only in part; then I will know fully, even as I have been fully known" (13:9–12). Paul's contorted arguments are actually a theological invitation to humility.

That is the posture of the practical, apocalyptic, hermeneutical theologian. Indeed, it may be that Paul's own efforts throughout the first twelve chapters of the letter—maybe especially in this section—lead him to the recognition and affirmation of his own limited knowledge in chapter 13. Theologians and pastors, Paul reveals, are, like the church, always on the way in the liminal space between the old age and the new. We need not fear the attempts, even the fractured, contradictory ones, to address the practical struggles and issues in the church, but we always do so with humility and love.

From this perspective discernment remains essential, as Paul suggests, even if ironically, in verse 13. He invites the Corinthians to "judge for yourselves," even though he makes the assertion rhetorically, almost shaming the Corinthians to agree with him. Ultimately, however, that is what the Corinthians and the contemporary church are always doing: judging, discerning for ourselves as best we can in our context but never writing our conclusions in stone, never making idols of them. Rather, we continue on the way, recognizing our limited perception and seeking for clearer vision. In this sense, Paul's convoluted arguments in 11:2–16 contain a profound theological affirmation about the journey of Christian theology, which never arrives but is always tempted by cultural configurations and is always seeking new and deeper perception along the way to the new creation.

FURTHER REFLECTIONS
Clothing and the New Creation

Paul's wrestling also holds up a mirror to the contemporary church. He invites us to continued theological reflection on the significance of clothing in worship leadership. The issue is not simply an ancient one limited to the Corinthian community, but it has continued throughout the history of the pulpit and remains significant today. Clothing continues to be a place where cultural convention and new creation often collide. Clothing today, as in Corinth, can be used as a vehicle of control and even subordination; it can be used as a means of affirming the male body as superior to the female in worship leadership. How many women are forced to wear certain kinds of culturally acceptable clothing in the pulpit and judged when they transgress these expectations? Indeed, clothing has itself been a symbol of the cultural oppression of women in the pulpit through the ages. The resistance of the Corinthian women around the matter of clothing—a resistance that continues today—represents an important theological challenge to the Christian pulpit.

Consider the extreme example of the eighteenth-century preacher Jemima Wilkinson, who became known as the Public Universal Friend and "one of the most notorious women in America."[22] As women have done throughout history, Wilkinson, excluded from the "masculine" authority to preach conferred by ordination, instead claimed the "feminine" (and Pauline!) authority of divine revelation and call.[23] Her call, however, took an extreme form. In 1776, she claimed to have died and been raised as a spirit sent by God. She was no longer a "she" but a genderless spirit, "her" female body simply a tabernacle for the Public Universal Friend. "She" was no longer Jemima Wilkinson, and "her" followers no longer used gendered pronouns to describe their Friend. The Public Universal Friend (P.U.F.), like the women in Corinth, modeled "her" life on Paul's promise: "there is no longer male and female."[24]

Unlike the women in Corinth, however, the P.U.F. dressed in clothes that disguised and veiled the female form, "long, loose gowns and cloaks that fastened at the neck and hid all but her hands, feet, and face from public view." Dressing more like a man than a woman, the P.U.F. "looked like a minister wearing clerical robes" and, in imitation of a popular style among men, knotted a handkerchief around "her" neck. One person described the P.U.F. as

22. Catherine A. Brekus, *Strangers and Pilgrims: Female Preaching in America 1740–1845* (Chapel Hill: University of North Carolina, 1998): 81. My account of Wilkinson is based on Brekus's work, 80–97.
23. Ibid., 82
24. Ibid., 93.

"a virtual cross dresser."[25] Clothing, not simply calling, apparently made the person:

> By cultivating a "masculine" appearance, Wilkinson imitated scores of other women, from medieval female saints to Revolutionary female soldiers, who dressed as men in order to gain greater social, political, economic, or religious authority. Historically, dress has always been connected to power: people declare their wealth, social class, race, and sex by what they wear, whether it be trousers and neckties or dresses and high heels. Because clothing draws visible boundaries between men and women, it has functioned as one of the primary means of representing sexual difference and perpetuating sexual inequality. It is not surprising, then, that women who have wanted to increase their status have appropriated visible signs of men's power: their pants, vests, shirts, and *even clerical robes.*[26]

Significantly, this "masculine" appearance increased the standing of the Public Universal Friend in the eyes of the world. In contrast to other women, who were excluded from pulpits, the P.U.F. was invited to preach in many respectable churches.[27] In this way, "she" subverted male authority and ridiculed men, "implying that their power lay in the trappings of dress, rather than in their natural superiority." By convincing people to allow "her" to preach simply by donning ministerial robes, the P.U.F revealed that clothing, not character, "made the man." "She" revealed that "the binary categories of male and female were not natural at all, but socially constructed."[28] Ironically, however, the P.U.F. also reinforced male authority, reaffirming "the principle of male supremacy by dressing as a man and denying that she was a woman. . . . Instead of defending female evangelism, she implicitly sanctioned the cultural and institutional structures that consigned her to a place of subordination and inferiority. In her eyes, a woman had to be beyond gender to preach

---

25. Ibid., 87.
26. Ibid., 87–88, italics mine. The P.U.F. came in for intense criticism for this "manly" appearance and was considered to be insane or a lunatic. "She" was mocked and slandered, even by many who came to hear "her" preach.
27. Ibid., 91.
28. Ibid., 90.

the gospel."[29] Preaching, she implicitly affirmed, "was a male privilege [women] could only achieve by renouncing their 'femininity,'" something the women in Corinth were pressured to do in a different way.[30]

The P.U.F.'s model of "masculine" religious leadership offered women one of their few opportunities to preach in Revolutionary America.[31] The model was inseparable from clothing. Though Paul does not demand that women wear men's clothing, the oppressive conjunction of women's subordination and distinctive clothing has continued in the Christian pulpit, deeply connected to suspicions about the inferiority and sexuality of women's bodies. The tensions between old-age cultural conventions and the new creation continue today, as women are still excluded from many pulpits and are often judged in terms of their clothing.[32]

Maybe the most profound theological response to 1 Corinthians 11:2–16 comes from a group of saints who took Paul's words in First Corinthians more seriously than most: the holy fools. It is perhaps not surprising that many holy fools, such as St. Basil the Blessed in Moscow and even St. Francis of Assisi, inspired by Paul's assertion that we are "fools for the sake of Christ" (4:10), often valued *nakedness*.[33] Indeed, they even preached naked. St. Basil the Blessed proclaimed the gospel naked on the streets of Moscow. St. Francis is reported to have entered a Christian pulpit naked one Sunday. In their nakedness, these holy fools created a liminal space, disrupting the world in which clothing was a symbol of social hierarchy, status,

---

29. Ibid.
30. Ibid., 95. In her meetings, however, the P.U.F. welcomed women to preach and testify in public, though "she" never justified their right to speak *as women*. The P.U.F. functioned with a one-sex model of gender that believed that women's bodies were inferior and incomplete versions of men's—a model similar to that in Paul's time (95–96).
31. Ibid., 96.
32. Today this issue is even more complex as the rigid binaries of male and female are being both challenged and reinforced by Christians. Gay, lesbian, and transgender pastors further subvert and challenge the binary assumptions about gender and appropriate clothing. They invite us to perceive in new ways the in-breaking of the new creation that breaks down the old-age binary between "male and female."
33. There were also women holy fools who went around naked, although usually not in public. For a more detailed account of the following discussion, see Charles L. Campbell, "Preacher as Ridiculous Person: Naked Street Preaching and Homiletical Foolishness," in Robert Stephen Reid, ed., *Slow of Speech and Unclean Lips: Contemporary Images of Preaching Identity* (Eugene, OR: Cascade, 2010), 89–108.

and security. Their nudity was a form of resistance that subverted the hierarchical powers of the world.

The nakedness of the holy fools was deeply theological. They embodied *both* the nakedness of humanity at creation *and* the shame of Jesus' nakedness on the cross. Combining allusions to both creation and crucifixion, their nakedness could be perceived, through an apocalyptic bifocal vision, as an enactment of the *new* creation that interrupted the world through the cross of Jesus Christ. Resisting the powers of this age and living into the new creation are simultaneously expressed in the nakedness of the holy fools, who embody the folly of the new age in an extreme and radical form.

> Nudity is abhorrent to the conventional because it violates the system of classification by which one can identify a person's place on the social map. Without clothes, the boundaries by which society is ordered and guarded are dissolved. Clothing signifies one's social location, gender, and status.
>
> Walter Wink, *Engaging the Powers: Discernment and Resistance in a World of Domination* (Minneapolis: Fortress Press, 1992), 317n16.

While it seems bizarre, the witness of the holy fools was actually enacted in early baptisms, which, as has been noted, possibly informed the freedom Corinthian women claimed in worship. People were baptized naked. Being drowned in the death of Christ involved being baptized into his nakedness on the cross. Being raised from the waters, one entered the new creation, like Adam and Eve, naked. Ironically, being "clothed" with the crucified and risen Christ in baptism was being clothed in a nakedness that broke down all the hierarchical arrangements associated with clothing. This baptismal practice is one of the "traditions" Paul undoubtedly handed on to the Corinthians (11:2). So the women in Corinth had excellent theological arguments for rejecting oppressive sartorial requirements in order to prophesy and pray. Women today appropriately challenge certain sartorial requirements for preaching, even as the church continues to wrestle with the need for order in Christian worship. As in Corinth, the church today continues to seek discernment amid the tensions between *communitas* and order present in Paul's opening words: "I commend you because

you remember me in everything and maintain the traditions just as
I handed them on to you. But . . ."

11:17–34
Sacrament: The Lord's Supper

Whereas in verses 2–16 Paul interrupts the new-creation traditions,
including probably the practice of baptism, with old-age cultural
conventions, in verses 17–34 Paul unequivocally interrupts the
dominant meal practices of the culture with the radical claims of the
gospel. Here there is no "but" when Paul declares, "Now in the following instructions I do not commend you" (v. 17). In the middle of
the text (vv. 23–26), the church's traditional words of institution for
the Lord's Supper become a radical political and theological subversion of economic and social hierarchies that divided and continue to
divide the church.

In countless ways, from large, public events to everyday interac-
tions, the powers of this age seek to ritualize relationships of dominant and subordinate. This ritualization is one of the most effective
ways in which the powers work; through repeated, everyday habits
and practices they create a "public transcript" that reinforces the
hierarchical arrangements of strong and weak, honored and shamed.
From matters of dress, discussed in the previous section, to gestures
of subordination, such as bowing, to deferential language (women,
for example, repeatedly apologizing), the "public transcript" of the
dominant is enacted and reinforced in a daily ritual theater.[34]

In the New Testament period this ritual enactment often occurred
around meals, which were intentionally arranged to honor some
people and shame others. In first-century Rome meals—particularly the evening meal—were some of the most important occasions
for social theater and ritual in the ancient world. Rich householders
would often stage a dinner for those whose favor they were seeking
to gain. The meal was designed to display one's own wealth and status ostentatiously and to honor the guest for the sake of anticipated

---

34. See James C. Scott, *Domination and the Arts of Resistance: Hidden Transcripts* (New Haven,
CT: Yale University Press, 1990).

future rewards. An important element at many of these meals was the presence of persons of lesser honor and status, who would be seated in different spaces and served lesser quality food, all as a way of shaming them in order to accentuate the honor of those in the chief seats. Often this dinner-theater took place in dining areas open to the streets, so that passersby could witness and comment on the affair. Meals, in short, were occasions publicly to reinforce the social hierarchy in a culture of honor and shame.[35]

Paul addresses this social context in verses 17–34. The Corinthian Christians have accommodated to these cultural practices. Their practice of the Lord's Supper is reinforcing the divisions among them (v. 18). So distorted are these practices that "it is not really . . . the Lord's supper" that they eat. "For when the time comes to eat, each of you goes ahead with your own supper, and one goes hungry and another becomes drunk. What! Do you not have homes to eat and drink in? Or do you show contempt for the church of God and humiliate those who have nothing?" (vv. 20–22). In the church's meals the wealthy, who host the meal in their homes and possibly see themselves as the patrons of the community, go ahead with their own meal before others arrive. When they arrive the poor receive little or nothing, while the wealthy not only get the best food, but even get drunk. The poor, that is, have too little (they are hungry) while the wealthy have too much (they get drunk). The dominant culture's table rituals of honor and shame have captured the table practices of the Christian community. The church's common meal has become a practice that reinforces social and class division. Paul consequently minces no words in his condemnation. He opens the section with an unequivocal statement: "Now in the following instructions I do not commend you, because when you come together it is not for the better but for the worse. . . . When you come together it is not really to eat the Lord's supper" (11:17, 20). He repeats himself for emphasis in verse 22: "In this matter I do not commend you."[36]

---

35. See Gerd Thiessen, *The Social Setting of Pauline Christianity: Essays on Corinth*, trans. John H. Schütz (Philadelphia: Fortress Press, 1982), 145–74. Also Hays, *First Corinthians*, 192–206.
36. As Thiessen notes, Paul does appear to offer a compromise, allowing the wealthy to eat as they like in their own homes (only the rich would have houses) but to behave differently in the common meal of the community. However, as Thiessen suggests, a logical trajectory of Paul's argument would involve a more radical sharing of food. See Thiessen, *Social Setting*, 164.

The ground of Paul's critique is twofold. First, he highlights the table fellowship of Jesus, particularly his words at the last supper with his disciples (vv. 23–26). Paul understands that Jesus' table fellowship was an act of resistance to the culture's divisive, oppressive hierarchies of strong and weak, honored and shamed. He recognizes that such practices, which stood at the heart of the culture, had implications for social and economic relationships. The apostle discerns that for Jesus the table was a place to enact the self-giving love at the heart of the new order he was bringing into the world. "This is my body that is for you. Do this in remembrance of me. . . . This cup is the new covenant in my blood. Do this, as often as you drink it, in remembrance of me" (vv. 24–25). These are not simply Last Supper words; they rather characterize the self-giving of Jesus at all meals throughout his ministry. This remembrance is not just a mental exercise. It is *anamnesis* (*anamnēsin*, vv. 24–25), through which the community actually embodies again the self-giving meal practice of Jesus. How, Paul wonders, can a community that repeats these radical words and remembers Jesus' self-giving love engage in meal practices that reinforce the status of some members over others?

The table was a Jubilee table, at which the social patterns of domination and subordination were to be broken down and a new community embodied. Table fellowship was to be an enactment of the new *communitas* of the baptized. In short, Jesus' table fellowship, which Paul seeks faithfully to carry forward into the life of the early Christian community, was a practice of resistance in the face of the powers of the world that use everyday ritual practices to enslave human minds and hearts in the old age.

Second, Paul's critique of the Corinthians' practice rests on what the community *proclaims* when it shares the Lord's Supper: "For as often as you eat this bread and drink the cup, you proclaim the Lord's death until he comes" (v. 26). The meal, like Jesus' death itself, interrupts the old age and sets the community in the liminal, liturgical space at the juncture of the ages—in between Christ's death and the eschatological fulfillment. The practice of the church at the table, like Paul's preaching discussed in chapter 1, *proclaims* Christ's weak and foolish death, which interrupts the powers of this age and subverts the world's understandings of power and wisdom.

Paul interprets the table through the lens of his foolish preaching. The Lord's Supper, rightly practiced, is as scandalous in the eyes of the world as Paul's preaching of the cross. At the table the church proclaims the folly and weakness of the cross. The church cannot proclaim this radically disruptive, apocalyptic message by continuing to accommodate to the hierarchical meal practices of the old age.

The consequences of this inappropriate practice are dire. As Paul writes, "all who eat and drink without discerning the body, eat and drink judgment on themselves" (v. 29). That is, those who participate in the Lord's Supper, those who proclaim Christ's death, without discerning the Body of Christ, remain captive to the powers of death. Paul again emphasizes discernment, the fundamental gift of the Spirit, which enables believers to perceive the new creation amidst the old age. Such discernment enables the church to discern the odd Body of Christ and to live into it, rather than simply accommodating to the culture's conventions. For the body Paul calls the Corinthians to discern is not Christ's body somehow mysteriously present in the bread but the body that is enacted when the church gathers at the meal. At the meal the church is to be the very Body of Christ, enfleshing his "weak" and "foolish" way in the world. The practice of the Lord's Supper, in which equality and mutuality are to be enacted in the community of faith, prepares the community to live into the kind of body Paul will write about in chapters 12–13. The primary gift of the Spirit—discernment—and the activity of the body are intimately linked because, as Paul will stress in the next chapter, it is the power of the Spirit that counters the powers of this age and makes possible the faithful Body of Christ.

Apart from this Spirit, there is the power of death: "For this reason many of you are weak and ill, and some have died" (v. 30). Paul's words need not be read as some kind of supernatural judgment, as if God is zapping people right and left who inappropriately participate in the meal. The powers of death are more realistic than that. Wherever a few people have too much and others have too little ("one goes hungry and another becomes drunk"), illness and death will follow. Those who are hungry and malnourished will suffer and die. Those who overindulge will likewise suffer from illness and even death. In a few words, Paul unmasks and judges the death that follows from the world's economic and social hierarchies. This judgment is a form of discipline (v. 32); it unmasks the church's captivity and calls the church to embody a different way of being in the world, one that begins with discernment in the power of the Spirit.

A profound understanding of ritual practice underlies Paul's words. Practice, Paul affirms, is intimately related to discernment, imagination, and perception. Through the practices of the Christian community, imaginations take shape; believers come to perceive the world and negotiate life in distinctive ways.[37] Perception is formed in critical ways through the practices that shape our communities. For this reason, the powers of this age use the theater of daily practices to reinforce the system of domination. Through such practices the system becomes normalized, taken for granted; it becomes the air we breathe. For this reason the church's practices are critical; the community of faith will not form imaginations or resist cultural accommodation simply by talking about alternatives or thinking about them; alternative practices are essential for resistance.

Paul's theology of the Lord's Supper is radical and possibly shocking. The apostle has little or no interest in theological niceties regarding whether the meal should be interpreted as transubstantiation, consubstantiation, or memorial. He would surely not commend the church for the ways his words about discerning the body have been dissected through the centuries, so dividing the church that we cannot all even sit at table together anymore. For Paul the table is an apocalyptic battleground where the new creation breaks in, but the powers of this age are at work seeking to take the table captive for their own deadly purposes. Like Christ's death that it proclaims, the

> For the imagination is not simply a container of images or ideas that we now entertain in preference to other images and ideas. Rather imagination is a set of habits and relations that can only be carried by a group of people in distinction from the world's habits.
>
> Stanley Hauerwas, *Against the Nations: War and Survival in a Liberal Society* (Minneapolis: Winston Press, 1985), 197.

---

37. Stanley Hauerwas, "The Politics of the Church: How We Lay Bricks and Make Disciples," in *After Christendom: How the Church Is to Behave If Freedom, Justice, and a Christian Nation Are Bad Ideas* (Nashville: Abingdon Press, 1991), 107.

table enacts a new social and political reality; it is an invitation to the radically subversive weakness and folly of Jesus.

Liturgists routinely use Paul's words from this chapter (vv. 23–25) as the words of institution at the Lord's Supper, often forgetting their radical social and political implications. We often ignore the fact that Paul used these words *precisely* to challenge cultural, social, and economic hierarchies. The words of institution proclaim the apocalyptic interruption of the gospel into the cultural accommodation of the Corinthian church. The Lord's Supper, for Paul, is a practice of the new creation; it subverts the social hierarchies of strong and weak, rich and poor, honored and shamed. Where this new creation, shaped by the hospitality and self-giving love of Jesus, is not embodied, it is not the Lord's Supper that we eat. It is, rather, a "ritual lie."[38]

The Lord's Supper, that is, does not function *ex opere operato* for Paul; the supper is not effective independent of the character of the church's practice. Simply gathering at the table, repeating ritual formulas, and trusting the work of Christ does not a Lord's Supper make. There is, in fact, a danger in making overly extravagant claims for the meal. Through inappropriate practice the meal can, in fact, become something other than the Lord's Supper. When the table honors some people and shames others—for example, by excluding women and LGBTQ+ persons from leadership—Paul invites the church to discern the Body and ask if it is really the Lord's Supper we are eating. When poor people are not welcomed at the table because churches have become segregated by class, the church should wonder if Paul would proclaim, "I do not commend you!" When the meal becomes a comfortable ritual that does not interrupt or disturb the hierarchical arrangements of the old age—whether based on race or ethnicity or gender or sexual orientation—the church must ask if it is truly proclaiming the foolishness and weakness of the cross or is it practicing a "ritual lie."

Paul's words present a striking challenge to both the Corinthian and the contemporary church. In the coming chapters Paul builds on his words about the ritual practice of the Lord's Supper by further

---

38. Michael Warren, *At This Time in This Place: The Spirit Embodied in the Local Assembly* (Harrisburg, PA: Trinity Press International, 1999), 13.

exploring the work of the Spirit in the church and the character of the Body of Christ. Turning to a discussion of spiritual gifts, the apostle further guides believers in our discernment of the kind of body the Christian community is called to be.

12:1-31
Theological Vision:
The Body of Christ

In chapter 12, building on his sacramental call to discern the body, Paul offers the theological vision of the Body of Christ that shapes the practical guidance that follows in 13–14. The chapter is, in fact, a theological tour de force. The various dimensions of Paul's theology, grounded in the cross, come to the fore in Paul's theological vision. While Paul is certainly affirming "unity in diversity" in the church, this affirmation is inseparable from Paul's apocalyptic theology. Indeed, it is the deep structure of this theology that underlies Paul's vision of the church as the Body of Christ.

First, Paul *interrupts* the common understanding of the "body politic." The analogy of the body, prevalent in Greco-Roman culture and rhetoric, was used to *reinforce* the status hierarchies of strong and weak. The analogy of the parts of the body, with some weaker (and uglier) and some stronger (and more beautiful), was employed to *maintain* the hierarchical arrangements given in the society. Such hierarchies were thought to be grounded in nature and necessary for the healthy functioning of the social order. Paul, however, interrupts this analogy and uses the image of the body to subvert those hierarchies; he raises up the weak and lowers the strong to challenge the hierarchical divisions in the church and to call the church to interdependence and mutuality. Paul's rhetoric "pushes for an actual reversal of the normal 'this worldly' attribution of honor and status. The lower is made higher, and the higher lower."[1]

Such a move is common in rituals that create the liminal space

---

1. Dale B. Martin, *The Corinthians Body* (New Haven, CT: Yale University Press, 1995), 96. See Martin's full discussion of this hierarchical reversal of the body analogy, 87–96.

of *communitas*. Hierarchies are reversed, as the secular structures of rank and status disappear and positions of higher and lower status are negated.[2] Paul's apocalyptic interruption of the body analogy thus creates the liminal space of *communitas* through which he seeks to overcome the divisions in the Corinthian church. This theological vision of *communitas*, central to ritual, is particularly significant because Paul continues to be concerned with the worship life of the community, as will become apparent when he returns to the matter of glossolalia in chapter 14.[3]

Second, Paul affirms that *God* interrupts the status quo to create a new and different kind of community. Whereas in the Greco-Roman world *nature* sets the status hierarchies to which everyone is to conform, for Paul God through the Holy Spirit interrupts nature and disrupts the entire framework. Just as on the cross, God in Christ reversed the status of weak and strong, so now the Spirit moves to generate the same kind of reversal in the Body of Christ. This body, like the Body of Christ on the cross, will enact a disruption of the "natural" values and hierarchies of the world and provide an alternative polity for life in the new creation. Paul's affirmation of the Spirit's work throughout the chapter reinforces his earlier assertions that the Spirit creates an alternative to the powers of this age (chapter 2). The Spirit moves in the space between the ages to challenge the powers of division and death and to create a new people. The Spirit subverts the analogy of the body employed by the culture and reframes the analogy for the new creation. Paul's apocalyptic theological vision, developed in chapters 1–2, shapes his vision of the church as the Body of Christ.

Third, Paul employs an apocalyptic rhetoric of unveiling or unmasking. In the chapter Paul deals with appearance and reality. Those parts of the body that *appear* to be weaker and more shameful are *in reality* most honored. The "normally conceived body hierarchy is actually only an apparent, surface hierarchy."[4] Similarly, the cross appears weak and foolish but in reality is the power and wisdom of

---

2. Victor Turner, *The Ritual Process: Structure and Anti-Structure* (New York: Aldine de Gruyter, 1995), 95–97.
3. Dale Martin has argued that chapters 12–13 are in fact meant to challenge the hierarchical status claims of those who speak in tongues. *Corinthian Body*, 87–103.
4. Martin, *Corinthian Body*, 94.

God. Just as the hidden reality of the cross must be unveiled and perceived anew, so the hidden realities of the Body of Christ must be unveiled so a new perception of weak and strong might emerge. With this new perception, a new way of living grounded in mutual respect and support may shape the community of faith. Unity in diversity may become an embodied reality.

12:1–3

Gifts of the Spirit

Paul's development of this theological vision of the Body of Christ is set up in the opening three verses, in which the apostle reiterates theological emphases with which he began the letter. Just as Paul opened the letter with an emphasis on the disruptive call of Christ, the gracious gifts of the Spirit, and a call to unity (1:1–8), so he returns to these themes to ground his vision of the Body of Christ. He does not want the community to be uninformed about *spiritual gifts* (v. 1). This opening presents the Corinthians with two essential theological reminders. First, all the activities Paul will discuss are *gifts*. They have not been earned but simply received from the giver. At the very outset, through his emphasis on gifts, Paul presents important theological assumptions: the initiative is from God; there is no room for boasting in a gift; there is no way to claim status from a gift. One can only receive a gift with gratitude and use it for the purpose for which it has been given. All these theological assumptions underlie Paul's emphasis on spiritual gifts.

Second, these are *spiritual* gifts. Paul does not simply mean that these gifts are purely in the spiritual realm; as will become clear, many of these gifts involve quite practical, bodily activities. Rather, Paul highlights the active role of the Spirit, who empowers the gifts and plays the central role in everything that follows. Paul repeatedly emphasizes the work of the Spirit throughout the chapter, and his opening words set the stage for this emphasis. He is talking about *spiritual* gifts—gifts of the Spirit. Also implicit in this emphasis is the work of the Spirit as counter to the powers of this age. Where the Spirit is moving, one can expect a different kind of power and a different kind of life from that shaped by the powers of death. By this point in the letter the phrase "spiritual gifts" is theologically loaded indeed.

Having set up the theme of the chapter, which will continue through chapter 14, Paul again reminds the Corinthians of God's calling that interrupted their lives and brought them into the community of faith. Although Paul does not use the term "call," he emphasizes God's initiative in disrupting the Corinthians' idolatry and enabling them to confess Jesus Christ as Lord. Paul also reminds the Corinthians—and contemporary readers—of one of the ways the powers of death work: they "entice" or "seduce" (*apagō*). The powers do not always work by oppressing or threatening; they lure people into paths that lead to idolatry and death.[5] They promise life and offer all kinds of benefits, but their way is the way of captivity and death.

Paul interrupts these powers using the mocking, satirical approach of Isaiah: these seductive powers that demand human worship cannot even speak (v. 2); their claims to power are a sham. As Isaiah writes:

> To whom will you liken me and make me equal,
>   and compare me, as though we were alike?
> Those who lavish gold from the purse,
>   and weigh out silver in the scales—
> they hire a goldsmith, who makes it into a god;
>   then they fall down and worship!
> They lift it to their shoulders, they carry it,
>   they set it in its place, and it stands there;
>   it cannot move from its place.
> If one cries out to it, it does not answer
>   or save anyone from trouble.
>
>   (Isa. 46:5–7)

---

5. In Revelation, for example, there is the Beast who oppresses and the Seducer (a term I prefer instead of "whore") who seduces. The term, *apagō*, actually suggests both aspects of the powers' work. It can mean being carried away by pleasures and desires, but it can also mean being led away to prison or execution. The element of captivity to the powers of death is inherent in the word, whether one is captured by seduction or threat. See *"apagō,"* in Frederick W. Danker, Walter Bauer, and William F. Arndt, *A Greek-English Lexicon of the New Testament and Other Early Christian Literature,* 3rd ed. (Chicago: University of Chicago, 2000), 95.

Mocking the idolatrous powers, Paul reminds the Corinthians that God has taken the initiative, interrupted their former lives, set them free from the enticing powers of death, and given them a new confession and a new community.

Finally, in this opening section Paul emphasizes that even this new confession is a gift of the Spirit: "no one can say, 'Jesus is Lord' except by the Holy Spirit" (v. 3). Confessional speech, contrary to the muteness of the idols, relies on the initiative and power of the Spirit. Here too Paul returns to the paradoxical theological claims with which he opened the letter. The confession that the crucified Jesus is Lord requires, as Paul stressed in chapter 1, "destabilizing pairs of opposites" (crucified Lord) that can be discerned and spoken only through the gift of the Spirit. Such a confession, which confounds the world's understandings of Lordship, interrupts the hierarchies and assumptions of the powers of death. Moreover, such speech is a radical expression of freedom from captivity to these powers. Indeed, the voiceless idols often demand silence in the face of their oppressive and seductive rule. The powers pursue their ways of death by silencing their victims and opponents, for silence is one of the ways the deathly status quo gets authenticated. As the LGBTQ+ community has rightly acknowledged, "Silence is death." So Paul offers Spirit-empowered, confessional speech—"Jesus is Lord"—as an alternative to the silent death of the principalities and powers. Through this confession, the powerful hierarchies of the world are interrupted and destabilized, and a space is created for new perception and new community. The initiative of God and the gift of the Spirit, which empower such disruptive speech, shape the theological vision of the Body of Christ that follows.

12:4–11
Unity in Diversity

Grounded in the initiative of God and the work of the Spirit, Paul emphasizes unity in diversity within the Body of Christ. He stresses unity that is grounded not in human efforts but in the Spirit, repeating "the one Spirit" or "the same Spirit" like a refrain throughout this section. Paul envisions a community animated by the dynamic initiative and movement of the Spirit. For theological traditions that have downplayed the Spirit by emphasizing Christology, Paul's strong pneumatology serves as a corrective. Highlighted at the beginning of the letter as animating resistance to the powers of this age (chapter 2), the work of the Spirit now receives further development. Two aspects of Paul's pneumatology can be highlighted.

First, the Spirit's work is the work of "the Lord" and "God" (vv. 4–6). Paul implicitly emphasizes the divine character of the Spirit in his proto-Trinitarian opening to this section. Through poetic parallelisms, Paul suggests the unity of the Spirit, the Lord, and God:

> Now there are varieties of gifts,
> but the same Spirit;
> and there are varieties of services,
> but the same Lord;
> and there are varieties of activities,
> but it is the same God who activates all of them in everyone.

Although Paul has no doctrine of the Trinity, and at times even seems to have a rather subordinationist Christology (see 11:3; 15:28), the equality among the Spirit, the Lord, and God is here apparent. In Paul's pneumatology, the work of the Spirit is the work of the Lord and of God.

Moreover, Paul assumes these three—Spirit, Lord, and God—are a unity. Otherwise there could be different sources of the spiritual gifts, creating the possibility of a hierarchy of gifts. Emphasizing their one divine source, Paul seeks to prevent any such hierarchy. The apostle would never want people to claim, "My gift is from God!" "Mine is from the Lord." "Mine is from the Spirit." Because there is no hierarchy of gift givers, there can be no hierarchy of gifts. Paul here subtly, but clearly, suggests the practical implications of the divinity of the Spirit in unity with the Lord and God.

At the same time, Paul asserts that the *work* of the Spirit is the *same work* as that of "the Lord," the crucified Christ. Paul establishes this relationship, again with Trinitarian implications, in the first two chapters of the letter, and he reemphasizes it here. The crucified

Christ provides the lens through which the work of the Spirit may be "tested," as all spirits must be tested. This relationship is affirmed earlier when Paul emphasizes that the Spirit enables the confession, "Jesus is Lord," while no one speaking through the Spirit can say, "Let Jesus be cursed" (v. 3). There is the test: Does the Spirit further the confession and work of Jesus Christ? The Spirit, in fact, may be understood as the living presence and activity of the curious *Kyrios*, Jesus. Indeed, this theological affirmation undergirds the entire chapter. For the Spirit shapes the community as nothing less than the *Body of Christ*. The Spirit creates a community that embodies the way of Christ in resistance to the powers of this age. The unity of the Spirit and the Lord is essential to Paul's theology. This unity is itself inseparable from the divine activity of God.

As Trinitarian theology would later develop, though, there is also diversity in this unity. Paul, after all, mentions three different "persons" (though that term is anachronistic here): the Spirit, the Lord, and God. While Paul does not develop in any detail the dynamic relationship among these three, beyond asserting their unity of action, he does implicitly suggest that unity in diversity characterizes God. In this sense, Paul's proto-Trinitarian theology actually undergirds his understanding of Christian community. Just as God exists in a dynamic, interdependent, mutual relationship of three equal persons, so the community of faith as the Body of Christ lives into this same dynamic relationship. There are many persons and many gifts in the church, but all are animated by the same Spirit, all are formed by the same Lord, all are activated by the same God. The unity in diversity that characterizes the divine also shapes the life of the community of faith, the Body of Christ. Indeed, to be formed by the Spirit into the Body of Christ is to participate in the unity and mutuality at the heart of God. Paul's pneumatology brings together the life of God and the life of the church.

Second, Paul affirms, where the Spirit is at work the common good of the community is pursued; the spiritual gifts are given *"for the common good"* (v. 7). In the midst of the divisiveness of the Corinthian church, often exacerbated by claims regarding the spiritual gifts themselves, Paul emphasizes the work of the Spirit in building up the church. Because one and the same Spirit is at work in all the gifts, they cannot be the source of hierarchies and divisions. Because the Spirit forms the Body of Christ—the one who gave himself for others, as Paul highlighted in the previous chapter—the spiritual gifts cannot be self-serving but are given for the building up of the community. Just as the three persons of the Trinity work together in unity, equality, and mutuality, so those taken up in God's life through the work of the Spirit will seek the common good of the church. Where the Spirit is really present the wounds of division are healed.

Following these theological affirmations, Paul provides a list of various spiritual gifts, punctuated by the refrains of "the same Spirit," or "the one Spirit" (vv. 8–11). Paul's list is part of his theological vision; it is not meant to be an exhaustive presentation of each specific gift required in the church. The point is that whatever the gift may be—from wisdom and knowledge to healing and miracles to speaking in and interpreting tongues—all are allotted by the one Spirit "as the Spirit chooses" (v. 11). Paul again emphasizes the activity and freedom of God, who is not under the control of the church or individual Christians. No matter what the gift, he declares, it is given by the Spirit; it is not a possession of the recipient or, as he repeatedly states throughout the letter, a cause for boasting. No one in the church can "corner the market" on spiritual gifts or claim that one particular gift is more important than another. The life of the church is the dynamic and free work of the Spirit for the common good.

12:12-13
The Body of Christ

Paul further emphasizes the inseparable relationship between Christ and the Spirit in verses 12–13. His initial theological move in this section is a startling and extraordinary one.[6] He radically identifies the Spirit-inspired church with Christ, emphasizing as strongly as possible that the church *is* the Body of Christ: "For just as the body

6. See Richard B. Hays, *First Corinthians*, Interpretation: A Bible Commentary for Teaching and Preaching (Louisville, KY: John Knox Press, 1997), 213.

is one and has many members, and all the members of the body, though many, are one body, *so it is with Christ*" (v. 12). One would expect Paul to conclude, "so it is with the church." But instead he declares, "so it is with Christ." Whether Paul is assuming some kind of mystical union between Christ and the church or speaking in a profoundly metaphorical way, he proclaims the essential identification of Christ and the church through the Spirit. Paul here speaks of the living Christ as the body with many parts. Through this body, Christ continues his presence and work in the world. The work of the Spirit is the work of Christ, and the community formed by that Spirit is the Body of Christ. It is difficult to imagine a more profound theological claim about the church—or a more challenging word to the church. You are Christ, Paul declares with a striking indicative, which brings with it an implicit imperative: now live into that reality!

The members of the body, Paul next proclaims, are incorporated into Christ through the Spirit in baptism (v. 13). Central to the church's faithful living is the baptismal identity of the members, which is also shaped by the one Spirit. This turn to baptismal identity is a critically important theological move in this section. The Spirit not only apportions the variety of gifts in the community but also creates a new identity for the members of the church through the concrete practice of baptism. Having emphasized the role of the Lord's Supper in forming the Body of Christ in the previous chapter, Paul here states the centrality of baptism as incorporation into that body—indeed into Christ himself.

Paul's move is significant because early in the letter he had disparaged baptism, asserting that his preaching was far more important (1:13–17). Baptism itself had become a source of division, as the members of the Corinthian church split into camps depending on who had baptized them. Paul thus criticizes the baptismal practice of the Corinthians and emphasizes his preaching of the cross. Now, however, Paul presents a positive, alternative vision of baptism, one that in fact, as was discussed in the previous chapter, may have created some of the tensions regarding the role of women in the worshiping community.

Everyone, Paul announces, has been baptized into the *one* Body of Christ through the *one* Spirit. Paul here counters any divisions based on the persons who performed the baptisms. The *one Spirit* is the primary actor in baptism, no matter who might perform the ritual. Through this Spirit all other identity markers are relativized, whether racial and ethnic markers (Jews or Greeks) or social and economic markers (slaves or free) (v. 13). By trajectory, as Paul's letter to the Galatians suggests (3:28), the markers of gender (male and female) would also be subordinated to baptismal identity.[7] Moreover, by the same trajectory, all other social or cultural identity markers that divide people and create hierarchies or exclusion in the community of faith, such as sexual orientation or gender identity, are also relativized by one's baptismal identity. In the community of faith, the primary identity is baptismal, which incorporates persons into the body as equal and interdependent members.

The issue here is privilege and hierarchy, as Paul has emphasized throughout the letter. Paul is not subsuming everyone into one homogenous, amorphous baptismal blob. Just as the particularity of different gifts remains, so the particularity of individual identities remains. In the community of faith, however, none of these non-baptismal markers of identity brings any special privilege; they are subordinated to the shared baptismal identity in the community. Baptism, that is, inaugurates the *communitas* between the ages, where notions of high and low, honored and shamed are overcome and a new form of community emerges, one shaped by the Spirit of Christ, rather than the powers of this age.

Indeed, the baptismal identity of Christians should lead the church not only to be a different kind of community itself, but to live into a trajectory that overturns all societal and economic hierarchies and practices. The church's participation in the abolitionist movement and the civil rights movement as well as the movements for women's and LGBTQ+ persons' equality represent, despite Paul's frequent hesitations, a faithful trajectory of the baptismal affirmations made by the apostle.

The implications of Paul's affirmation for the church are clear and possibly surprising in chapter 12. Paul's emphasis on both the freedom of the Spirit and baptismal identity account for what is

7. Again, as mentioned in the previous chapter, Paul possibly omitted this affirmation here because of the freedom being claimed by women in the community's worship.

strikingly absent in his delineation of the diversity of spiritual gifts. Throughout both lists of gifts (vv. 8–11, 28–30), Paul never divides them according to categories of people. That is, Paul does not reserve certain gifts for some categories of people, some for others. To be certain, there are different functions for different people within the community, but those different functions cannot be assigned to or limited by cultural categories such as Jew or Greek, slave or free, male and female.

Paul, for example, does not limit being a prophet or a teacher— or even an apostle—to men. Nor does he reserve church leadership to heterosexuals. The gifts are distributed freely "just as the Spirit chooses." They are given to members of the body whose baptismal identity is of primary significance. The gifts are part of a liminal *communitas* of mutuality and interdependence. Limiting certain gifts and responsibilities to different categories of persons is a denial of Paul's theological vision. Reserving preaching for men or ordination for heterosexuals represents an illegitimate trajectory of Paul's vision. Such a "division of labor" denies the freedom of the Spirit and the primacy of baptismal identity; it represents a form of captivity to the categories and hierarchies of the powers of this age. Such an approach is a way for those in power, for whom the *communitas* of the Body of Christ may appear dangerous and anarchical, to hedge it around "with prescriptions, prohibitions, and conditions."[8] Although Paul's own practical conclusions are at times at odds with his underlying theology, Paul's theological vision sets the church on the path of *communitas*. Formed by this vision, the church does not think in terms of human categories imposed by the powers of this age. Rather, the church considers the gifts given "as the Spirit chooses" to those whose primary identity comes from baptism.

12:14–27
Playful Theology

In the longest section of this chapter (vv. 14–27), Paul invites theologians to something too rarely practiced: playfulness and humor.

---

8. Turner, *The Ritual Process*, 109.

Throughout the letter, as has been noted, Paul employs a variety of rhetorical moves, from parody to sarcasm to irony, to make his theological points. Now he turns to humor. In overturning the cultural metaphor of the body, which was used to reinforce the social hierarchies, Paul becomes playful. To make his theological point he lampoons the powers of this age, who would use the image of the body to reinforce social hierarchies.

In order to affirm his central point that the Corinthians "are the body of Christ and individually members of it" (v. 27), Paul develops some quite comical imagery within his primary metaphor of the body. He depicts talking body parts. Initially the parts of the body speak for themselves. The foot ridiculously declares it does not belong to the body because it is not a hand; the ear similarly states it does not belong to the body because it is not an eye (vv. 15–16). Paul's talking body parts playfully and humorously depict the incongruity of dismissing certain parts of the body because they are different from others.

Then, making pointed use of absurdly obvious rhetorical questions, Paul takes his comical imagery a bit further, inviting the Corinthians to envision the entire body as just one part: one giant eyeball or one enormous ear (v. 17). The image is hyperbolic and ridiculous but serves to remind the reader of the importance of each body part. If the entire body were an eyeball, "where would the hearing be?" If the body were one big ear, "where would the sense of smell be?" Not to mention the fact that the big eye and the huge ear would just lie on the ground, unable to move around or pick anything up without legs and feet or arms and hands. It is a comical image, mocking those who would make their own gifts of highest importance to the body. Without the other parts, where would you be, Paul asks, drawing the reader into his conclusion through his rhetorical questions. So, echoing his emphasis on the Spirit allotting gifts *as the Spirit chooses*, Paul reemphasizes God the creator who forms the body *as God chooses*: "God arranged the members in the body, each one of them, as [God] chose" (v. 18). The apostle draws out the glaringly obvious conclusion: If the entire body were a single member, where would the body be? It would just be a big eye or a big ear flopping around on the ground, that's where.

Paul is not done yet. Next he presents different body parts *talking to each other*. Imagine the eye saying to the hand, "I have no need of you;" or the head saying to the feet, "I have no need of you" (v. 21). Through this imagery, Paul exposes the silliness of the Corinthians' divisiveness over spiritual gifts, as well as the absurdity of their boasting about the superiority of some gifts over others. Paul's comical image invites the Corinthians to see the inappropriateness of their divisions and even to laugh at themselves.

Finally, through playfully ambiguous language, Paul takes the incongruities one more step, elevating the "weaker" members of the body to the places of honor (vv. 22–25). As Dale Martin notes, the word *anankaia*, used of the genitals and translated "indispensable," can imply both high status (referring to the most necessary and nonexpendable parts of the body) *and* low status (the penis, for example, was euphemistically called the "necessary" member). As at other places in the letter, Paul's language here is intentionally tensive; it is language that lives and moves at the turn of the ages, unveiling the realities beneath appearances and creating a liminal space for new perception. As Martin writes, "Paul admits that the genitals, the 'necessary' members, seem to be the weaker; but, by their very necessariness, they can demand high status. They have a legitimate claim, therefore, to honor and care from the other body members. Through his play on words, Paul both admits and denies the low status of the weaker members of the body."[9]

Paul's playful, mocking language functions in the space where the struggle between the Spirit and the powers of this age is underway. Nevertheless, Paul's conclusion is clear: in the new age one must discern beneath appearances. The "normal connection between status and honor should be questioned; and we must recognize that those who, on the surface, occupy positions of lower status are actually more essential than those of higher status and therefore should be accorded more honor."[10] Shaped by the weakness and folly of the cross, the Body of Christ necessarily takes the paradoxical, ambiguous form of foolish wisdom and weak power.

9. Martin, *Corinthian Body*, 95.
10. Ibid., 95–96.

In this liminal space, driven by the work of the Spirit, real mutuality, genuine unity in diversity—*communitas*—becomes possible. Within this kind of body, there will be no dissension and "members may have the same care for one another" (v. 25).

There is really no other option at the conclusion of Paul's humorous and revealing depiction of the body: "If one member suffers, all suffer together with it; if one member is honored, all rejoice together with it" (v. 26). That is because the church, first, is the Body of Christ. Believers, secondarily, are "individually members of it" (v. 27). Paul here reverses the assumption that is often prevalent in the North American church: the community of faith is a collection of individuals that make up a body. Paul's order is different: You are the Body of Christ and *only then* individually members of it. Paul is closer to the African tradition of *Ubuntu* than to North American individualism. According to *Ubuntu*, human beings are part of a "delicate network of interdependence,"[11] grounded in the belief that one is a human being through others: "I am because you are."[12] One begins not with the individual but with the community. *Ubuntu*, in fact, provides a helpful conception of Paul's goals for the Corinthian community, especially the way in which he calls believers to relate to each other. *Ubuntu* suggests the kind of *communitas* that Paul seeks through his playful, comical treatment of the body.

> *Ubuntu* could also be translated as: A human being is a human being through the otherness of other human beings. This implies: if you try to alter or manipulate the otherness of others, you yourself end up being someone other than yourself. You have to face others unreservedly in order to see your own face. *Ubuntu* is the art of interfacing, of finding meaning within the liminal space of interfacing.
>
> Campbell and Cilliers, *Preaching Fools*, 50.

11. Michael Battle, *Reconciliation: The Ubuntu Theology of Desmond Tutu* (Cleveland: Pilgrim Press, 1997), 35.
12. Charles L. Campbell and Johan H. Cilliers, *Preaching Fools: The Gospel as a Rhetoric of Folly* (Waco, TX: Baylor University Press, 2012), 49; see 48–52 for a discussion of *Ubuntu*.

FURTHER REFLECTIONS
Laughter and Apocalyptic Theology

Paul's choice of humor at this point in the letter is not simply a rhetorical trope. It is theologically significant. Laughter is a critical means of *interrupting* the status quo and unmasking the powers of this age. Theologians might want to take laughter more seriously. Just as Paul's "foolish" apocalyptic theology interrupts and fractures the cultural assumptions of his day, so does laughter. Indeed, the idioms we use to speak about laughter are revealing. We say we "break up" laughing. Or we exclaim that a joke really "cracked me up." Or we report that the crowd *erupted* with laughter. Laughter shatters. It breaks up; it cracks up. It interrupts the neat totalities by which we often seek to control and make sense of our lives.[13] Laughter disrupts, even if for a moment, the myths and rationalities by which the world is neatly ordered and managed. Like the fool, laughter tends to "melt the solidity of the world"; it interrupts the conventions and assumptions that are supposedly written in stone; it keeps reality fluid. In just this way, Paul comically "melts" his culture's assumptions about the use of the body metaphor.[14] Laughter becomes an appropriate vehicle for Paul's apocalyptic theology.

This disruptive laughter exposes the powers for what they are: not the way of life but the powers of death. In so doing, laughter may create a space in which people are set free from captivity to the old age. Although laughter can, of course, be used destructively to exclude and demean people, when it is directed at the powers, unmasking their deadly absurdities and incongruities, it can be a force for liberation. Paul's use of laughter in his discussion of the body disrupts the powers of death

> Humor oils the joint where contradictions meet. If humor evaporates, then ambiguity becomes polarized and conflict follows.
>
> Lewis Hyde, *Trickster Makes This World: Mischief, Myth, and Art* (New York: North Point Press, 1999), 274.

---

13. D. Diane Davis, *Breaking Up [at] Totality: A Rhetoric of Laughter* (Carbondale: Southern Illinois University Press, 2000).

14. On laughter and fluidity, see Davis, *Breaking Up.*

and seeks to set the Corinthians free from the divisions that hold them captive.

Paul suggests the church's service of the free and living God will often be characterized by laughter, for, as is clear throughout Paul's letter, no one controls God. The Spirit allots the gifts where the Spirit chooses—blows where the Spirit wills (John 3:8)—disrupting the Christian community when it becomes closed, dogmatic, and idolatrous. The crucified Christ continues to work through the Spirit, interrupting, fracturing, cracking up in order to move people toward the fulfillment of God's purposes. Consequently, the Christian community remains open to the disruptive surprises of the Spirit. Faithful Christians can laugh, welcoming life that is not complete but is always on the way, always being saved in the dynamic and fluid movement at the joint between the old age that is dying and the new that continues to be born.[15]

12:28-31
"The Last Shall Be First"

Paul concludes the chapter with yet another subversive irony. At first glance Paul appears to return to a hierarchy of offices or gifts. He speaks of "first," "second," and "third"—"first apostles, second prophets, third teachers" (v. 28)—and he encourages the Corinthians to seek "the greater gifts" (v. 31). However, the irony of this ranking becomes clear when one remembers Paul's comment about apostles earlier in the letter: "I think that God has exhibited us apostles as *last of all*, . . . because we have become a spectacle to the world, to angels and to mortals. We are fools for the sake of Christ . . ." (4:9–10). Paul here, as throughout the chapter, reverses normal status rankings.[16] The one who is "last of all," the "fool for the sake of Christ," is the one who is "first." As Jesus put it, "So the last will be first, and the first will be last" (Matt. 20:16). The social and cultural rankings of the Corinthians are thoroughly upended. The "foolish" and "weak"

---

15. See the discussion of open seriousness, which is closely related to laughter, in chapter 4, p. 75. Also the discussion of resurrection laughter in chapter 15, pp. 254–56.

16. Martin, *Corinthian Body*, 102–3.

> "You know that the rulers of the Gentiles lord it over them, and their great ones are tyrants over them. It will not be so among you; but whoever wishes to be great among you must be your servant, and whoever wishes to be first among you must be your slave; just as the Son of Man came not to be served but to serve, and to give his life a ransom for many."
>
> Matthew 20:25–28

ones, like the crucified Christ, are "first." The cruciform way of Christ, empowered by the Spirit, shapes the priorities of the community of faith, including all the spiritual gifts and offices in the church.

Consequently, when Paul encourages the Corinthians to strive for the greater gifts, he is not speaking of status or rank in any normal sense of the term. Nor is he talking about specific positions or offices in the church. Rather, the "greater gifts" refer to the "more excellent way" that Paul turns to in chapter 13—the way of love. This way further subverts the Corinthians' boasting and rankings. The way of love qualifies and gives shape to every spiritual gift.

13:1-13

The Greatest Gift

Paul's familiar chapter on love, as with the rest of his letter, needs to be interpreted within his practical, apocalyptic theological framework. Paul's praise of love (*agapē*), including his implicit critique of the divisions among the Corinthians, is a call for *communitas* in the liminal space between the ages. His words are addressed to the church as it seeks to live together in the new creation, which has interrupted the world in Jesus Christ but has not yet been fulfilled. Unfortunately, the chapter has often been tamed and sentimentalized; it has been interpreted as a beautiful, inspiring idealization of marital love or individual love. Paul's words, however, are addressed to a divided community and offer a stinging critique and challenge, as well as promise, to that community. Replete with hyperbole (vv. 1–3), and even mockery (v. 11), the text is far from a sentimental "Hallmark" moment or inspiring wedding sermon.

Paul does not offer a general treatise on love but practical theology addressed to the specific situation of division in the Corinthian church. The characteristics of love he highlights are directed at the challenges and conflicts in the Corinthian church. He praises distinctive characteristics of love as a corrective to the division in the community of faith at Corinth. In addition, Paul addresses the *community*, not individuals, and certainly not marital relationships. Paul calls for the church to live as the Body of Christ at the turn of the ages.

Paul's words are christological. The way of love, Paul declares, shapes the Body of Christ; it enacts Jesus' way of self-giving that interrupts the world's power and wisdom on the cross. Love performs the words of institution at the table: "this is my body that is for you" (11:24). This love shapes the life of the Body of Christ in resistance to the powers of this age, which revel in hierarchies and honor and domination. This love, which enables unity and mutuality within the church, represents an odd way of living together in a world governed by the powers of death that crucified Christ.

Paul calls the church to become a school for love. By engaging in certain practices within the community, believers are formed in the way of love. The communal practice of love is like the practice of becoming a musician. Great musicians have a vision they seek to express through their music, but that vision becomes a musical reality only after hours and weeks and years of constant practice—so much practice that the playing comes naturally. The often-glorious musical vision expressed at a concert is grounded in the rather routine, daily practice of the scales and chords and techniques that enable the musician to play. Paul has similarly offered the Corinthians a vision of the church as the Body of Christ (chap. 12). Now he points to the scales and chords of love so the vision might become a reality. One note at a time. One chord at a time. One measure at a time.

Through these practices the church grows as a people in whom others may see the Body of Christ in the world. Indeed, in the early years of the church the practice of love served as a primary way of proclaiming the gospel. Often the gospel wasn't spread first through preaching or theology but through the church's form of life.[1] "See how they love one another," outsiders often said as they looked at Christian community.[2] Unbelievers would notice the love among those in the church and would come to check out this odd community. Then the church would share the gospel with them. The church would share, that is, the source and power of its love.

Through these practices the church itself lives as an alternative to the powers of this age. And grounded in these practices, believers are formed and empowered to resist the ways of death that hold people captive and govern the larger world.

1. George A. Lindbeck, *The Nature of Doctrine: Religion and Theology in a Postliberal Age* (Philadelphia: Westminster Press, 1984), 132.
2. Tertullian, *Apologeticum*, 39.7, http://www.tertullian.org/anf/anf03/anf03-05.htm#39_7.

This formative power of practicing love can be seen in the witness of the Christians in Le Chambon, France, during World War II. During the war five-thousand Christians sheltered five-thousand Jews right in the shadow of the Nazi threat. It was a dangerous act of hospitable love. The Chambonaise risked their lives to provide sanctuary. What is fascinating, however, is the response the people of Le Chambon gave when a documentary filmmaker asked how they decided to provide this kind of dangerous sanctuary. The villagers looked at him with puzzled expressions on their faces. They replied with comments like these: "It happened so naturally, we can't understand the fuss. It happened quite simply." "It's a normal thing to do." Finally, when one woman was asked why her family risked their lives in this way, she replied, "I don't know. We were used to it."

"We were used to it." That was a true statement. For generations that little community in France had been offering hospitality to all kinds of people who came to their village. They had repeatedly practiced scales and chords of hospitality in non-threatening situations. Hospitality had become their way of life. So when Jewish people came knocking at their doors during World War II, there was no dramatic decision to be made. Loving others by providing hospitality was the "normal thing to do."[3]

This is Paul's goal for the church as well. He calls the church to be the Body of Christ by practicing the love of Christ in their life together. As that love becomes the "normal thing to do," the church not only embodies the way of Christ in its life together, but also is prepared to resist the powers of death in the world. By practicing love in everyday ways in the community of faith, the church is schooled to be ready when the great challenges come. Practicing love among themselves, the church is equipped to live as the Body of Christ in and for the world.

Paul's words are pneumatological as well as christological. The way of love enacts the living presence of Christ through the Spirit who forms the Body of Christ. This emphasis on the Spirit is central to Paul's treatment of love. Paul emphasizes love as the "more excellent" way of the Spirit that governs the use of all the other spiritual

3. *Weapons of the Spirit*, prod. and dir. Pierre Sauvage, 1hr. 30 min., First Run Features, 1989, videocassette.

gifts. In the midst of the divisiveness caused by the spiritual gifts themselves, Paul highlights the more essential unity that life in the Spirit inspires through love. This unity, characterized by the mutuality of *communitas*, is the goal of Paul's letter, and his call for this kind of community reaches its climax in chapter 13.[4] From the beginning of the letter, Paul has affirmed the power of the Spirit as the alternative to the powers of this age; now the apostle states most fully the way of Spirit that forms the Body of Christ.

Paul's practical theology of love also has an apocalyptic, eschatological character. The way of the Spirit, as Paul repeatedly affirms, is the way of life in the liminal space between the ages. Paul here is concerned with life on the way, with being-saved life in the time and space created by the interruption of the cross, which nevertheless still moves toward fulfillment. The final verses of this chapter (vv. 8–13) emphasize the provisional character of life at the turn of the ages. Paul depicts the dynamic movement of the community in this in-between space. Gifts that are important now will come to an end (v. 8); "we know only in part, and we prophesy only in part" (v. 9); "the partial will come to an end" (v. 10); "now we see in a mirror, dimly" (v. 12). In this liminal time and space, love is the way of both living into the new creation and moving toward its fulfillment.

13:1–3
The Interruption

Revealing the practical, apocalyptic character of Chapter 13, Paul begins with a striking *interruption* directed at the specific divisions in the Corinthian church. Love, like the word of the cross, becomes the great "but" that interrupts everything:

If I speak in the tongues of mortals and of angels,
but do not have love, I am a noisy gong or a clanging cymbal.
And if I have prophetic powers, and understand all mysteries
and all knowledge,

---

4. Richard B. Hays, *First Corinthians*, Interpretation: A Bible Commentary for Teaching and Preaching (Louisville, KY: John Knox Press, 1997), 222.

and if I have all faith, so as to remove mountains,
but do not have love, I am nothing.
If I give away all my possessions, and if I hand over my body
so that I may boast,
but do not have love, I gain nothing.[5]

The call of love interrupts the divisions over spiritual gifts within the community of faith.

Rhetorically, as he does elsewhere, Paul uses hyperbole to achieve his radical interruption. In the opening verses he highlights the precise issue he will address in chapter 14: speaking in tongues and prophesying. First he addresses speaking with the "tongues of mortals and of angels," which involves the remarkable gift of speaking with the heavenly world.[6] Without love, Paul declares, even this remarkable gift is just a noisy gong or a clanging cymbal. While Paul's references here are not completely clear, the hyperbole is obvious. This highly valued speech is simply worthless, clanging noise.[7] Because, as will be discussed in the next chapter, the "tongues of angels" was an elitist form of speech, reinforcing social hierarchies, Paul's interruption here is sharp and unequivocal. Such hierarchies of honor and importance are contrary to the way of Christ, the way of the Spirit, the way of love.

The apostle does not stop there. He next interrupts even prophesy. In the next chapter Paul will emphasize the importance of prophecy, intelligible speech that brings a word from God for the present situation. Before making that turn, however, Paul reminds the community, and possibly himself, that even this gift without love is nothing— *nothing*. Other seemingly important gifts are nothing as well: the gift of understanding mysteries and all knowledge is also nothing without love. On the one hand, Paul may here be referring to the kind of popular philosophical knowledge of mysteries that he has critiqued throughout the letter, which would be understandable. By mentioning

---

5. Note the similar repetition of the disruptive "but" in 1:18–31.
6. Hays, *First Corinthians*, 223.
7. Richard Hays suggests the "noisy gong" is actually a bronze amplification device used in the theater and the "clanging cymbal" was associated with the wild, ecstatic worship in the cult of Cybele. As he paraphrases, "your high-toned speech has become like the empty echo of an actor's speech or the noise of frenzied pagan worship." Ibid., 223.

all mysteries, though, he may also be including the Spirit's gift of discernment, which enables believers to perceive the new creation in the weakness and folly of the cross (2:6–16). He may be referring to the "apocalyptic seer" who can unveil the hidden work of God that the powers of this age seek to obscure.[8] Even this essential gift of the Spirit—the gift of bifocal discernment—is *nothing* without love. The hyperbole continues. Paul doesn't simply say these important gifts are made less without love or distorted without love. They are *nothing*.

So is faith—even faith that "removes mountains," as Jesus himself suggested genuine faith could do (Matt. 17:20). Even such extraordinary, miracle-producing faith, without love, is nothing. Paul has not simply qualified gifts that are critical for the life of the community—the very spiritual gifts he has highlighted in chapter 12 and will discuss in chapter 14. He has hyperbolically dismissed them if they are exercised without love. Indeed, he has suggested that these gifts *cannot* be faithfully exercised without love. Paul employs the hyperbolic rhetoric of interruption, which is necessary to shock the Corinthians, to unsettle their assumptions and to unmask their divisions. In order to affirm the centrality of love for the exercise of the gifts, Paul interrupts the community as sharply as the cross interrupts the powers of this age.

Finally, Paul applies his hyperbole to the most extreme forms of discipleship. Even extraordinary acts of self-sacrifice, such as giving away all one's possessions or handing over one's body, can be worthless.[9] The very acts that would seem to carry forward the self-sacrifice of Jesus on the cross gain one *nothing* without love. Paul's ethical insight here is profound. One can perform even the most extreme acts of discipleship not out of love for others, but in order to gain a reward and be able to boast. Self-giving itself can be practiced with self-serving motives, but such misdirected motivation gains one *nothing*. Love is the necessary dynamic driving the cruciform life.

Paul here implicitly makes a critically important theological and ethical point about the cross. The cross can never be celebrated as

---

8. Ibid., 224.
9. The exact meaning of giving away one's body is disputed. It could possibly refer to martyrdom, or it may refer to selling oneself into slavery in order to ransom others. Either way, the emphasis on self-sacrifice is clear. See ibid., 225.

a call to sacrifice for the sake of sacrifice or as a glorification of suffering for the sake of suffering. In themselves, suffering and sacrifice are of no value; they are neither a cause for boasting nor the means of eschatological rewards. Rather, Paul suggests, the cross is the *consequence* of Jesus' active, engaging love that resists the deadly powers of this age. His death does not glorify suffering and sacrifice but rather embodies the way of love.

The same is true for the community of faith. Love is the overarching ethical dynamic within which any sacrifice or suffering must be considered. Sacrifice and suffering have no value in and of themselves; in fact, they can be demonic when they are used to pacify those who are being abused or oppressed. The only sacrifice worth affirming is that which results from the way of discipleship, the way of active, loving resistance to the powers of death. Apart from this kind of love, suffering and sacrifice are to be rejected; from them one "gains nothing." Far from a sentimental idealization of love, Paul's hyperbolic opening words not only interrupt the specific divisions within the Corinthian church, but also subvert understandings of the cross that glorify sacrifice and lead to abuse or passivity.

13:4–7
A Practical Encomium to Love

One way of calling the church to new practices without falling into the trap of moralism is through praise or encomium. In his *Rhetoric* Aristotle recognized the close connection between praise and advice: "Praise and counsels have a common aspect; for what you might suggest in counseling becomes encomium by a change in the phrase. . . . Accordingly, if you desire to praise, look what you would suggest; if you desire to suggest, look what you would praise."[10] New Testament scholar David DeSilva has highlighted this approach in the book of Hebrews. By providing a host of exemplars of the virtues of trust and firmness in 10:32–12:3, the author of Hebrews "sets out

---

10. Aristotle, *Rhetoric* 1.9.35–36. Quoted in David A. DeSilva, *Perseverance in Gratitude: A Socio-Rhetorical Commentary on the Epistle "to the Hebrews"* (Grand Rapids, MI: William B. Eerdmans Publishing Co., 2000), 355.

to praise those who have embodied the course he is advising. The effect of this encomium should be the arousal of the emotion of emulation: the hearers are encouraged and even made ambitious to embody the same virtue as these figures who have attained a praiseworthy resemblance."[11] Encomium, that is, provides a redemptive way of calling the community of faith to a new way of life.

In verses 4–7, Paul engages in such an encomium. He offers praise to life set free from the powers of this age. Paul's encomium, however, does not celebrate the virtues of any particular person or saint. Rather, Paul praises the virtues of a personified love, and he hopes to inspire emulation. Moreover, Paul praises precisely those aspects of love that run counter to the practices creating division in the Corinthian church. Paul's encomium to love is a targeted, practical encomium, through which he addresses the wound at the heart of the church and seeks to move the Corinthians from divisiveness to mutuality and unity.

The encomium is framed by a celebration of virtues appropriate to a community that lives in the liminal space between the ages: patience (v. 4), and faith, hope, and endurance (v. 7). Patience, in this context, does not only refer to patience with others in the community, though that is certainly involved. Patience also highlights the character of the Christian life between the ages. The virtue of patience is an essential characteristic of the practice of love, which often seems to be a weak and foolish way of resistance in the face of the powers of this age. Patience enables the Christian community to continue to grow in love without becoming demoralized by the persistent challenges and attacks of the powers. Patience enables the church to continue creating the space—note by note and chord by chord—for mutuality and community in the midst of a culture characterized by hierarchy and domination.

Patience is, moreover, grounded in the character of God, who works through folly and weakness, who does not coerce human obedience, but who nurtures the church with "steadfast love [that] endures forever" (Ps. 136). Indeed, Paul's opening emphasis on patience and kindness may itself be a pastoral reminder of the

11. DeSilva, *Perseverance in Gratitude*, 355.

steadfast love of God, on which the community relies on its way to the new creation. As the way of embodying the new age in a hostile world, while awaiting the coming of the Lord, love is necessarily characterized by patience.[12]

The intimately related virtues of faith, hope, and endurance are similarly necessary characteristics of the practice of love between the ages. In the apocalyptic, eschatological context in which the community lives, love "bears all things, believes all things, hopes all things, endures all things" (v. 7). Paul is not saying that love is gullible or indiscriminate in believing and hoping. Rather, Paul affirms that there are no limits to the faith, hope, and endurance of love.[13] As the order of Paul's words highlights, hope, rooted in faith, provides the ground for patient endurance, enabling the church to "bear all things" in the face of the powers of this age. In the face of the powers, faith and hope sustain the practice of love. Trusting that Jesus has already overcome the powers of death with the power of life (faith), and living with the assurance of the ultimate fulfillment of God's purposes of redemption (hope), Christians can engage in the daily practice of love with patience and endurance. Receiving both life and the future as a gift, the community is set free from the desire for boasting and the need for control. The being-saved community is liberated to grow in love on the way to the new creation.

Paul's encomium to love is dynamic, not static. Having interrupted the old-age ways of the community in verses 1–3, Paul places his praise of love in the liminal context of life between the ages by framing the encomium with the virtues of patience, faith, hope, and endurance in verses 4 and 7. Love, for Paul, is not settled or comfortable or easy; through the Spirit it lives and moves in the space where

> Hope is reliance upon grace in the face of death; the issue is that of receiving life as a gift, not as a reward and not as a punishment; hope is living constantly, patiently, expectantly, resiliently, joyously in the efficacy of the Word of God.
>
> William Stringfellow, *An Ethic for Christians and Other Aliens in a Strange Land* (Waco, TX: Word, 1973; repr. Eugene, OR: Wipf & Stock, 2004), 138.

12. Hays, *First Corinthians*, 228.
13. Ibid.

the new creation has broken into the world, even though the powers of this age continue their deadly work. Love, for Paul, is a dynamic and active way of living in resistance to the powers of death. It shapes the life of the being-saved community that is always on its "weak" and "foolish" way to the coming fulfillment of God's purposes.

Having highlighted the dynamic, liminal character of love in verses 4 and 7, Paul stresses what love is *not* in verses 4b–6. His encomium is worded in the negative, possibly calling to mind the "Thou shalt nots" of the Ten Commandments (Exod. 20). With each "not" Paul directs a pointed and practical challenge to the community of faith. He strikingly suggests that everything about their life together contradicts the way of love. He concretely addresses the wound at the heart of the community, calling the church away from division to unity in the Body of Christ. The very structure of this section, with the challenging "nots" framed by patience, faith, hope, and endurance, highlights the tensive character of life between the ages; on the way, new-creation love continues to exist in tension with old-age practices opposed to it.

Paul's list of "nots" is virtually a cross-reference back to earlier parts of the letter.[14] The community, Paul has earlier charged, is envious (jealous, *zēlos*; 3:3), boastful (1:29–31; 3:21; 4:7; 5:6), arrogant (puffed up, *physiousthe*; 4:6; 4:18–19; 5:2), and rude (actually, engaged in shameful behavior; 7:36).[15] Counter to all these previous critiques, Paul presents the way of love, which is "*not* envious or boastful or arrogant or rude" (vv. 4–5a). And he continues that love is *not* self-seeking, echoing his earlier critiques of selfishness in 10:24 (in response to the idol-meat controversy) and his earlier self-description in 10:33 ("not seeking my own advantage, but that of many"). Going to the heart of the divisions in Corinth, Paul declares that love does not insist on its own way and is not irritable or resentful (v. 5).[16]

Paul concludes this section with a remarkable statement: "[Love] does not rejoice in wrongdoing [*adikia*, injustice], but rejoices in

<hr/>

14. The following is based on ibid., 227.
15. Hays also suggests Paul may be referring to other forms of shameful behavior (5:1–2; 6:12–20; 11:2–16; 11:20–22), though the word does not appear in those places. Ibid.
16. Hays suggests that the NIV translation is stronger: love is "not easily angered" and "keeps no records of wrongs." Ibid.

the truth" (v. 6). Paul's conclusion with "truth" at first glance seems awkward. One might expect him to say, "rejoices in righteousness" or "rejoices in justice." But with the word "truth," Paul returns the reader not only to a positive characteristic of love, but to *practical theology*; he explicitly affirms the character of theology that shapes his entire letter. Inherent in theological truth are ethical practices, in this case the practices that characterize love. Theological truth is never simply an intellectual exercise. Theological truth is practiced, not just thought. Paul again emphasizes a central affirmation of Reformed theology: "Truth is in order to goodness; and the great touchstone of truth, its tendency to produce holiness. . . ."[17]

In his concluding words to this section, Paul echoes another central tenet of Reformed theology: "The chief end of humans is to glorify God and enjoy God forever."[18] The way of life Paul describes is not dour or oppressive; it *rejoices* in the truth. Truth about God, enacted in the life of the community, goes "on its way rejoicing," even in the face of the powers of death. Love is a practice of rejoicing in the odd truth of a "weak" and "foolish" Messiah. Love rejoices in the truth that believers have been set free from the powers of death, which seek to hold people captive through their deceitful promise of life. Love rejoices in the truth that discerns the way of God that the powers of this age seek to mask and deny. Love is the way of living "joyously in the efficacy of the Word of God."

13:8-13
Eschatology and Humility

Paul's declaration in verse 8 is a central eschatological claim for the church: "Love never ends." Here is Paul's ultimate affirmation about love. It is the Christ-shaped embodiment *now* of the new creation that will come to fulfillment when God is all in all (15:28). The Spirit-empowered *communitas* of which he has been speaking

---

17. *The Constitution of the Presbyterian Church (U.S.A.)*, Part II, *Book of Order* (Louisville, KY: Office of the General Assembly, 2015), F-3.0104.

18. Westminster Shorter Catechism, in *The Constitution of the Presbyterian Church (U.S.A.)*, Part 1, *Book of Confessions* (Louisville, KY: Office of the General Assembly, Presbyterian Church (U.S.A.), 2016), 7.001 (altered).

throughout the letter is a foretaste of and witness to God's final purpose for the world. Love is the "already" of God's new age present in the midst of the old. When one glimpses the work of love—even when it appears "weak" and "foolish," even when it happens only "here and there and now and then"[19]—one glimpses the new creation. For love never ends.

Paul's claim is ultimately an affirmation about God. It is the apostle's way of saying, "God is love" (1 John 4:8). For this unending love is not a principle or power independent of God, the One who will finally be all in all (15:28). There is no dualism here. If love never ends, then God indeed is love. This implicit claim pulls together much of what Paul has been saying about God throughout the letter. Through his proto-Trinitarian affirmations, as has been noted, Paul depicts God, Christ, and the Spirit living and working together in mutuality and equality—in love. God's interruption of the old age, embodied in the self-giving of the crucified Christ, is an act of love. The work of the Spirit between the ages takes the form of *communitas*—the self-giving mutuality and equality of love. In the Spirit, as the Body of Christ, the church participates in the very life of God, which is the life of love. Both God's person and God's work are love. When God is all in all, the fragments of *communitas* enacted now will be fulfilled, and human divisions and hierarchies will cease. Because love never ends.

Paul's theological claim here is daring, even foolish. In a world in which for millennia the old-age powers of violence and domination seem to rule, love appears to be a weak and ridiculous alternative. The power of love often seems as hidden as the work of God on the cross. Love, like the cross, paradoxically gives life by resisting death and control through vulnerability and apparent insignificance.[20] How can love overcome the powers of this age?

In response to a book telling the story of the people of Le Chambon who sheltered Jews during World War II, someone wrote a letter to the author, Philip Hallie. The writer of the letter honestly named

---

19. Stringfellow, *An Ethic for Christians*, 60.
20. L. Susan Bond, *Trouble with Jesus: Women, Christology, and Preaching* (St. Louis: Chalice Press, 1999), 127.

the seeming weakness and folly of love—the same weakness and folly that hides the power of God on the cross.

> Dear Professor Hallie,
> There is only one important thing to say about the Holocaust. It was merely a geological-type almost inanimate event (physical event). No one was responsible. No one started it. No one could stop it.
> Le Chambon wasn't even in the war. Nothing happened west of National Route 7 in southern France. The obscurity should be an insight. Reverend Trocmé [the pastor in Le Chambon] has a miniscule number of equally eccentric kindred spirits . . .

"And," as Hallie writes, the letter "went on to say that only vast forces like great armies 'make history,' make and break human institutions. The story of a few nonviolent eccentrics who did nothing to stop Hitler's armed forces mattered only to a few mushy-minded moralists like me."[21]

How, indeed, will love ever "win" in the midst of a world shaped by armies and weapons of mass destruction, by global technology and economy, by principalities and powers that overwhelm by their seductiveness and their threat? Love does seem to be a foolishly fragile and vulnerable way to bring in the new creation.

At precisely this point, Paul's *theological* affirmation is essential. If the triumph of love depended on human efforts, it would be impossible. As the Corinthian church reminds us, the Christian community falls far short of the love of God, all too often aligning itself with the powers of this age and succumbing to destructive divisions. "Love never ends," not because of "mushy-minded moralists" but because of God. The one who lasts is God. That theological promise alone sustains the church as it seeks to embody the hidden, vulnerable way of love in resistance to the seemingly overwhelming powers of this age.

There is an important corollary to Paul's claim that love never ends: all the other spiritual gifts *do end.* Even the most significant

21. Philip Hallie, *Lest Innocent Blood Be Shed: The Story of the Village of Le Chambon and How Goodness Happened There* (New York: Harper and Row, 1979; repr. HarperPerennial edition, 1994), xiv.

of the spiritual gifts—prophecies, tongues, knowledge—come to an end (vv. 8–10). All of them are partial. In themselves, they do not embody the presence of the new creation; they are not the things that last, for they will pass away. Even faith and hope, which are essential to life in the liminal space on the way to the new creation, are secondary to love, which is the greatest gift (v. 13). Faith and hope abide for now, but, unlike love, they are not the foretaste of the new creation; they come to an end. For in the end human beings will know God fully, even as God already knows us fully; we will participate in the life of God, intimately knowing and being known in love. Faith and hope will no longer be necessary because then we will see God face to face (v. 12).[22]

Paul sharply emphasizes this partial character of all the spiritual gifts by returning to his image of the child (v. 11). Earlier Paul had critiqued the Corinthians because they were acting like infants who needed milk not solid food (3:1–2). Now he returns to that image to interrupt them yet again. Here the image of the child is not simply a critique of the situation in Corinth but also a reminder of the character of all our speaking and thinking and reasoning in the liminal space between the ages. All of it is mere "child's play," a kind of squinting in the mirror dimly before we see God face to face, a partial knowing until we know fully.[23] Paul's words again are hyperbolic and disruptive, even mocking; he subverts all the extravagant claims about the spiritual gifts by asserting they are merely the activities of a child. Only children, he seems to suggest, think they know it all. Becoming an adult involves coming to terms with the partial character of all human knowledge and speech in the liminal space between the ages.

Here Paul also reaches the climax in his understanding of theology itself—his understanding of words (*logoi*) about God (*theos*). For theology, love expresses itself as humility. In the liminal space between the ages, in which all knowledge and speech are partial, theological humility is essential. Indeed, in this section Paul "fractures" his own theology, confessing that it too is partial, on the way, not yet complete. Paul confesses that he cannot master theology

---

22. Hays, *First Corinthians*, 231.
23. Ibid., 233.

because it can never exist as a final system or totality.[24] Paul unabashedly uses the first person here, confessing his own limitations. "When I became an adult," he states, "I put an end to childish ways" (v. 11). As an adult, Paul confesses, he recognizes the partial character of knowledge and speech—the partial character of theology. He concludes, "Now I know only in part; then I will know fully, even as I have been fully known" (v. 12). The only one who currently knows fully, Paul confesses, is God. All others, including the apostle himself, know only humanly, not divinely. Paul claims here a theological humility that casts a light back over his entire letter. Such humility clarifies those times when he confesses that he does not have a word from the Lord. It cautions all interpreters about writing Paul's practical conclusions in stone, as too many have done. Such an approach is at odds with Paul's confession in chapter 13. Paul's theology—and certainly our interpretation of that theology—occurs in a liminal space between the ages, in which theology itself is partial and on the way. There is no room for boasting, but only humility—and love.

Theologians, for Paul, are like the madman in Dostoevsky's short story, "The Dream of a Ridiculous Man."[25] The man has a vision in a dream, and he *must* share it; he must *preach.*[26] But there is a problem. The ridiculous man cannot find the words: "I do not know how to put it into words," he says. "After my dream I lost the knack of putting things into words. At least, into the most necessary and important words. But never mind. I shall go on and I shall keep on talking, for I have indeed beheld it with my own eyes, though I cannot describe

> We should not try to master the text. The Bible will become more and more mysterious to real exegetes. They will see all the depths and distances. They will constantly run up against the mystery before which theology is like trying to drain the ocean with a spoon.
>
> Karl Barth, *Homiletics*, trans. Geoffrey W. Bromiley and Donald E. Daniels (Louisville, KY: Westminster/John Knox Press, 1991), 128.

---

24. Roy A. Harrisville, *Fracture: The Cross as Irreconcilable in the Language and Thought of the Biblical Writers* (Grand Rapids, MI: William B. Eerdmans Publishing Co., 2006), 108.
25. Fyodor Dostoevsky, "The Dream of a Ridiculous Man: A Fantastic Story," in *The Best Short Stories of Fyodor Dostoevsky*, trans. David Magarshack (New York: Modern Library, 2001), 263–85.
26. Ibid., 283–84.

what I saw."[27] Like the ridiculous man, faithful theologians—and preachers—foolishly seek to bear witness to a mystery enacted and hidden on the cross, a mystery that simultaneously claims us and confounds us. Words about God are always unfinished language, provisional speech.

At the same time, however, as Paul makes clear throughout the letter, theologians must, paradoxically, speak boldly. Although always a provisional attempt, theology nevertheless calls us to speak truth—to risk, to dare, to testify. Indeed, as William Stringfellow has noted, the denial of truth is one of the strategies of the powers, which creates a situation of babel.[28] Theologians thus resist the powers of this age by "speaking truth,"—including "speaking truth to power"—but, paradoxically, speaking it humanly and provisionally.

This tension characterizes theology at the turn of the ages, which discerns the new creation that has broken into the world, but also recognizes its ongoing struggle with captivity to the powers of this age. This deep and profound tension lies at the heart of practical, apocalyptic theology, just as it shapes Paul's letter to the Corinthians; such theology involves *both* speaking humbly *and* speaking with élan. It involves speaking without fear of the wrong note while confessing there will always be wrong notes. The glue that holds together humility and boldness is love. Indeed, as Paul has noted earlier, theological truth is itself inseparable from the practice of love; theologians speak truth with bold humility only as they speak out of love (v. 6; Eph. 4:15). Theology finally gestures beyond itself, relying not on human knowledge and speech alone but trusting the grace and promise of the living God to build up the community in the love that never ends.

By the end of chapter 13, Paul has returned with a deepened sense to his earlier claim: "knowledge puffs up, but love builds up" (8:1). Theological humility creates room for love. No one needs to impose his or her theological conclusions on others or put others down because of their limited or misguided knowledge. Rather, faithful theology is shaped by the love that seeks to build up. As Augustine noted about biblical hermeneutics, any theology that does not build

27. Ibid., 285.
28. Stringfellow, *An Ethic for Christians*, 98–100.

up the love of God and neighbor is misguided.[29] Theology, like all other spiritual gifts, is itself *nothing* without love. When theology humbly and boldly pursues the way of love, it too may participate in the life of the new creation.

29. *De doctrina Christiana* I.35.40.

14:1-36
Pursuing Love in Worship

Having shared a theological vision of the Body of Christ and empha-sized the essential ethical practice of love, Paul turns now to the implications for Christian worship in Corinth, which has become a site, not of *communitas*, but of contention. He spells out in spe-cific details what pursuing love in the Body of Christ looks like in Christian worship. In particular, Paul addresses the divisive and disruptive issue of speaking in tongues. Indeed, many interpreters argue that this issue has driven Paul's argument throughout chapters 12–14. While speaking in tongues is clearly an important issue in the Corinthian church, Paul's address of this issue has broader theo-logical implications.

The practical dynamic of Paul's theology, integrating chapters 12–14, comes through in the opening words of this chapter. "Pursue love," he writes, echoing the ethical practice he has emphasized in chapter 13; "and strive for the spiritual gifts," he continues, return-ing to the theological vision of chapter 12; "and especially that you may prophesy," he concludes, revealing the direction in which his theological vision and ethical practice will lead in chapter 14. He then proceeds to develop the implications for the life of the worship-ing community in Corinth. The implications for worship are clear from what has preceded: through love, the spiritual gifts build up the Body of Christ rather than contributing to hierarchies and divisions. Consequently, intelligible prophecy is more important than speak-ing in tongues in Christian worship.

The movement of Paul's letter in chapters 12–14 is a concise example of the kind of practical theology that shapes Paul's entire

letter. As was noted in the introduction, Paul's creative theological thought takes place at the site of a wound. The divisions in the
Corinthian church, in this instance divisions in worship surrounding speaking in tongues, drive his theological and ethical reflections.
In response, Paul offers a theological vision of the Body of Christ
(chapter 12) and an encomium to the ethical practice of love that
counters the divisions in the church (chapter 13). Now, in chapter
14, Paul addresses the specific problem of the liturgical divisions in
Corinth. This dynamic represents the essential character of practical theology. The wound in Corinth, in this case the divisions in
worship, has led Paul to some of his most creative and beautiful
reflections on the Body of Christ and the centrality of love. Apart
from the wound and the need to address it, Paul might never have
penned these inspiring chapters; they emerged in the urgency of the
messy conflict, not in the abstract. Creative theology emerges from
the wound and seeks to describe it and transform it. While this pattern shapes Paul's letter as a whole, it is concisely evident in chapters
12–14. The contentions in communal worship lead to his theological and ethical reflections, which Paul now brings to bear on worship
practices.

The context of communal worship is critical. Paul does not criti-
cize speaking in tongues itself. On the contrary, he values this esoteric speech that communicates directly with God in the language
of the heavenly angels.[1] Paul says he would like everyone to speak
in tongues (v. 5). He thanks God that he speaks in tongues "more
than all of you" (v. 18). Indeed, he affirms that believers may speak
in tongues in public worship as long as there is an interpreter—and
indeed the person may be his or her own interpreter (v. 13). Nothing Paul says should dismiss the value of speaking in tongues; he
celebrates this extraordinary spiritual gift. Just as he made a distinction in chapter 11 between people eating in their homes and people
sharing the Lord's Supper together, so Paul here makes a distinction
between communal worship and individual practice. Here, too, one
must discern the body (11:29) and seek to build it up (*oikodomein*

---

1. Glossolalia was a different language spoken by superior angelic beings. See Dale B. Martin, *The
Corinthian Body* (New Haven, CT: Yale University Press, 1995), 88–89.

[*v.*]/*oikodomē* [*n.*]; vv. 4, 5, 12, 17, 26).[2] Prophecy builds up the church more faithfully than speaking in tongues. It is thus given priority in communal worship.

Paul's concerns about speaking in tongues are deeply rooted in his theology of the cross, which undergirds his vision of the Body of Christ and subverts hierarchies and status in the community. In two different ways, speaking in tongues reinforced the status divisions in the Corinthian church. First of all, speaking in tongues carried with it implications for social status. Such divine speech that dealt in mysteries was not the practice of uneducated marginal people—the "low and despised"—but was associated with high-status persons.[3] As a result, just as the table practices of the community reinforced social hierarchies within the church, so did the elevation of speaking in tongues above other spiritual gifts. In challenging the priority of tongues within the community, Paul once again challenges a church that has become captive to the old-age social hierarchies. Such hierarchies should not characterize the Body of Christ.

Second, in addition to the social hierarchy, there was a hierarchy of spirit (*pneuma*) over "mind" (*nous*) in the popular understanding of the human body.[4] The elevation of *pneuma* over *nous* represented the hierarchy of the special over the common. Consequently, Paul's treatment of the relationship between spirit and mind is not simply about intelligibility but about status (vv. 13–19). In fact, Paul here makes the same move with the individual human body that he has made with the communal Body of Christ. Just as the "lesser" members of Christ's Body are valued and elevated in order to engender cooperation and mutuality, so the same is true in the body of each person. Rather than elevating *pneuma* (spirit) over *nous* (mind), which was considered to be a lower aspect of the body, Paul elevates *nous* in order to encourage mutuality and cooperation between these two aspects of the human being in Christian worship. In a striking reversal, Paul calls on *pneuma* to submit itself to *nous* for the sake of intelligibility in the Christian community.

2. See the discussion of *oikodomein* in chapter 3, pp. 62–64.
3. My discussion of the status character of speaking in tongues is based on Martin, *Corinthian Body*, 87–92.
4. This section is based on ibid., 96–103.

Paul thus raises the status of the common over the esoteric. He "appeals to the higher member (*pneuma*) to submit to an equal partnership with the lower member (*nous*)."[5] He "disrupts these assumptions of higher-class ideology by arguing that the *nous* and the *pneuma* must work together."[6] In terms of his larger metaphor for the body, Paul disrupts the "status expectations of the two 'politicians' who rule the *polis* of the human person."[7] Paul's approach to *pneuma* and *nous* is thus consistent with his emphasis on the folly and weakness of the cross, which subvert all hierarchies within the community of faith. Just as he had done with the communal body, so Paul does now with the individual body. He breaks down the hierarchy between these two aspects of the human being and encourages cooperation between them so that genuinely spiritual speech may also be intelligible within the community. This dynamic, cooperative relationship between *pneuma* and *nous* guides the prophecy that builds up the Body of Christ.

FURTHER REFLECTIONS
The Prophethood of All Believers

While prophecy, for Paul, is a "spontaneous, Spirit-led encounter of the community with God," and not the same as composing and preaching a sermon,[8] Paul's words about prophecy nevertheless offer important emphases for a theology of preaching. Although more spontaneous and immediate than most (not all!) sermons, prophecy expresses essential aspects of preaching. To prophesy is not to foretell the future but to speak a word from God to the community of faith through the Spirit for the building up of the church.

Three aspects of Paul's theology of prophecy that have implications for preaching can be emphasized. Preaching, like prophecy, is, first of all, a gift of the Spirit. Whether spoken spontaneously in the moment or prepared carefully beforehand, speaking a word from

---

5. Ibid., 101.
6. Ibid.
7. Ibid., 102.
8. Richard B. Hays, *First Corinthians*, Interpretation: A Bible Commentary for Teaching and Preaching (Louisville, KY: John Knox Press, 1997), 234.

God for the community depends on the movement of the Spirit. As Jesus announced, quoting the prophet Isaiah in his inaugural sermon in Nazareth: "the Spirit of the Lord is upon me, because [the Spirit] has anointed me to bring good news . . ." (Luke 4:18). Preaching is a gift of the Spirit to be received from God; it is not simply a task to be mastered. Preachers can never rely on their own efforts but always trust in God as the source and the end of preaching. In this sense, all preaching, as Karl Barth has noted, is a "provisional attempt" to speak God's Word that begins and ends in prayer.[9]

Moreover, as the work of the Spirit, preaching itself lives in the liminal space between the ages, and its character is shaped by the Spirit's movement in resistance to the powers of this age.[10] Such Spirit-inspired preaching has several important characteristics. Like the Spirit itself, such preaching *interrupts*. It employs, as Paul demonstrates throughout his letter, transgressive rhetoric that disrupts the myths and conventions and rationalities of the old age, which lead to death. Such preaching engages in creative resistance to the powers of this age that hold people captive and often prevent them from even imagining alternatives to the ways of the world. Indeed, building up the Body of Christ as an alternative to the old-age cultural hierarchies explicitly calls forth homiletical interruptions, just as Paul's words in chapters 12–13 interrupt the powers of this age to build up the community of faith.

In addition, Spirit-inspired preaching builds up a being-saved community in the unsettled, *liminal space* between the ages. Such preaching keeps the community moving with the Spirit from the old age to the new; it repeatedly seeks to form and re-form the church, as Paul does throughout his letter. Such preaching seeks to keep the community of faith on the way.

Further, such preaching is concerned with *perception* and *discernment*. The Spirit-inspired preacher, like Paul himself, is an apocalyptic figure who simply seeks to unmask the deadly ways of the old age and help people discern the in-breaking new creation. Not surprisingly, prophecy is closely related to speaking a "revelation"

9. Karl Barth, *Homiletics*, trans. Geoffrey W. Bromiley and Donald E. Daniels (Louisville, KY: Westminster/John Knox Press, 1991), 47–55, 71–75.
10. See the discussion of the Spirit in chapter 2, pp. 52–57.

(*apokalypsis*, vv. 6, 26); indeed, at one point revelation is placed in direct parallel to prophecy: "If a revelation [*apokalyphthē*] is made to someone else sitting nearby, let the first person be silent. For you can all prophesy one by one, so that all may learn and all be encouraged" (v. 30–31). Prophecy is apocalyptic, seeking to unveil the often-hidden new creation through words. God has already invaded and changed the world through the cross and resurrection of Jesus Christ. Preaching, as the work of the Spirit, seeks to create the space where new discernment becomes possible.

Finally, Spirit-inspired preaching does not take itself too seriously. It is content with the role of the fool or the farmhand or the construction worker or the servant or the steward—the "low and despised" person who can always be dismissed as a moron (chaps. 3–4). Such preaching knows that discernment is the gift of the Spirit. No eloquent words or wisdom, as Paul earlier affirmed (1:17), can give the mind of Christ, but only the power of the cross through the movement of the Spirit. Again, God is both the source and the end of Christian preaching; there is no room for boasting by the preacher or the prophet.

In addition to being a gift of the Spirit, preaching is, second, speech oriented to others. Shaped by the cross and inspired by the Spirit, preaching is for the good of others; it is never self-serving speech but rather seeks to speak a word that will build up the church. For this reason, preaching, unlike speaking in tongues, is intelligible speech. It is speech in which *pneuma* (spirit) and *nous* (mind) cooperate for the good of the community. Preaching is never esoteric speech, including the esoteric language of theological jargon! Rather, it is common speech—speech in the language and idiom of the people. In the contemporary church, such speech would include sign language, intelligible for persons who are deaf, as well as language accessible to persons with mental disabilities. The church's speech should be intelligible to all so the community may be built up.

Importantly, this intelligible speech is not simply for the benefit of believers within the church, but also for outsiders and unbelievers who may be present (vv. 16, 23–25). There is an evangelistic aspect to Paul's emphasis on intelligible speech. No one, Paul states, should feel like a foreigner in worship, unable to understand the strange language being spoken (v. 11). Possibly Paul is translating the miracle of Pentecost for the everyday life of Christian worship. Whereas at Pentecost everyone miraculously heard and understood in their own language, now speech in the Spirit must be intelligible for everyone who enters. Such speech may directly address the unbelievers in the church's midst. Or the outsiders may simply "overhear" the gospel as it is spoken for believers in the church.[11] Either way, the church's speech in worship should be common language, intelligible and accessible to unbelievers and outsiders when they appear. The goal, Paul reminds the church, is that any outsider who comes will "bow down before God and worship [God], declaring, 'God is really among you'" (v. 25). That is an extraordinary and challenging theological guidepost for planning the language of Christian worship.

Even as common, intelligible speech, however, faithful preaching retains a surplus of meaning provided by the Spirit. *Pneuma* and *nous cooperate*; neither is discounted. With a positive twist on Paul's musical imagery (see vv. 7–9), William C. Turner has captured this dynamic relationship between *pneuma* and *nous* in his discussion of the musicality of black preaching:

> The music of black preaching can be understood as sort of a way to "sing praise with the spirit [*pneuma*]" (1 Cor. 14:15). The surplus expressed in the sermon's music accompanies its rational [*nous*] content, which is expressed in words literally. The rational [*nous*] portion is contained in the formal structure of the sermon, which represents the homiletical and doctrinal tradition in which the preacher stands. The surplus portion is achieved when the preacher becomes an instrument—a flute through which divine air is blown, a harp whose strings are plucked by God. For the sake of the audience, the preacher becomes an oracle through whom a divinely inspired message flows.[12]

11. Fred B. Craddock, *Overhearing the Gospel: Preaching and Teaching the Faith to Persons Who Have Already Heard* (Nashville: Abingdon Press, 1978).
12. William C. Turner, "The Musicality of Black Preaching," in *Performance in Preaching: Bringing the Sermon to Life*, ed. Jana Childers and Clayton J. Schmit (Grand Rapids, MI: Baker Academic, 2008), 204–5.

As Turner notes, the dynamic between *pneuma* and *nous* does not create "lifeless instruments" that simply produce "indistinct sounds" (vv. 7–8). Rather, this dynamic produces intelligible speech that nevertheless retains a surplus of meaning. As poets remind us, simple, everyday language—the idiom of the people—can indeed be immediately intelligible while also inviting the hearers into a surplus of meaning that can never be fully contained in human words. Paul's own letter, with its regular use of metaphor, irony, and paradox, itself offers an example of this surplus of meaning.

Third, Spirit-inspired preaching is, finally, the work of the entire community. While Paul calls for everything to be done "decently and in order" in worship (v. 40), his understanding of order might be quite unsettling for much Christian worship today. Paul's words might actually seem rather indecent and disorderly to many congregations. Worship, as Paul envisions it, is a lively, participatory affair in which "each one" is encouraged to contribute: "When you come together, each one has a hymn, a lesson, a revelation, a tongue, or an interpretation. Let all things be done for building up" (v. 26). Indeed, Paul wants *all* the members to *prophesy*, as long as participants speak "one by one" (v. 31). Worship, for Paul, is the participatory activity of the entire community; it is not governed by one ordained preacher, while others sit passively and listen.

In essence, Paul proclaims "the prophethood of all believers." He reminds the church that one never knows whom the Spirit will use to speak the Word. The preaching office is not reserved for those with ecclesial education or ordination or status but is bestowed by the unpredictable movement of the Spirit in the liminal space between the ages. Paul reminds the church that one never knows whom the Spirit will call to speak the Word. The Spirit blows where the Spirit will, and even the "low and despised" may be given a word

> I will pour out my spirit on all flesh;
> your sons and your daughters shall prophesy,
> your old men shall dream dreams,
> and your young men shall see visions.
> Even on the male and female slaves,
> in those day, I will pour out my spirit.
>
> Joel 2:28–29

for the community. As long as the prophecy builds up the church, and as long as the speaking proceeds in an orderly fashion, in which members respect each other and speak one by one, anyone may prophesy or preach in the church.

In a radical way, Paul undercuts hierarchical notions of ordination within the community of faith. Ordination does not confer a higher status on the minister; nor does it give that person a corner on the Spirit or preaching. Indeed, in his treatment of Christian worship in chapter 14 Paul depicts the essence of the Reformation doctrine of the priesthood of all believers. The doctrine does not simply affirm that each person is his or her own priest, with direct access to God. Rather, the doctrine asserts that every believer is a priest to other believers. The doctrine is thoroughly communal; it subverts all exclusive and priestly hierarchies. It is a rich image of the Body of Christ, in which each member serves as a priest to others in the community for the building up of the church.

In his discussion of prophecy, Paul suggests the contours of this doctrine, which is consistent with his vision of Christ's body. The implications for the church's ministry, as well as for our understanding of the gospel itself, are significant. Every believer, as inspired by the Spirit, is called to be a prophet to others in the community for the building up of the Body of Christ. "Prophethood," like priesthood, is a thoroughly communal activity, the responsibility of all believers. No one prophet has control of the gospel, just as no one priest controls access to God. Rather, the fullness of the gospel emerges only in the communal, multivocal, Spirit-inspired prophetic speech of the church. In the give and take of many different prophetic utterances, the multifaceted gospel lives and moves in the church and builds up the Body of Christ. Here is an image of gospel, as well as church, that is rich and polyvalent, not narrow or univocal. The dialogical character of Paul's letter itself, as well as his dynamic image of the body, reflects this lively, Spirit-inspired dynamic in the church.

Pursuing love in worship thus not only involves speech that builds up the church (prophecy), rather than simply edifying the individual (tongues). Such love also involves *listening* to the prophetic speech of others and learning from them. This dialogical edification is the goal of the love Paul desires in worship. This love involves respecting others' gifts of speech, allowing them the time to speak and being open to the word they offer. It involves humbly and patiently hearing a Word of the Lord from someone else, someone different: "Let two or three prophets speak, and let the others weigh what is said. If a revelation is made to someone else sitting nearby, let the first person be silent. For you can all prophesy one by one, so that all may learn and be encouraged" (vv. 29–31). No one person or group of persons is to dominate the church's prophetic speech. This communal practice, however, also involves the discernment of spirits. When someone speaks, others must "weigh what is said," for "the spirits of prophets are subject to the prophets" (vv. 29, 32). Paul is not here seeking to stifle the Spirit but to create a peaceful environment in which lively speech and discernment can take place.

To borrow Paul's musical metaphor, the church's worship should not become a random collection of cacophonous instruments producing indistinct sounds (v. 8) but rather form a harmonious, dynamic interchange among various well-played instruments. Possibly the image of a jazz quartet is helpful. All four instrumentalists improvise together, each musician listening to and responding to the others as they play in a kind of call and response manner. At different times, different members of the group will step forward for inspired solos—first the saxophonist, then the pianist, then the drummer. But the entire time the other members of the group listen and respond to the individual's improvisation. All of this happens in the spontaneity of the Spirit, as each member of the group—in orderly fashion!—takes his or her turn with a solo.

> Preaching's goal is to gather the community of faith around the Word where the church's central conversations are refocused and fostered. . . . The preacher and the congregation are colleagues, exploring together the mystery of the Word for their own lives, as well as the life of the congregation, the larger church, and the world.
>
> Lucy Atkinson Rose, *Sharing the Word: Preaching in the Roundtable Church* (Louisville, KY: Westminster John Knox Press, 1997), 4.

Each one contributes a distinctive improvisation, even as the purposeful harmony of the whole remains.

Such an understanding of preaching shaped the worship in the Christian base community in Solentiname, Nicaragua. Each week the priest, Ernesto Cardenal, would set a text before the worshipers, who themselves were "low and despised" *campesinos*. The members of the church would then contribute their own insights and interpretations. In this sharing the gospel emerges, often in startling ways, from the dialogue of the community rather than from a single preacher. Consider, for example, the Sunday on which the text is Mary's Magnificat. Cardenal asks the community "what they thought Herod would have said if he had known that a woman of the people had sung that God had pulled down the mighty and raised up the humble, filled the hungry with good things and left the rich with nothing." The following conversation ensued:

NATALIA	laughed and said: "He'd say she was crazy."
ROSITA:	"That she was a communist."
LAUREANO:	"The point isn't that they would just *say* the Virgin was a communist. She *was* a communist."
[CARDENAL]:	"And what would they say in Nicaragua if they heard what we're saying here in Solentiname?"
Several voices:	"That we're communists."
Someone asked:	"That part about filling the hungry with good things?"
A young man answered:	"The hungry are going to eat."
And another:	"The Revolution."
LAUREANO:	"That is the Revolution. The rich person or the mighty is brought down and the poor person, the one who was down, is raised up."
Still another:	"If God is against the mighty, then he has to be on the side of the poor."
ANDREA, Oscar's wife, asked:	"That promise that the poor would have

those good things, was it for then, for Mary's
time, or would it happen in our time? I ask
because I don't know."

One of the young
people answered: "She spoke for the future, it seems to me,
because we are just barely beginning to see
the liberation she announces."[13]

Here the community in Solentiname enacts a contemporary version of "the prophethood of all believers." There is an orderly exchange of insights, in which each is given the opportunity to speak and listen. There is active participation by all members; *campesinos* are given voice, subverting the hierarchies present not only in the culture but also in the church. There is discernment of the spirits, as questions are asked and clarifications are given, and a fitting, contemporary word emerges for the building up of the church.

Although the focus in chapter 14 has often been on speaking in tongues, Paul's understanding of the "prophethood of all believers" has radical implications for the church's worship and preaching. In Paul's understanding of the loving Body of Christ, hierarchies are broken down and *communitas* is encouraged. The proclamation of the gospel itself becomes the work of the community speaking and listening to each other while discerning the Word in the Spirit. In a time in which old forms of the institutional church are dying, Paul's vision encourages new directions for the contemporary church.

14:33b–36
One More Time: Women

Paul's dynamic communal theology of worship in chapter 14 is interrupted by one of the most notorious texts in the New Testament, in which women are prohibited from speaking in church and are counseled simply to ask questions and learn from their husbands at home. Unfortunately, verse 37, in which Paul claims to have a

13. Ernesto Cardenal, *The Gospel in Solentiname*, vol. 1, trans. Donald D. Walsh (Maryknoll, NY: Orbis Books, 1987), 30–31.

command from the Lord, has often been applied directly to these verses, as if these words alone constituted that command. This text, which has been used for generations to keep women outside the pulpit, demonstrates the danger of isolating passages of Scripture from their larger context. It also, as I have noted earlier, highlights the importance of a *theological* reading of Paul's letter, rather than a narrow focus on specific directives addressed to presenting issues.

Within the larger context of Paul's letter, these verses radically contradict other clear statements the apostle has made about the participation of women in worship. In chapter 11, as has been discussed, Paul assumes women will speak in worship; all he requires is some form of head covering. In addition, in chapter 12 Paul does not give any external qualifications for exercising different spiritual gifts; no gift is limited to a certain category of person, but the exercise of every spiritual gift is open to anyone. Earlier in chapter 14, Paul has affirmed that he wants *"all of you"* to prophesy (v. 5). Moreover, Paul's "command" in verse 37 is directly addressed to those who *are* prophets—a calling he has not previously limited to men: "Anyone who claims to be a prophet, or to have spiritual powers, must acknowledge that what I am writing to you is a command of the Lord." For these reasons, verse 37 should be interpreted as a concluding word related to Paul's larger vision of the Body of Christ worshiping together in love guided by the particular gift of prophecy, not specifically to the directive in verses 33b–36. When Scripture interprets Scripture, the specifics of Paul's larger witness belie the directives in verses 33b–36.

In addition, the underlying theology of Paul's letter, as I have noted earlier, undercuts these directives. As Paul argues repeatedly, one cannot follow a crucified Messiah and continue to maintain the old-age cultural hierarchies. Nowhere is this clearer than in chapter 12, the theological vision undergirding Paul's counsel about prophecy in chapter 14. In chapter 12, as has been discussed, Paul argues that, just as the "weak" Christ was elevated on the cross, so the members of the body who appear to be weaker are actually to be more highly valued. In Paul's culture women were considered "weaker." Therefore, from the perspective of Paul's theological vision of the Body of Christ, women should be highly valued as speakers in public worship. Paul's theological vision of the Body undercuts the directives in verses 33b–36.

For these and other reasons, many interpreters have argued that these verses were inserted into the letter at a later time. As a result, they need not be heard as the words of Paul. While this may get Paul off the hook, it doesn't solve the problem. These verses appear in English Bibles, and people read them as Scripture. These words have been used to oppress women throughout church history, and they are still used in this way today. Although correctly dismissed by scholars, these verses continue to exercise a profound influence in denominations and churches around the world. A deeper *theological* and *hermeneutical* engagement with these words is required. Paul's own letter, which places us in the liminal space between the ages, actually provides a helpful lens for this task. Within Paul's apocalyptic theological framework, we can recognize that these verses are themselves an interruption—an interruption of the old age hierarchies into Scripture itself. They highlight the church's ongoing captivity to and struggle with the powers of this age.

As I have noted throughout this commentary, Paul and the church continue to live in the tension between the old age and the new. The community of faith continues to seek to discern the work of the Spirit in particular situations. This quest for discernment is evident throughout Paul's letter. At times, Paul recognizes that he has no command from the Lord. Finally, in the climactic chapter on love, Paul affirms in general theological terms that all of us now see in a glass dimly and know only in part (13:12). His own letter, Paul recognizes, is itself on the way; it is part of the being-saved life of the church between the ages.

Just as Paul is a hermeneutical theologian, seeking to discern and interpret the work of Christ for the community of faith, so contemporary interpreters and theologians continue to do the same. That means individual texts must be interpreted both within the larger Scriptural witness and the underlying theological affirmations. Paul's own apocalyptic theology, that is, invites contemporary interpreters to discern when Scripture is in fact *not* a "command of the Lord." As has been noted, Paul himself makes this very claim about his letter at several points, usually in relation to very specific directives (see e.g., 7:12, 25). Paul himself thus calls the being-saved church to discern and name the continuing distortions of the old age even when they appear in Scripture. From this perspective, the counsel about women in verses 33b–36 should be seen as one such distortion. Moreover, Paul's theological vision calls the church to develop hermeneutical *trajectories* that continue to move the community of faith on the way to the new creation, to the genuine *communitas* that will be fulfilled when God is "all in all" (15:28). This trajectory points not to more rigid and exclusive rules but to an ever-more-inclusive pulpit within the church.

Having concluded this lengthy section of the letter concerning the worship life of the community, Paul, in the following chapter, reemphasizes the being-saved-community (15:2). He reaffirms the core theological confession of the church: "that Christ died for our sins in accordance with the scriptures, and that he was buried, and that he was raised on the third day in accordance with the scriptures" (15:3–4). He offers a vision of the end when Christ has overcome every principality and power (15:24). Until then, the cruciform struggle between the ages continues; the church is on the way, and the risky task of discernment remains—even with regard to Scripture itself.

15:1–58
The Resurrection of the Body

Christ's resurrection, like his crucifixion, is a radical interruption of the powers of this age, particularly the power of death—the "last enemy" (v. 26). Whereas the crucifixion unmasks the powers of this age as the agents of death, not life, the resurrection sets people free from the tyranny and fear of death. Resurrection is not simply about hope for the future. Rather, resurrection empowers life now in the liminal space between the ages. Through the resurrection Christ sets believers free from the power of death so we might take up the foolish way of the cross. The resurrection, that is, empowers the kind of life that Paul and the church enact as "fools for the sake of Christ."

Indeed, the resurrection *constitutes* the cross as the weak power and foolish wisdom of God. Apart from the resurrection, Jesus' crucifixion is simply the horrific death of one more "low and despised" person, never to be heard from again. The resurrection, however, confirms the crucified Christ as the way of God in the world. One might even say the cross *becomes* foolish on Easter Sunday. For then the cross can be seen as the scandalous wisdom and power of God. Appropriately, in the confessional material shared in 15:3–4, crucifixion and resurrection belong inseparably together.

Chapter 15 is thus neither the center of the letter nor simply a response to a query by the Corinthians.[1] Rather chapter 15 and chapter 1 serve as brackets or bookends for the letter. The Christian life discussed in chapters 2–14 is lived in the dynamic relationship between crucifixion and resurrection. This "weak" and "foolish" life

---

1. Karl Barth interprets chapter 15 as the center of the letter. See Karl Barth, *The Resurrection of the Dead*, trans. H. J. Stenning (Eugene, OR: Wipf & Stock, 2003).

moves toward the future fulfillment when the crucified and risen Christ ultimately overcomes the last enemy. The structural and theological parallels between chapter 1 and chapter 15 are striking. The chapters mirror each other in many ways. In each chapter Paul emphasizes his disruptive call, which transformed him into an apostle, even though he "persecuted the church of God" (15:9). By the grace of God alone, Paul declares at the beginning and the end, "I am what I am" (15:10; cf. 1:1). Both sections also emphasize preaching. The letter opens with the proclamation of the cross and concludes with the proclamation of the resurrection. In both cases, the content of preaching is at issue, and the proclamation of the gospel shapes and undergirds the central theological claims. Beginning with preaching, both sections also employ ascriptive logic, which identifies Jesus through his particular story rather than seeking to describe Jesus through generally available categories or common sense. In resurrection, as in crucifixion, Jesus cannot be defined by general truths that people know through other means (e.g., "there is no resurrection of the dead," v. 12). Rather, one begins with the identity of Jesus rendered through the particular stories about him.[2] Ascriptive logic creates the "destabilizing pairs of opposites" (e.g., crucified Messiah, resurrected body) that shape each chapter and highlight the radical interruption of the old age by the crucified and risen Christ. Moreover, in both sections Paul emphasizes the being-saved community (1:18; 15:2). Both crucifixion and resurrection place the Corinthian church on the way in the liminal space between the ages. Consequently, both chapters also point to "the end" (*telos*; 1:7–9; 15:24) toward which believers are moving, a future in which God will overcome the powers of this age and be all in all (15:28). A closer look at chapter 15 will highlight these central theological aspects of Paul's treatment of resurrection.

Everything Off Balance

The Roman Catholic American short-story writer Flannery O'Connor penned extremely odd and even grotesque stories that

---

2. See the discussion of ascriptive logic in chapter 1, p. 29.

were provocatively Christian. Indeed, the New Testament scholar J. Louis Martyn has argued that O'Connor's grotesque Southern fiction actually echoes in remarkable ways the apocalyptic gospel of the apostle Paul.[3] The stories are frequently characterized by destabilizing interruptions.

In one of her stories, titled "A Good Man Is Hard to Find," O'Connor presents a character called the Misfit. He is not a good person. In fact, he spends the entire story methodically directing the murder of six members of a single family, one after the other. At one point in the story, amid all the killing, the Misfit makes this comment: "Jesus was the only One that ever raised the dead . . . and He shouldn't have done it. He thrown everything off balance."[4] In this comment, the Misfit names the disruptive character of resurrection. Resurrection *interrupts* the old age, which is governed by the powers of death; it throws everything off balance. If the resurrection is true, it changes everything. If it is not, as the Misfit starkly claims, the power of death reigns supreme, and we might as well serve as its acolytes. Or as Paul puts it, we might as well "eat and drink, for tomorrow we die" (v. 32).

Resurrection throws everything off balance. We see this disruptive role of the resurrection throughout chapter 15. Most basically, the resurrection interrupts the conventions and rationalities that hold the Corinthians captive. Like Jesus' crucifixion, resurrection melts the solidities of the world, the assumptions that are supposedly written in stone. The sophisticated Corinthians cannot even imagine the resurrection Paul proclaims.

The Corinthians have apparently shared their assumptions about resurrection with Paul, asserting that there is no resurrection from the dead (v. 12). And Paul anticipates their deeply skeptical question: "How are the dead raised? With what kind of *body* do they come?" (v. 35). That is the real issue. The *body*. The phrase "resurrection of the dead" (*anastasis nekrōn*; vv. 12–13) literally means the "rising of the corpses." For the spiritually sophisticated Corinthians

---

3. J. Louis Martyn, "From Paul to Flannery O'Connor with the Power of Grace," in *Theological Issues in the Letters of Paul* (Nashville: Abingdon Press, 1997), 279–97.

4. Flannery O'Connor, "A Good Man is Hard to Find," in *The Complete Stories of Flannery O'Connor* (New York: Farrar, Straus and Giroux, 1971), 132.

this notion was, as Richard Hays puts it, "crass and embarrassing." "It was not the stuff of Christian hope; it was a scenario for a horror story;" it sounded "like the superstitious foolishness of popular legends" held by the uneducated masses.[5] "Resurrected body" presented a "destabilizing pair of opposites" just as radical and disruptive as "crucified Messiah." The resurrection of the *body* was simply inconceivable to most of the Corinthians. It was not part of the philosophical or cultural air they breathed. Nor was it compatible with their spiritualized understanding of the Christian faith. The entire chapter is a deep and profound interruption of this conventional way of thinking. Paul seeks to interrupt the Corinthians and throw their world off balance so they might perceive and live in the world in a new way.

The way Paul interrupts the assumptions and conventions of the Corinthians is instructive for preachers. In fact, Paul actually *begins* with preaching. It is the same here as in chapter 1, where the *preaching* of the cross is the great interruption. The *preached* word interrupts everything and counters the Corinthians' assumptions:

> Now if Christ is proclaimed as raised from the dead, how can some of you say there is no resurrection of the dead? If there is no resurrection of the dead, then Christ has not been raised; and if Christ has not been raised, then our proclamation has been in vain and your faith has been in vain. We are even found to be misrepresenting God, because we testified of God that he raised Christ—whom he did not raise if it is true that the dead are not raised. (vv. 12–15)

Christ's resurrection should not be questioned because it has been *preached*, as Paul emphasizes by using three key terms for preaching: *kērussō* (to proclaim), v. 12; *kērygma* (proclamation), v. 14; and *martyreō* (to testify or witness), v. 15. At the beginning of the chapter Paul similarly begins his entire argument with preaching, using other central terms: *euangelizō* (to proclaim good news, v. 1–2); *euangelion* (good news, v. 1); and *logos* (message or word,

---

5. Richard B. Hays, *First Corinthians*, Interpretation: A Bible Commentary for Teaching and Preaching (Louisville, KY: John Knox Press, 1997), 253; see also Dale B. Martin, *The Corinthian Body* (New Haven, CT: Yale University Press, 1995), 106.

v. 2).[6] Rarely, if ever, do so many different and repeated terms for preaching come together to emphasize a message: *Preaching is the starting point from which everything else follows.*

The disruptive preached word leads to theological reflection, not *vice versa*. In fact, chapter 15 represents a fascinating moment in the life of the Christian church and Christian theology. We witness the threshold between preaching and theology. The Word has been proclaimed—*and received* (v. 1); now theological reflection on that proclamation ensues. The order is important. Preaching is primary theology, and secondary theological reflection seeks to explicate the content of the church's preaching.

Up until this time in Corinth, Paul has proclaimed the community's gospel of Christ crucified and risen—the gospel, as he notes in primary, confessional language, that he has received and passed on (vv. 3–11). Now questions and challenges about the character of resurrection have arisen within the church in Corinth. So Paul engages in theological dialogue with the community; he begins to work out the theological implications of his proclamation of the risen Christ. The preaching nevertheless remains primary. Indeed, there is a blurring between preaching and theology; the chapter itself would probably have been read out loud as a kind of sermon. So here we get a kind of homiletical theology. The preaching of the church shapes its theology.

Paul begins by reminding the Corinthians of the good news (*euangelion*) that he proclaimed (*euangelizō*) to them (v. 1). That good news is the story of Jesus, focused on Jesus' crucified and risen body. So Paul recounts that story briefly: Christ died, he was buried,

6. These different Greek terms have different nuances. *Kērussō* emphasizes the act of preaching; it is the term from which we get the image of the herald who goes ahead of the ruler to share an announcement; there is little emphasis on the content or the person of the preacher. *Euangelizō*, as is clear in v. 1, includes not simply the act but the content of the "good news," the story of Jesus. *Martyreō*, more than the other terms holds together the person of the preacher and the message preached. It is the word both for martyr and for witness; it is a message for which one would be willing to risk one's life. The English word "witness" in fact captures some of the dynamics: a witness first sees (or witnesses) something; then the witness witnesses to what he or she has seen; and in the process the person becomes a witness. The message of the witness depends on the trustworthiness or the character of the person. See Dietrich Bonhoeffer, "The Proclaimed Word," in Richard Lischer, ed., *The Company of Preachers: Wisdom on Preaching, Augustine to the Present* (Grand Rapids, MI: William B. Eerdmans Publishing Co., 2002), 31–37.

he was raised on the third day. Then, Paul emphasizes, he appeared *four* different times (vv. 3–11). It is significant that Paul repeats four times that Jesus appeared to various people. That is central to his theological move. In emphasizing Jesus' appearances, Paul does not seek to *prove* the resurrection. Everything still depends on *testimony* (*emartyrēsamen*, "we testified"; v. 15); there is no other proof for the Corinthians or for us than the preaching of these initial witnesses. Moreover, in emphasizing Jesus' appearances, Paul asserts that Jesus, a buried corpse, appeared in the form of some kind of recognizable body (vv. 1–11). He was raised as a body.

Resurrected corpse. Resurrected body. These are incommensurable realities for those Corinthians shaped by the popular philosophies of their day. The opening of chapter 15, like chapter 1, is a fascinating study of the disruptive character of ascriptive theo-logic. Paul begins with the preaching he has done, and he recounts the narratively rendered particularity of Jesus in that preaching. Jesus died, he was buried (that is, he really died; he was a corpse), but he was raised from the dead, and he *appeared*. Then, in the theological reflection that follows Paul appropriates that story through ascriptive logic as he addresses questions about the resurrection of the body. This logic is in fact the link between story and argument— preaching and theology—in Paul's letter. Even the Misfit recognizes this logic; he knows you have to begin with the unique particularity of Jesus' resurrection—"Jesus is the only one that ever raised the dead," he says. That's what throws everything off balance.

Paul begins his secondary theological reflection in verse 12. "Now if Christ is proclaimed as raised from the dead [as a risen body], how can some of you say there is no resurrection of the dead [of the body]?" He continues: "If there is no resurrection of the dead, then Christ has not been raised; and if Christ has not been raised, then our proclamation has been in vain and your faith has been in vain.... But in fact Christ has been raised from the dead" (vv. 12–14, 20). The argument sounds a bit circular, but that is the point. One cannot begin with a general understanding that bodies are not raised—and then move to interpret Jesus in those terms. One has to move in the other direction, from the particularity of Jesus, who *has* been raised, to theological reflection on resurrection.

In chapter 15, as in chapter 1, Paul uses the term "fool," now in the Old Testament sense of the person who has failed to take God into account. Someone will ask, he says, anticipating questions from the Corinthians: "How are the dead raised? With what kind of body do they come?" Again, these questions assume no resurrection of the body; it is really unimaginable—ridiculous. Paul responds, "Fool!" (*aphrōn*, rather than the more perjorative *mōros* as used earlier; vv. 35–36; cf. 3:18; 4:10). As with the message of the cross, the word of resurrection makes foolish the wisdom of the world, the wisdom that cannot imagine the resurrection of the body. Through his exclamation, "Fool!" Paul interrupts the conventions and rationalities of the sophisticated Corinthian Christians as radically as he does earlier with the word of the cross. One cannot begin with general understandings of life after death (e.g., life after death as an escape of the soul from the prison of the flesh). Jesus defines resurrection— not *vice versa*. From his primary theology of preaching, Paul explores the character of the resurrected *body* as a kind of *transformed* body (vv. 36–54).

Through his use of ascriptive logic, Paul issues a profound theological challenge to preachers. Ascriptive logic, Paul suggests, is often what makes preaching interesting and bold. If preachers simply plug Jesus into acknowledged wisdom and common sense, if we simply seek to describe Jesus according to the given conventions and rationalities of the day, preaching becomes predictable and boring, not to mention theologically problematic. There are no interruptions. Jesus simply fits into common sense. Consequently, sermons have no really interesting movement; there are no twists, no turns, which are at the heart of interesting, engaging sermonic movement. Our sermons simply move "and, and, and, and . . . " "So, so, so . . . " "Therefore. . . ."

Ascriptive logic, however, is the logic of Paul's interruptions and of disruptive preaching. It is the source of the repeated "buts" in chapters 1 and 15. It is the source of the "buts" in sermons. "But" may actually be the most important word in Scripture and the most important word in preaching. It is the word through which the gospel breaks into the wisdom of the world and interrupts the powers of this age; it is where the new age breaks into the old and something new becomes possible. The gospel is a "but." When we're dealing with resurrection, we're dealing with the most important "but" of all. Luke 24:1 captures this reality perfectly. After relating all the events of Jesus' crucifixion and burial, chapter 23 concludes with the women preparing spices and ointments for the dead body; then they rest on the Sabbath. They have reached a dead end. There is nothing but a corpse to deal with. Then 24:1 begins: "*But* on the first day of the week. . . . " The world turns on that "but."

> God encounters us "not with a natural Therefore, but with a miraculous Nevertheless. . . . "
>
> Karl Barth, *Church Dogmatics*, II/2, trans. G. W. Bromiley, et. al. (Edinburgh: T & T Clark, 1957), 315.

This "but" throws everything off balance. Paul in 1 Corinthians does the same thing as Luke; he interrupts the world's assumptions about the power of death with a great "but." After going through his various arguments challenging the Corinthians' assumptions about resurrection in verses 1–19, Paul makes his positive turn in verse 20 like this: "*But* in fact Christ has been raised from the dead. . . . " The Greek phrase translated "but in fact" (*nyni de*) is a strong one; it introduces the real situation after an unreal one has been described.[7] Death, Paul declares, is a radical end; there is a real corpse with no future; death relativizes everything human. But resurrection is a radical new beginning through the act of God alone.[8] In that "but," God does God's work with no help from us. Resurrection not only disrupts the power of death; it also interrupts the human desire to be in control, to assure our own future, to avoid depending completely on God's act of grace. Resurrection is so radical, even the word "but" is probably inadequate. "But" is a conjunction, whereas resurrection is thoroughly disjunctive. In a deep sense, there is not even any narrative continuity between death and resurrection. Christians often move from death to resurrection as if there is a nice smooth story line. There is, however, no plot-like

---

7. "*nyni*," in Frederick W. Danker, Walter Bauer, and William F. Arndt, *A Greek-English Lexicon of the New Testament and Other Early Christian Literature*, 3rd ed. (Chicago: University of Chicago, 2000), 682.
8. Barth, *Resurrection of the Dead*, 201, 207, 209.

connection between death and resurrection. Just the radical interruption of God, just the radical "but" of the resurrected body.[9]

Resurrection Life at the Turn of the Ages

Resurrection, then, like crucifixion, is a destabilizing interruption. More specifically, as I have already suggested, resurrection is
an *apocalyptic* interruption. It is an interruption of the old age by
the new. In conjunction with the cross, the resurrection inaugurates the new age or new creation right in the midst of the old.
Paul's words about resurrection simply confirm what he has been
proclaiming all along: as a result of this apocalyptic interruption,
Christians live at the "juncture of the ages" or the "turn of the ages."
Believers live in-between, in the liminal, threshold space where the
two ages overlap, where the old is passing away while the new has
not yet fully come.

In chapter 15, as he does throughout the letter, Paul moves in this
apocalyptic, in-between space and time created by Jesus' crucifixion
and resurrection. There are three indicators of the character of this
space in 1 Corinthians 15. The first two are quite specific images;
the third is a more general, dynamic movement that captures the in-
between, liminal character of this space.

First, Paul employs the metaphor of first fruits. This metaphor
is the first positive theological claim Paul makes about the resurrection in verse 20: "But in fact," he says, "Christ has been raised
from the dead, the first fruits of those who have died." Christ's resurrection is the "first fruits." This metaphor powerfully accentu-
ates the threshold character of the Christian life at the turn of the
ages. The metaphor itself has a liminal character. It is taken from
Scripture (Lev. 23:9–14), where it refers to consecrating the first
fruits of the harvest to God. It is a scriptural image that has been
passed on, but it takes on a fresh hermeneutical life in the new
age. Paul is not just interested in its former use. Rather, he transforms "first fruits" into a metaphor. For Paul first fruits points to

---

9. See Richard Lischer, "The Limits of Story," *Interpretation* 38 (January 1984): 33.

"the first of the harvest serving as a kind of guarantee for the full harvest."[10]

Even in Paul's choice of the image, there is dynamic movement, which characterizes Paul's hermeneutical theology. As he does throughout the letter, Paul takes a text from the past and speaks through it to a new context. Here Paul takes the legal directive to consecrate the first fruits to God, and he turns it into a fluid metaphor that takes on a distinctively eschatological character. The metaphor proclaims the resurrection as a fundamentally eschatological event that carries the future within it. Christ's resurrection is the first fruits—it is the first of its kind that guarantees a full harvest. Of course that also suggests that for now it remains only the first—the rest are promised but not yet gathered. The metaphor holds out great promise but leaves believers in an unsettled space between the ages. It keeps the Body of Christ on the way, living with hope amid the tension between the old age and the new.

In addition, the metaphor incorporates all humanity into Christ's resurrection (as Paul again affirms through the metaphor of Adam; vv. 45–49). Jesus' resurrection, as Barth notes, encompasses the horizon of the entire world. If the resurrection does not include us, Barth boldly claims, if the resurrection concerns only Jesus himself, then the resurrection would be no more significant than if it had not happened at all.[11] The metaphor of first fruits, that is, incorporates humanity into the new age that has broken into the old in Christ's death and resurrection. We continue to live in that threshold space at the juncture of the ages. The first fruits have been presented, the new age has broken into the old, but we continue to live in the tension until all the fruits have been gathered. "First fruits" thus becomes a metaphor through which we may begin to perceive the world in new ways; it becomes a metaphor for life between the ages, life on the way from the old age that is dying to the new that is being born.

The second phrase has been highlighted earlier. In 15:2 Paul

---

10. Gordon D. Fee, *The First Epistle to the Corinthians*, New International Commentary on the New Testament (Grand Rapids, MI: William B. Eerdmans Publishing Co., 1987), 749.
11. Barth, *Resurrection of the Dead*, 144–45, 154.

speaks of the good news, "through which also you are *being saved.*" This extraordinary phrase, also used in 1:18, captures the character of the Christian life and the Christian community at the juncture of the ages. The phrase is dynamic and filled with movement. Believers are being saved. This theological affirmation runs directly counter to questions some Christians often ask: "Are you saved?" "When were you saved?" Implicit in those questions is a quest for security, certainty, solidity. The notion of being saved, however, places believers and the church directly in a liminal space, where there is dynamic movement from one place to another—from the old age to the new. Nothing is finished or final. We remain on the way. Salvation cannot be separated from this eschatological tension, movement, and hope. That is the space inaugurated by Christ's crucifixion and resurrection.

First fruits. Being saved. These two loaded little phrases set believers again into the liminal space at the juncture of the ages. Even more important is the overall dynamic of chapter 15. In Paul's language throughout the chapter, one gets a sense of life at this threshold where the old age, governed by the power of death, and the new age, shaped by God's odd new creation, intersect, overlap, and conflict. The tensions and paradoxes in the chapter are extraordinary, and they reveal the ongoing struggle of life at the juncture of the ages—even in the power of the resurrection.

> Our present relationship to God, even the Christian one, is a provisional state, an episode, an episode indeed of the transition and the struggle. . . . The error of the Corinthians may be understood in this wise: they comprehended what had happened in Christ in the world as something finished and satisfying in itself. In reality it is only a beginning, in fact only an indication.
>
> Barth, *Resurrection of the Dead,* 168.

On the one hand, for example, in his powerful, climactic affirmation, Paul can boldly and sarcastically mock the power of death: "'Death has been swallowed up in victory.' Where, O death, is your victory? Where, O death, is your sting?" (vv. 54–55). Paul invites us to laugh at death. He actually offers a theology of resurrection laughter, which has been developed in the church through a specific ritual: the *risus paschalis* or Easter laughter.[12] In this tradition, often practiced on the second Sunday of Easter, the minister tells jokes and uses *double entendres* and humorous antics, including obscenities and sexual innuendo, to mock death and incite the Easter laughter.[13] Laughter thus becomes an embodied response to resurrection and a liturgical symbol for Easter.[14]

Although often criticized for its abuses and superficialities, the *risus paschalis* has been widely recognized and celebrated. In a sermon about Easter on Bavarian radio, for example, Joseph Cardinal Ratzinger, Pope Benedict XVI, recognized the importance of the *risus paschalis* and highlighted the central role of laughter in Easter celebrations. This laughter, he proclaims, testifies "to the freedom of the redeemed" from the power of death. His sermon, entitled "Sarah's Laughter," concludes, "Like Sarah, people who share an Easter faith can say: 'God has made me laugh; everyone who hears me will laugh with me'" (Gen 21:6).[15]

The Protestant theologian Jürgen Moltmann has written affirmatively about the *risus paschalis*, suggesting that Paul exorcistically laughs at death in 1 Corinthians 15:54–55. Easter, he proclaims, "begins the laughter of the redeemed, the dancing of the liberated... even if we still live under conditions with little cause for rejoicing."[16] Celebrating Easter's homiletical jokes, Moltmann affirms Easter laughter as an expression of resistance to the powers of death. This laughter displays our freedom from the powers of this age; it is the "beginning of the rebellion of the liberated against the bonds of their slavery."[17] Such laughter shapes our eschatological hope: "The

12. For a helpful account of the history and character of the *risus paschalis*, see Michael O'Connell, "Mockery, Farce, and *Risus Paschalis* in the York *Christ before Herod*," in *Farce and Farcical Elements*; Ludus: Medieval and Early Renaissance Theatre and Drama 6, ed. Wim Hüsken and Konrad Schoell (Amsterdam: Rodopi, 2002), 45–58.

13. Jacqueline Bussie, *The Laughter of the Oppressed: Ethical and Theological Resistance in Wiesel, Morrison, and Endo* (New York: T. & T. Clark, 2007), 20. See also Charles L. Campbell, "Ministry with a Laugh," *Interpretation* 69 (April 2015): 196–208.

14. Joseph Cardinal Ratzinger (Pope Benedict XVI), "Sarah's Laughter," in *Images of Hope: Meditations on Major Feasts*, trans. John Rock and Graham Harrison (San Francisco: Ignatius Press, 2006), 51.

15. Ratzinger, "Sarah's Laughter," 51, 52.

16. Jürgen Moltmann, *Theology and Joy*, trans. Reinhard Ulrich (London: SCM Press Ltd., 1973), 50–51.

17. Ibid., 51.

laughter of the universe is God's delight. It is the universal Easter laughter."[18]

This laughter at death, whose power has been defeated, remains in tension throughout chapter 15 with the powers of the old age, which continue to oppress people and make the way of discipleship the way of the cross. Without confidence in the reality of the resurrection, Paul asks, "Why are we putting ourselves in danger every hour? I die every day. . . . If with merely human hopes I fought with wild animals at Ephesus, what would I have gained by it?" (v. 30–32). And, of course, there are his well-known words, "If for this life only we have hoped in Christ, we are of all people most to be pitied" (v. 19). Paul has no illusions about the realities of the old age that continue to exercise the power of death in our world. Resurrection, Paul proclaims, frees us from the fear of death. We can laugh at death. Resurrection, however, frees us, ironically, to take up the way of the cross in resistance to the powers of this age that still seek to rule the world. Indeed, following his words mocking death, Paul's final word in the chapter calls believers to the challenging journey of the

> How can the resurrection be proclaimed in the midst of the cross? That is just the point. The cross is the epistemological crisis for the simple reason that while it is in one sense followed by the resurrection, it is not replaced by the resurrection.
>
> J. Louis Martyn, "Epistemology at the Turn of the Ages," in *Theological Issues in the Letters of Paul* (Nashville: Abingdon Press, 1997), 109.

Christian life, a journey empowered by the hope of the resurrection: "Therefore, my beloved, be steadfast, immovable, always excelling in the work of the Lord, because you know that in the Lord your labor is not in vain" (v. 58).

Paul reminds believers again of the powers of death in his extraordinary comments about "the end" (vv. 24–28). Here too we find both a ringing affirmation of God's new creation and simultaneously an underlying recognition of the continuing reality of the old age. "Then comes the end," Paul declares, "when [Christ] hands over the kingdom to God the Father, after he has destroyed every ruler and

18. Jürgen Moltmann, *The Coming of God: Christian Eschatology*, trans. Margaret Kohl (Philadelphia: Fortress Press, 1996), 339.

every authority and power [archēn; exousian; dynamin]. For he must reign until he has put all his enemies under his feet. The last enemy to be destroyed is death" (vv. 24–26). At "the end" (telos, goal) the powers of this age will finally be overcome. Implicit in this ringing affirmation, however, is a recognition that these powers continue to be active in the world, as everyone knows from simply looking around. Even in the light of the resurrection, there continues to be an ongoing struggle at the juncture of the ages—a struggle between the old age governed by the powers of death and the new age inaugurated by the crucified and risen Christ.

In his words about the end Paul recognizes that the powers of this age depend on death for the order and control they seek in the world. Death—the last enemy—is the ultimate power and sanction of the institutions and systems and structures and myths that seek to maintain their domination and control over human beings. The powers that be will finally put to death any who seek to resist their will to domination, just as they did to Jesus (2:8). That is why the comment of the Misfit is so significant. From the perspective of the Misfit, the ultimate power in the world remains the power of death—the power to kill. Interrupt that, and everything is thrown off balance.

The Gospel of John depicts this power of death when Jesus raises Lazarus from the dead (11:1–44). From that moment the religious authorities formally plan to put Jesus to death (11:45–53). They plan to kill Lazarus too—to destroy the evidence of resurrection (12:9–11). The religious authorities know the empire will not put up with anyone who raises the dead. The powers of this age will not tolerate people who believe in resurrection and live free from the fear of death. The powers of this age have too much riding on the threat of death. Resurrection subverts the whole system. The religious authorities know that their well-being depends on keeping the empire happy. They dare not resist the threats and the power of Rome: "If we let him go on like this," they say, "everyone will believe in him, and the Romans will come and destroy both our holy place and our nation" (11:48). The threat of death keeps everyone—even religious authorities—under control.

So the authorities plot to kill Jesus—and Lazarus too. It is rather stupid—trying to stop the one who has power over death by killing him—but that's the only option imaginable. Someone's a threat— kill him. It is simply the Misfit writ large. As theologian and activist Bill Wylie Kellerman has put it, "Resurrection is against the law."[19] Resurrection subverts the order of things. It throws everything off balance. The Gospel of John thus provides a subtle narrative account of Paul's extraordinary insights about the power of death that lies behind the work of the powers of this age as they seek to dominate the world. Both John and Paul agree: resurrection leads to the way of the cross—a reversal of our normal thinking; resurrection empowers the way of cruciform resistance because it frees us from the threat of death posed by the powers that be. The way of resurrection is the way of the cross. Such is the struggle at the juncture of the ages.[20]

Paul not only names the power of death; he also names the reality of sin. Sin is living captive to the power of death, as the religious authorities do in the Gospel of John. Sin involves ceding ultimate authority to death rather than to God. That is why sin is "the sting of death" (v. 56); sin is the painful, debilitating reality in which people live in captivity to death. Sin, for Paul, is not simply a list of individual sinful acts, but our captivity to the powers of this age that are killing us. Sin is the human inability or refusal to step into the freedom of the new age created by Jesus' cross and resurrection; it is the result of weakness as much as active evil. Driven by the fear of death, sin is living under the spell of the last enemy. For the Misfit, that involves carrying out literal acts of murder. For Paul, it can also be the assumption that death has the final word, so all resistance is futile. There is no point in taking up the way of the cross; we simply tend to our own security and desires—we eat and drink for tomorrow we die.

Even Paul's extraordinary affirmations about the resurrection of the body contain this same tension between the deathly realities

---

19. That is the point of the seal over the tomb: the seal didn't keep the tomb literally secure; it was a statutory seal; breaking it was against the law. See Bill Wylie Kellermann, "Easter: Resurrection Is Against the Law," in *Seasons of Faith and Conscience: Explorations in Liturgical Direct Action* (Eugene, OR: Wipf and Stock, 2009), 184–88.

20. In John the resurrected Jesus bears the wounds of crucifixion (John 20:27). See also John 21:18–19, where the resurrected Jesus tells Peter that his new postresurrection faithfulness will lead to crucifixion.

of the old age and the powers of life in the new. "What is sown is perishable, what is raised is imperishable. It is sown in dishonor, it is raised in glory. It is sown in weakness, it is raised in power" (vv. 42–43). These stirring phrases—"imperishable," "glory," "power"— remain in tension with old-age realities—"perishable," "dishonor," "weakness." Even in the power of the resurrection, the struggle with sin and death remains.

It is thus no wonder that one haunting phrase runs like a thread throughout the chapter. Indeed, Paul begins and ends the chapter with this phrase (and he repeats it five times throughout the chapter): "in vain" (vv. 2, 10, 14 [twice], 58). There is a poignancy in that repeated phrase, reflecting the tensions of life at the juncture of the ages. At the beginning of the chapter Paul recognizes that in the face of the powers of death, our faith is in vain without the resurrection (v. 2). And at the end of the chapter, in his final affirmation, he returns to assure believers that in the Lord—who is the first fruits and in whom we are being saved—our labor is *not* "in vain" (v. 58). The great challenge for believers, the great temptation of sin, is to consider our resistance to be in vain, even though it often feels that way, and to surrender to the power of death.

Throughout the chapter, then, there is deep hope and assurance that sets believers free from the powers of death. There is also a recognition of the ongoing activity of those powers. At the juncture of the ages, the way of God continues to appear weak and foolish. That is why Paul's proclamation of Jesus' crucifixion and resurrection frames his letter to the Corinthians and provides the lens through which to read everything else. Paul begins with Jesus' crucified body in chapter 1. Paul concludes with the resurrected body in chapter 15. In between, at the juncture of the ages created by Christ's crucifixion and resurrection, Paul addresses the being-saved community of faith, the church—the *Body* of Christ, crucified and raised with Jesus, which itself is called to *embody* an interruption in the world. The resurrection thus points back to the crucifixion of Jesus as the wisdom and power of God. It points ahead to the end when the power of death will be overcome. It also points in-between, to the unsettled, often cruciform journey of the Body of Christ at the juncture of the ages.

FURTHER REFLECTIONS
Metaphorical Theology

In addition to emphasizing the disruptive character of the resurrection, which, along with crucifixion, shapes the Christian life at the turn of the ages, Paul also seeks to answer the Corinthians' possibly sarcastic question: "How are the dead raised? With what kind of body do they come?" (v. 35). Paul responds with metaphorical theology. He does not even attempt a logical argument but rather piles metaphor upon metaphor and image upon image. He seeks to stir imaginations that have become captive to the power of death while recognizing the inadequacy of language ever to capture the reality of resurrected bodies. He speaks of a seed that has to die and be transformed into a new kind of body (vv. 36–38). He highlights different animals having different kinds of flesh, and he extols the differences between earthly and heavenly bodies (vv. 39–41). He mentions the first human, Adam, made from dust, and the second, Christ, made of heaven (vv. 45–49). In the midst of all these metaphors, he simply turns to a series of poetic juxtapositions:

> So it is with the resurrection of the dead.
> What is sown is perishable,
> what is raised is imperishable.
> It is sown in dishonor,
> it is raised in glory.
> It is sown in weakness,
> it is raised in power.
> It is sown a physical body,
> it is raised a spiritual body.
>
> (vv. 42–44)

Throughout his many different gestures toward the character of resurrected bodies, Paul suggests that theology does not only pursue rational, abstract argument. Theology also needs to be poetic, metaphorical. Indeed, when dealing with resurrection, there may be no other way to speak. One can only gesture with words that can never fully capture the reality. One can only speak with humility, knowing only in part, in order to create the space in which new imagination and new life might be born.

In a broader sense metaphor itself is deeply theological; it is actually an appropriate mode for apocalyptic theology at the threshold of the ages. For metaphor is an unsettled figure of speech—a kind of in-between form of rhetoric. Metaphors do not have fixed meanings, and their effect cannot be precisely predicted or controlled. Bringing together two seemingly disparate realities, metaphors have a decidedly open character.[21] They tenuously suggest a new reality rather than establishing absolute dogmas or certain proofs.[22] Metaphors do not provide a fixed or final delineation of truth but rather an openness and freedom, a space in which surprising, imaginative discoveries and insights are possible. Using "conventional language unconventionally," metaphors call for discernment and new perception; they move us "to see our ordinary world in an extraordinary way."[23] Metaphors interrupt and "rearrange the world," which is precisely what resurrection does. In the threshold space between the ages, in which believers discern with bifocal vision, metaphors are an essential mode of speech. Metaphorical theology is essential at the juncture of the ages. It is the kind of theology Paul actually practices throughout the letter, for it is theology that seeks to unveil the new creation that has interrupted the old age so new perception and new life might be born.

River inside the river.
World within the world.

All we have is words

To reveal the rose
That the rose obscures.[24]

21. For an excellent treatment of metaphor see Janet Martin Soskice, *Metaphor and Religious Language* (Oxford: Oxford University Press, 1985).
22. Rodney Kennedy, *The Creative Power of Metaphor: A Rhetorical Homiletics* (Lanham, MD: University Press of America, 1993), 32, 36.
23. Sallie McFague, *Speaking in Parables: A Study in Metaphor and Theology* (Philadelphia: Fortress Press, 1978), 4. McFague defines metaphor as "a word used in an unfamiliar context to give us new insight" (4). See also Sally McFague, *Metaphorical Theology: Models of God in Religious Language* (Minneapolis: Augsburg Fortress Press, 1982).
24. Gregory Orr, "River inside the River," in *River inside the River: Three Lyric Sequences* (New York: W. W. Norton and Company, 2013), 124.

16:1–24

Concluding Pastoral Concerns

Chapter 16 reveals the pastoral character of Paul's work that provides the context for the letter. We get a glimpse into the day-to-day activities and plans within which his theological reflections take place. Before his closing words, Paul organizes a collection for the saints in Jerusalem, details his travel plans, recommends servants to the Corinthian community, and shares greetings from other churches. Because his letter would have been read at the community's gathering, it is as if Paul, at the end of his letter, shares announcements and concerns, as many pastors currently do each week in worship. This active pastoral life is the context of Paul's theology. Even in these concluding, seemingly trivial announcements, important theological affirmations are apparent.

A Connectional Church

Throughout the chapter Paul reminds the Corinthians of the connectional character of the church. No congregation stands alone but each one is part of the larger church, the larger Body of Christ. The apostle began his letter with this reminder: "To the church of God that is in Corinth, to those who are sanctified in Christ Jesus, called to be saints, together with all those who in every place call on the name of our Lord Jesus Christ, both their Lord and ours ..." (1:2). Now, having focused on the particular challenges in the Corinthian community, Paul concludes by again reminding the congregation of its connection to the larger church. Paul's ecclesiology is not simply congregational but more broadly connectional.

Paul highlights this connectional character of the church in several ways. He begins by giving the Corinthians detailed instructions for preparing a monetary collection that will be taken to the saints in Jerusalem, who are poor and need the resources (vv. 1–4). Like the churches of Galatia, the Corinthians are invited to remember their brothers and sisters in Jerusalem through the weekly practice of setting aside money for them. Paul here applies to the larger church the ecclesiological affirmation he has earlier shared with the Corinthians themselves: "if one member suffers, all suffer together with it" (12:26). The suffering of the Jerusalem church impinges on the life of the Corinthian congregation. The weekly collection is a concrete practice of lovingly giving oneself to another member of the body.

Not only does this daily practice connect the Corinthians with other churches, both those in Galatia and Jerusalem; it also enacts a new-age reality that Paul has affirmed earlier in the letter: in the Spirit, through baptism, Jews and Greeks are one body (12:13). Through this concrete practice of solidarity by the Gentile Christians in Corinth, the Body of Christ resists the divisions of the old age; the binary divisions between Jew and Greek are broken down, and the church embodies the boundary crossing realities of the new creation. This specific, weekly practice enacts Paul's theological vision of baptismal identity and enables the church to grow as the Body of Christ.

In addition, Paul highlights the connectional character of the church through his travel plans (vv. 5–12). Through his itinerant missionary work, Paul himself actually embodies the larger church in his own life. He serves as a personal connection among the various churches he serves. The details of his travels remind the Corinthians that they are not an isolated congregation but part of a larger church. Before coming to Corinth, Paul will stay in Ephesus until Pentecost, continuing the dangerous but promising work there (vv. 8–9; 15:32). He will pass through Macedonia, visiting the churches in that region. Paul places the church in Corinth in a larger context. It is simply one small member of the larger Body of Christ. This affirmation brings with it the assurance that the Corinthians are not alone. It also calls for humility because the Corinthian congregation is not the whole story and does not possess all the wisdom and faithfulness. There are other churches who serve not only as examples but also as correctives for the Corinthian congregation.

Finally, through his various greetings and recommendations Paul affirms the connectional character of the church (vv. 10–20). Paul is not the only one ministering in various congregations. There is considerable sharing among the various churches, as different people minister in a variety of places. Timothy is working with Paul and may come as his representative to Corinth. Apollos, whose presence in Corinth had created some divisions (1:10–17), remains a coworker with Paul. Indeed, Paul has even urged Apollos to return to Corinth, though for some reason—either the will of God or his own choice—Apollos cannot come. Stephanas and his household have been serving the saints in Achaia. Fortunatas and Achaicus have apparently come from Corinth to support Paul's work. Aquila and Prisca, who had worked with Paul in Corinth, are now working with him in Ephesus—and he sends greetings from them. Indeed, beyond these believers Paul gestures to an even larger family of coworkers: "all the brothers and sisters send greetings" (v. 20). While these various greetings and recommendations may seem like a simple set of formalities, they are a profound affirmation of the connectional character of the church. Through these various servants, the congregations are joined in a common ministry. No congregation stands alone, but all are intimately woven together into a rich tapestry of shared service.

Theology and the Trivial

As the above rather routine activities and announcements suggest, the church's theology is often enacted in what may seem to be trivial practices. Taking up a monetary collection may actually embody the solidarity in suffering characteristic of the Body of Christ, and it may enact the new creation in which there is neither Jew nor Greek. An itinerant ministry, which is never settled in any one place, may personally embody the boundary-crossing, connectional character of the church. Simple greetings may witness to the mutuality of a shared ministry and vocation. Seemingly trivial acts may, in fact, be the daily means through which the new age interrupts the old and one gets a glimpse of the new creation. Trivial activities may be forms of resistance that shape our imaginations and enable us to grow as disciples.

In his final words before closing the letter with his own hand, Paul further emphasizes the ethical significance of the trivial in a one-sentence directive: "Greet one another with a holy kiss" (v. 20b). As was noted earlier, daily gestures and rituals often reinforce the hier-archies of dominant and subordinate.[1] In this context, Paul's direc-tive for the Corinthians to greet each other with a holy kiss is actually a radical disruption of gestures and rituals that reinforce the "public transcript" of the dominant. The holy kiss was a "sign of greeting among those who love one another." It was a gesture of reconcilia-tion that countered the divisions and hierarchies in the community through a "simple, radical, embodied" practice of love.[2] When the "low and despised" share a holy kiss with the elites in the church, the old age is interrupted by something new; the mutuality and equal-ity of *communitas* is enacted in a concrete way. It is easy to overlook the significance of such seemingly trivial gestures. A handshake, for example, which has become something perfunctory, was originally a way of signaling with open palm that one did not have a weapon; it was a sign of peace. And the same is true with the holy kiss, which has often lost its power as it has been adapted into a routine "passing of the peace."

Coming at the end of Paul's letter, this seemingly trivial practice takes on profound theological significance. Indeed, it becomes a ges-ture that actually embodies and enacts the fullness of Paul's letter: love, reconciliation, mutuality, equality. It becomes a singular prac-tice of being saved on the way to the new creation. Each holy kiss provides a momentary glimpse into the reconciled community, the *communitas*, that is the goal of Paul's letter. In a sense, Paul's entire letter provides the theological underpinning for this simple eccle-sial practice. By the time one gets to these words, the holy kiss is theologically loaded. The apostle thus suggests the importance of

---

1. See chapter 11, p. 188.
2. Richard B. Hays, *First Corinthians*, Interpretation: A Bible Commentary for Teaching and Preaching (Louisville, KY: John Knox Press, 1997), 291.

theologically *redescribing* what appear to be trivial activities that the church often takes for granted.

I have suggested this kind of "redescription" above in my discussion of the collection. That weekly activity may in fact enact the news that there is no longer Jew or Greek. Indeed, the simple act of giving away money, understood theologically, may itself be an act of resistance to one of the powers of this age—mammon—that holds so many captive today.[3] Given away, money becomes a sign of grace ("giving") rather than of domination.[4] The practice reflects the very character of God as gift-giver, which Paul emphasizes throughout the letter.

Paul himself actually provides an additional, if subtle, redescription of this collection. He directs the Corinthians to set aside money for the collection "on the first day of every week" (v. 2). It is easy to rush by this temporal designation, but it is theologically important. The first day of the week is the Lord's day, the day on which Christ was raised; it is a "little Easter." In Christian liturgical history, it has often been called the eighth day—the first day of the new creation that has interrupted the old age. It is the day on which the church, from the beginning, has gathered for worship. According to some calculations, it is the day on which the Spirit was poured out on Pentecost. Whether or not Paul is calling for the collection to be taken at worship, the theological significance of his reference should not be overlooked. The collection is a form of worship, a Spirit-inspired offering to God, not simply to the Jerusalem church, on the Lord's day. Far from being simply a routine, practical matter, the collection is a "token of the resurrection";[5] it is a concrete way in which the being-saved community enacts and anticipates the new creation when God will be all in all.

Whether it be the kiss of peace or the collection, Paul's sharing of concerns and announcements presents an important theological reminder to the church. Nothing is really trivial; all of our daily

3. Jacques Ellul, *Violence: Reflections from a Christian Perspective*, trans. Cecelia Gaul Kings (New York: Seabury Press, 1969), 166.
4. Jacques Ellul, *The Subversion of Christianity*, trans. Geoffrey W. Bromiley (Grand Rapids, MI: William B. Eerdmans Publishing Co., 1986), 180.
5. William Stringfellow, *An Ethic for Christians and Other Aliens in a Strange Land* (Waco, TX: Word Books, 1973), 139.

practices are theologically loaded. They may embody the hierarchies and divisions of the old age, or they may be practices of resistance that seek to enact "tokens of the resurrection" in the face of the powers of death. Practical theologians seek to redescribe these everyday practices so their deep theological significance is named, either positively or negatively. In the process, the being-saved life might actually become more interesting, even exciting, as people begin to discern the radical, though often hidden, implications of the gestures and rituals that shape the common life of the Body of Christ.

16:21–24
Concluding Words

Paul concludes the letter with words written in his own hand. While the remainder of the letter was probably dictated to someone else, Paul at the end signals the intimacy and love he desires with the community by writing his final greeting himself. His concluding words express love and grace for the church that lives at the juncture of the ages awaiting the fulfillment of God's purposes.

Paul's initial words about love come in the form of a curse: "Let anyone be accursed who has no love for the Lord" (v. 22). Significantly, Paul focuses on *love* for the Lord. He does not write, "cursed be those who do not *believe* in the Lord." The issue is love. As has become clear throughout the letter, love for the Lord entails love for the Body of Christ and the members of that body. One does not love the Lord without discerning and loving the body. Indeed, it is the lack of love that has puffed up some of the Corinthians with knowledge and created divisions in the church. Paul's words thus reflect his pastoral concern for the congregation. His curse upon those who do not love and who therefore divide the church is itself rooted in his own love for the congregation.

While Paul's words seem harsh here, they reflect the reality he has presented throughout the letter. Love is "the more excellent way" of the Spirit in resistance to the powers of death. Love is the one gift that lasts; it is the way that participates in the life of God and the freedom of the new creation. Failing to love not only wreaks destruction in the church; it also represents a person's ongoing captivity to the powers of this age. Failing to love is itself a form of curse, for it is existence under the power of death.

Paul follows up his curse with the church's cry for Christ to come: "*Marana tha*: Our Lord, come!" (v. 22b). Paul once again sets the Corinthians at the juncture of the ages, on the way to the fulfillment of God's purposes. In that fulfillment, when "the Lord comes," the last enemy will be defeated and God will be all in all. Speaking these words immediately after the curse sets the curse in a larger context of hope. As was seen throughout the letter, when Paul curses someone the purpose is redemptive; the goal is to bring the person back into the community (e.g., 5:3–5). When Paul cries, "Our Lord, come," he is calling for the curse to be overcome, the power of death to end, and God to be all in all. He is calling for that day when all will be set free from the powers of this age and all will love the Lord.

The cry is also a final reminder of the struggle that continues at the turn of the ages. It is a cry for the redemption of the powers of this age, which continue their deadly work. Indeed, the urgency of the cry highlights the depths of the struggle and the challenges of the cruciform life. In the liminal space between the ages, there is a longing, even at times a lament, for the Lord to come so believers will know their labor is not in vain. There is a longing for the steadfast love of the Lord to "strengthen you to the end, so that you may be blameless on the day of our Lord Jesus Christ" (1:8). "Our Lord come" is a cry of faith and hope that nevertheless reveals that the "greatest of these"—love—has not yet arrived in its fullness.

In this liminal space where one cries "Our Lord come," the church is sustained by the grace of God alone, as Paul immediately reminds the Corinthians: "The grace of the Lord Jesus be with you" (v. 23). Paul began his letter by reminding the Corinthians that their life together is grounded in the gift of God's grace (1:3–4). Now he concludes the letter with the final blessing that God's grace will sustain them on the way. This final word also reminds them that it is *God's grace* that sustains them, not their own power or wisdom. Standing in that grace, as Paul suggested at the beginning of the letter, there is no room for boasting but only humble reliance on the God who will strengthen them to the end. Here too there is the indicative of God's gift but also the imperative of living on the basis of that gift, rather than on one's own accomplishments.

Finally, in a poignant closing, Paul shares his own love with the community: "My love be with all of you in Christ Jesus" (v. 24). Paul has spoken some harsh words throughout the letter, but here he makes his motive clear: love. His love for the church has shaped the letter, and all of it should be read in that light. Like a good, if frustrated, pastor, Paul has sought to speak the truth in love. Now he reminds the Corinthians of that. He shares his love with *all* of them, even those who have rejected him and criticized him, even those whom he has cursed and told the community to put outside the church. This love is not simply Paul's personal act. Rather, it is love in Jesus Christ, love given by God's grace in the Body of Christ. So Paul's final words are "Christ Jesus." For it is only in him that the church loves; it is only in him that the wound in Corinth will be transformed.

Postscript: What Have I Learned?

The question "What have I learned?" seems inadequate after ten years of engaging with 1 Corinthians. The letter works on the interpreter at a deeper level than that. I haven't just "learned." I have discovered and changed and grown. So I will instead address these questions: "What have I discovered?" and "How have I grown?"

First, I discovered that this letter has actually informed much of my work through the years. While on the surface I have tended to focus on the Gospels, I have been fascinated to discover the many ways 1 Corinthians has been there all along, a thread running through my theological and ethical reflections. More than any other epistle, this letter has shaped my theology. From my emphasis on the scandal of particularity and building up the church (*oikodomein*) in *Preaching Jesus* to my exploration of the principalities and powers in *The Word before the Powers*, Paul's words to the Corinthians have been there as a companion influencing and shaping my thought and my life. More recently, in *Preaching Fools*, coauthored with my South African colleague Johan Cilliers, I turned directly to Paul's letter to develop a theology of preaching. Indeed, *Preaching Fools*, which was written in conjunction with my work on this commentary, may be read as a companion to this book. A few sections of the earlier book appear here in further developed form. The theological orientation developed in *Preaching Fools* continues through this commentary. I am grateful to have had the opportunity to recognize how much I owe to 1 Corinthians, and I am thankful that this commentary has given me an opportunity to pull together some threads that weave throughout my work.

Second, 1 Corinthians has revealed the limitations of my earlier work. In particular, the letter challenged the narrow christological focus of my earlier books. Paul repeatedly confronted me with the question "Where's your pneumatology?"—a question others have posed before him. This challenge produced the most significant area of theological growth for me. The commentary—of necessity—contains a much more robust pneumatology than I have previously explored. The role of the Spirit in discerning the new creation, resisting the powers, building up the church, and living as fools for the sake of Christ has now taken its rightful place in my theological and ethical reflection. As a consequence, my theology moves toward a more Trinitarian orientation, as opposed to my previously rather narrow focus on Jesus.

At a deeper level, Paul's letter has revealed another limitation of my earlier work: it was too neat. It wasn't dynamic enough or unruly enough. It didn't reflect the folly and scandal of the gospel. It wasn't adequately "on the way" or *being*-saved. In 1 Corinthians I have encountered the apocalyptic interruption of the crucified and risen Christ, who fractures all theological systems. I have been unsettled by paradoxical "destabilizing pairs of opposites" that will never be resolved—and that I now see everywhere in Scripture, not just in this letter. I have been blown off balance by the rushing wind of the Spirit, who blows where the Spirit will and is constantly moving to form and re-form the church. The goal of the Christian life and Christian theology has changed significantly for me. I am no longer concerned about certainty or security but am rather seeking to live into that always unsettled, liminal space at the turn of the ages.

Third, I have renewed my Reformed commitment to practical theology. Through my engagement with Paul's letter I have claimed more fully my conviction that faithful theology is practical. I have come to value in a new way a central Presbyterian principle of church order, which I have quoted more than once in the commentary: "Truth is in order to goodness; and the great touchstone of truth, its tendency to produce holiness."[1] As a homiletician and preacher, I have necessarily been a practical theologian. I have always been concerned about the ways theology takes form in Christian preaching. Paul, however, has convinced me that practical theology is not a secondary or derivative form of theology but is in fact the very heart of theology.

Fourth, the assignment to write a *theological* commentary has invited and clarified a fresh hermeneutical approach to Scripture. My engagement with Paul's letter has challenged me to look beneath the presenting issues, on which interpreters so often focus, in order to explore the underlying theological concerns, which may at times contradict Paul's specific directives. In particular, I have explored in this commentary a kind of "hermeneutics of trajectory" in order to discern the contemporary implications of Paul's theological emphases. While as preacher I have undoubtedly taken this approach on many occasions, Paul's apocalyptic theology has provided a new grounding for this hermeneutic. The apostle's theology invites this kind of discernment because tensions and contradictions are inescapable characteristics of theology at the turn of the ages. Such contradictions and tensions are no longer aspects to ignore or explain away. Rather, they are simply part and parcel of practical, apocalyptic theology, which simultaneously involves glimpses of the new creation and captivity to the old age. Admittedly, such discernment is dangerous. Some, possibly many, readers will disagree with my critiques of Paul and the trajectories I have suggested. Theological interpretation, however, calls for such risk if Paul's theology is not to become a static set of dogmas and rules.

Finally, and perhaps most important, I have come to a deep appreciation of an affirmation made a few years ago by Pope Francis at the beatification of Pope Paul VI, who implemented the vast changes of Vatican II: "God is not afraid of new things." It is difficult for me to imagine how radically new the gospel of the crucified and risen Christ was for the apostle Paul. And it is hard to imagine how disruptive and unsettling this gospel must have been for the church

1. *The Constitution of the Presbyterian Church (U.S.A.),* Part II, *Book of Order* (Louisville, KY: Office of the General Assembly, 2015), F-3.0104.

in Corinth and the larger culture. Throughout the letter Paul echoes the words of the Pope: "God is not afraid of new things." Rather, God in Jesus Christ through the Spirit repeatedly *instigates* newness, interrupting those places where human beings are held captive by the static, oppressive systems and structures of the world. As believers and preachers and theologians, we do not need to fear change and transition. Dynamic, unsettled change is at the heart of our lives as a covenant people who seek to serve the living God. "Fear not," Paul declares. We have been set free for risky theology, preaching, and discipleship, assured that the grace and love of God will sustain us to the end.

For Further Reading

Barth, Karl. *The Resurrection of the Dead*. Translated by H. J. Stenning. New York: Fleming H. Revel, 1933. Reprint Eugene, OR: Wipf and Stock, 2003.

Bassler, Jouette M. "1 Corinthians." In *The Women's Bible Commentary*, edited by Carol A. Newsom and Sharon H. Ringe, 321–29. Louisville, KY: Westminster/John Knox Press, 1992.

Boeve, Lieven. *God Interrupts History: Theology in a Time of Upheaval*. New York: Continuum, 2007.

Brown, Alexandra R. *The Cross and Human Transformation: Paul's Apocalyptic Word in 1 Corinthians*. Minneapolis: Fortress Press, 1995.

Campbell, Charles L. *The Word before the Powers: An Ethic of Preaching*. Louisville, KY: Westminster John Knox Press, 2002.

Campbell, Charles L., and Johan H. Cilliers. *Preaching Fools: The Gospel as a Rhetoric of Folly*. Waco, TX: Baylor University Press, 2012.

Fee, Gordon D. *The First Epistle to the Corinthians*. The New International Commentary on the New Testament. Grand Rapids, MI: William B. Eerdmans Publishing Co., 1987.

Gench, Frances Taylor. *Encountering God in Tyrannical Texts: Reflections on Paul, Women, and the Authority of Scripture*. Louisville, KY: Westminster John Knox Press, 2016.

Harrisville, Roy A. *Fracture: The Cross as Irreconcilable in the Language and Thought of the Biblical Writers*. Grand Rapids, MI: William B. Eerdmans Publishing Co., 2006.

Hays, Richard B. *Echoes of Scripture in the Letters of Paul*. New Haven, CT: Yale University Press, 1989.

_____. *First Corinthians*. Interpretation: A Bible Commentary for Preaching and Teaching. Louisville, KY: John Knox Press, 1997.

Marcus, Joel. "Crucifixion as Parodic Exaltation." *Journal of Biblical Literature* 125, no. 1 (2006): 73–87.

Martin, Dale B. "*Arsenokoitēs* and *Malakos*: Meanings and Consequences." In *Biblical Ethics and Homosexuality: Listening to Scripture*, edited by Robert L. Brawley, 117–36. Louisville, KY: Westminster John Knox Press, 1996.

_____. *The Corinthian Body*. New Haven, CT: Yale University Press, 1995.

Martyn, J. Louis. "The Apocalyptic Gospel in Galatians." *Interpretation* 54 (2000): 246–66.

_____. "Epistemology at the Turn of the Ages." In *Theological Issues in the Letters of Paul*. Nashville: Abingdon Press, 1997, 89–110.

_____. "From Paul to Flannery O'Connor with the Power of Grace." In *Theological Issues in the Letters of Paul*. Nashville: Abingdon Press, 1997, 279–97.

Mitchell, Alan C. "Rich and Poor in the Courts of Corinth: Litigiousness and Status in 1 Corinthians 6:1–11." *New Testament Studies* 39 (October 1993): 562–86.

Powery, Luke A. *Dem Dry Bones: Preaching, Death, and Hope*. Minneapolis: Fortress Press, 2012.

Resner, Andre. *Preacher and Cross: Person and Message in Theology and Rhetoric*. Grand Rapids, MI: William B. Eerdmans Publishing Co., 1999.

Saward, John. *Perfect Fools: Folly for Christ's Sake in Catholic and Orthodox Spirituality*. Oxford: Oxford University Press, 1980.

Thiessen, Gerd. *The Social Setting of Pauline Christianity: Essays on Corinth*. Translated by John H. Schütz. Philadelphia: Fortress Press, 1982.

Turner, Victor. *The Ritual Process: Structure and Anti-Structure.* New York: Aldine de Gruyer, 1995.

Stringfellow, William. *An Ethic for Christians and Other Aliens in a Strange Land.* Waco, TX: Word, 1973. Reprint Eugene, OR: Wipf & Stock, 2004.

Venable-Ridley, C. Michelle. "Paul and the African American Community." In *Embracing the Spirit: Womanist Perspectives on Hope, Salvation, and Transformation,* edited by Emilie M. Townes. Maryknoll, NY: Orbis Books, 1997, 212–33.

Welborn, L. L. *Paul, the Fool of Christ: A Study of 1 Corinthians 1–4 in the Comic-Philosophic Tradition.* London: T. & T. Clark, 2005.

Wilson, Brittany. *Unmanly Men: Refigurations of Masculinity in Luke–Acts.* New York: Oxford University Press, 2015.

Wink, Walter. *Engaging the Powers: Discernment and Resistance in a World of Domination.* Minneapolis: Fortress Press, 1992.

_____. *Naming the Powers: The Language of Power in the New Testament.* Philadelphia: Fortress Press, 1984.

Index of Scripture

Index of Subjects